EXECUTIVE
TEMP

D1548338

EXECUTIVE TEMP

DIANE L. THRAILKILL

RANDOM HOUSE
NEW YORK

Executive Temp

Copyright © 1999 by Diane L. Thrailkill

All rights reserved under International and Pan-American Copyright Conventions. No part of this book may be reproduced in any form or by any means, electronic or mechanical, including photocopying, without the written permission of the publisher. All inquiries should be addressed to Reference & Information Publishing, Random House, Inc., 201 East 50th Street, New York, NY 10022–7703. Published in the United States by Random House, Inc., New York and simultaneously in Canada by Random House of Canada Limited.

Random House and colophon are registered trademarks of Random House, Inc.

This book is available for special purchases in bulk by organizations and institutions, not for resale, at special discounts. Please direct your inquiries to the Random House Special Sales Department, toll-free 888–591–1200 or fax 212–572–4961.

Please address inquiries about electronic licensing of this divisions's products, for use on a network or in software or on CD-ROM, to the Subsidiary Rights Department, Random House Reference & Information Publishing, fax 212–940–7370.

Visit the Random House Web site at www.randomhouse.com

Typeset and printed in the United States of America.
Typeset by ComCom, an RR Donnelley & Sons company

Library of Congress Cataloging-in-Publication Data

Thrailkill, Diane. 1935–
    Executive temp Diane Thrailkill.
        p.   cm.
    Includes bibliographical references and index.
    ISBN 0–679–78014–9 (pbk.)
    1. Temporary employment. 2. Part-time employment.
  3. Supplementary employment. 4. Self-employed. I. Title.
  HD5854.T477   1999
  331.25'72—dc21

                                       99-11346
                                        CIP

0 9 8 7 6 5 4 3 2 1

First Edition
ISBN 0–679–78014–9
February 1999
New York   Toronto   London   Sydney   Auckland

*To Lucille Kelsey and
Maureen Sams, kindred spirits
and treasured friends.
Always in my heart, babes.*

Acknowledgments and Thanks

Many people freely gave their time, talent, and knowledge to benefit this book; I would like to mention a few of them and their contributions.

My literary agents, Sheree Bykofsky and Janet Rosen, for believing in the project and finding the right publisher for it;

Megan Schade, assistant editor at Random House, for her boundless enthusiasm and untiring efforts on behalf of the book;

Susan Weinstein and Ann Cefola, for their continuing encouragement, manuscript reading and valuable commentary;

Renee Cohen, my "sanity check," for her precise and thoughtful editorial comments;

My friend and daughter Susana, who acted as a sounding board and patiently read numerous drafts of the manuscript, always providing me with useful comments and a different slant; and her sidekicks Chloe, Ophelia, and young Willie, for their critical comments at each stage of the project;

Bruce Steinberg at *Staffing Industry Report;* Dawn Greco, Krissy Eby, and Ed Lenz at NATSS; Julia Rabig at Working Today; Preston Connor at NAPTE for furnishing much of the information on current legislation that affects our world of work;

Those who allowed me to quote from their work and include their stories as a part of this book;

The many people along the way who were generous with information and sources.

My heartfelt thanks to all of you.

Contents

Preface

How I Became a Temp Before It Was Fashionable

Once upon a time (it seems a lifetime ago) I became a temp in an emergency. I had started a consulting business and had chosen to subsidize it by holding down three undemanding jobs (sequentially, not simultaneously). The last job was as the office manager for a newly formed investment partnership.

At the time I accepted the position, I didn't know that "Loathsome & Schlock," as I came to call them, wasn't a real business. The head partner was a certifiable lunatic who frequently formed and terminated partnerships and had hired and fired five office managers in the two years before I joined the staff. The newest "new" partner was a glib dilettante who dabbled in business and "power" volunteer work. But as I said, I didn't know that.

My employment with them lasted ninety days. They ended their partnership of six months one weekend and fired me that Monday with no notice, no severance pay, and no payment of the "guaranteed bonus" that was one of the terms of my employment agreement. Along with the normal financial obligations of single parenthood, I had a daughter in college. I became an office temporary because I needed money—and quickly.

Why have I remained a temp? In spite of everything that was going on in my life, my consulting business grew steadily. However, I had begun writing a book. As I became more involved in the writing, I found I couldn't put in sixty hours a week for a client and still have enough energy left to write. I also became used to calling the shots in my work and having a personal life as well. I liked both.

I have settled into a lifestyle that includes teaching the *Temp Strategically!* seminars, writing (including fiction that *will* get published one of these days), occasional computer consulting, and flexible temping. Working as a temp takes nothing from me emotionally; yet it subsidizes work that I care about passionately.

Over the years I have learned how to be a successful temp with a minimum of effort. Some of this knowledge was gained the hard way, some through helpful tips others have shared with me. When the recession of the late 1980s hit, I began passing this information along in workshops given through college and community adult and continuing education programs (the *Temp Strategically!* seminars) and eventually ended up writing a book, *Temp by Choice.*

About This Book

I am a voracious reader and an admitted information junkie. Having made it to the post-ingenue/pre-senescence stage of life, I find I've collected a lot of information along the way. Part of the joy of collecting is then sharing the stuff. Wherever possible, I have mentioned by name those whose ideas or writings have helped me find the answers to whatever I was looking for at the time. If I wax enthusiastic about a particular book, product, or service, it is because I am just that. I always think maybe someone else will benefit from knowing about it too. I don't give my recommendations indiscriminately or for profit.

Most resources mentioned within the text will be found in Appendix A, or under the Further Reading section at the end of the chapter where they appear. There are a few exceptions:

- Medical and disability insurance resources appear at the end of Chapter 9. I felt health-related topics would be easier to find all in one place, rather than scattered throughout Appendix A. I encourage you to look over the membership organizations offering affordable health insurance, whether or not you need insurance. These groups have a variety of agendas and are worthy of your attention.

- Sample temporary agency tests, including computer skills tests, are found at the end of Chapter 3.

- Web sites useful for checking out the progress of state and federal legislation appear at the end of Chapter 10.

How were the resources chosen for Appendix A? Very carefully. I included those I have used over the years, as well as those I learned about through the experiences of colleagues, or through research. I have personally verified the services and information of any outside my personal acquaintance. If the resource cited is a book, I have read it, or at least looked through it carefully to see if I found the bulk of the information useful. If it is a service, I have called and talked to representatives about it and gathered additional printed information when it was available. In the case of online services and Web sites, I have browsed to see what was there. At the time of publication, all of the addresses and telephone numbers were current and correct; but as we all know, change is constant. I have tried to record several selections under each topic. If there are only one or two choices, then, *of the ones I knew about,* they represent all I felt were worthy of inclusion. There may be many more in existence that I just didn't know of.

Before parting with money for any product or service, no matter how highly recommended, I would encourage you to check out what *Consumers Reports* has said about its quality, and what the Better Business Bureau and your state or local department of consumer affairs has to say about the reputation of the company providing it. The first page of Appendix A enumerates all of its topics. Within this appendix, I have grouped together books, organizations, and Web sites. Resources mentioned throughout the book appear there under the appropriate alphabetized subject listing. If there is a free sample or service, it is marked ☺ **Free** to alert you.

Some of the temping-related forms and agency material in the body of the book are ones I have been using in my workshops, updating and revising as times have changed. They appear in one form or another in *Temp by Choice* (Career Press, 1994).

Whenever I present a long list of possible options, I do so to get you thinking about different ways to approach a problem and, I hope, to help you to come up with creative solutions. The lists are never intended to be a "to do" list, unless they are labeled as such.

There are two additional appendices: Appendix B lists the twenty IRS qualifying rules for independent contractor status. Appendix C summarizes the Tax Reform Act of 1986 (TRA) as it pertains to temporary employment.

So there you have it. Bon Appetit.

INTRODUCTION *The New World Order Where No One Is Safe*

*T*oday's career strategists put their professional survival first. New realities demand they do so. The past few years of corporate restructuring, job exportation, defense industry contraction, workplace automation, spiraling costs, wage stagnation, and shift to a contingent work force have wrought havoc with the American Dream. Old company loyalties and the career tactics they produced are as dated as they are ineffective. The new adjectives alone now used with the words "manager" or "executive" are astonishing in number. Instead of corporate executive or corporate manager, we have the flexible manager, the portable executive; project, provisional, and supplemental managers; interim, contract, and temporary executives; short-term, migrant, itinerant managers; throwaway and troubadour executives. Then there are consultants, flexecutives, business commandos, rent-a-bosses, stopgap or just-in-time staffing, headrenting, temporaries, and of course temps. These language changes are not describing a transitory aberration. Anyone expecting to climb the success ladder in this decade had better plan on constructing it first.

When my book *Temp by Choice* was published in 1994, I wrote in its introduction, "This book is about options and choice." At the time, I had hoped to show temporaries how to use contingent employment to *their* advantage by running it as a business. Over the years I had noted that the most successful temporaries—the ones getting the highest rates and best assignments—did just that. Whether they used contingent employment to subsidize a new business venture, conduct a job search, or supplement other freelance or consulting income, they considered themselves presidents of their own small companies. They viewed the agencies placing them on assignments as business colleagues and talent bookers, then conducted themselves accordingly. Another portion of my agenda was to educate those who had never considered temporary work about some of its opportunities. Little did I know *The Economist* had already predicted that by the turn of the century 50 percent of all jobs would be temporary. Nor did I suspect that three years later, the U.S. Department of Labor statistics would show another ten million jobs disappearing from the economy; or that economists would begin speculating that within the next decade, 95 percent of all jobs in the United States would be contractual—that is, for a negotiated fee and a set period of time. If these forecasts turn out to be even partially true, an individual's business fortunes will become tied to a portable bundle of skills, and one's aptitude in securing remuneration for them— "employability"—will be the new employment security. The "options and choices" are a little more compelling now.

In a volatile economy where positions may have disappeared, but not necessarily their functions or their work, a person's employment value is tied to marketable skills that cut across industry lines. This means a successful career will require knowing how to juggle long- and short-term employment periods along with skillfully moving in and out of freelance and/or temporary jobs without financial penalty or loss of ground. Willingly or not, you must assume the presidency of your "career business," your "permanent" job for the next decade or two, and operate it accordingly.

Let's look at some of the numbers and statistics that are generating this market. In February 1993, which the U.S. Department of Labor hailed as the point when the economy began to turn around, 90 percent of the 385,000 new jobs generated were part-time or temporary. It is no secret that for the past few years people who have lost jobs are *taking longer* to find *lower-paying jobs* with *fewer growth opportunities.* The yearly rate of job loss peaked at 3.4 million in 1992 and it has remained close to that number ever since, in spite of periods of growing economy and a booming stock market. A *New York Times* analysis of Labor Department statistics shows that more than 43 million jobs have been erased since 1979. The "new jobs" created by the "growing economy" are continuing the trend of paying less, or being part-time.

What happens to the work or the functions that didn't disappear? They are outsourced to specialty service providers and temporary help companies, exported to cheaper towns and countries, or automated out of existence. While effecting these sweeping changes, corporate America has blamed fiercely competitive world markets and bloated and/or lazy work forces.

The reality is that this is happening because it is possible. Permanent layoffs continued to occur in the same large numbers during our purported five-year economic recovery, even among companies that did well. *The reality is,* approaching the millennium and beyond, corporations will continue to employ core workers only until they can replace them with technology or someone cheaper. As former Secretary of Labor Robert Reich said of steady employment in this decade, "Nobody is safe."

When the recession first provoked massive layoffs in the late 1980s, newly downsized managers followed time-honored job search techniques. Graduates of outplacement counseling, they researched and they networked. They wrote succinct and perfect cover letters for their freshly updated resumes, followed up with telephone calls to schedule interviews, and sent thank-you notes after the interviews took place. Yet these formerly successful practices soon collapsed under the weight of sheer numbers. Too many people were out of work. Human resources departments, paper-intensive in the best of circumstances, assumed the elegance of Postal Service dead letter offices. During this same period, as a professional temporary and writer uninterested in a permanent job, I was averaging one or two offers a month—either to take the position I was filling in for or to join the company in another capacity. The irony of that situation didn't escape me. The upshot was that I put together a three-hour seminar to show unemployed managers how to work successfully as temps so that they could get these job offers. The seminars led to my writing *Temp by Choice*. Now, here I am again, writing another book.

Continuous change seems to be our new norm. There may never be a return to a steady state of employment, or to a recognizable resemblance to the way things used to be. In and of itself, that necessitates rethinking our perceptions of career strategy and success. Whether this period will go down in history as the "Decade of Dysfunction" or the "Downsized Decade," the corporate family in its downsize-dissolve-merge-acquire-restructure (dysfunctional?) frenzy has pushed out of the nest millions of its employee "family members" and now seems intent on stomping on the fingers of any remaining edge-of-the-nest clutchers. Technology has redesigned job functions to render many of them obsolete or useful only for robotic tasks, and it has changed the social structure of the workplace as well. The once paternalistic, hierarchical corporation is metamorphosing to a network configuration that can retrieve information instantly and share it with customers or other divisions throughout the world. The status formerly conferred by titles and positions is now more likely to be granted by the portfolio of portable skills that keeps us employed. In the process, the nature of work itself has changed, and many of today's working professionals find, to their dismay, that they may have already reached, or passed, the summit of their corporate careers if they have remained employed by one company. The new successful career may be a series of short-term engagements. At this juncture, to engage in traditional thinking by focusing inwardly on a particular job or an immediate group (no doubt emitting a sigh of relief for having survived numerous cutbacks) avoids confronting the future and immeasurably limits opportunity.

In this new climate, it is imperative that *we* determine the essential qualities of the work we engage in rather than have that work define and delimit us. Those who take the helm of their career businesses, to navigate it with creativity and aplomb, will be the ones defining success for this decade.

As the temporary worker population has swelled, the competition for any job or project has increased correspondingly. Economists note that contingent workers fall into two broad but very different categories—the haves and the have-nots. In such a climate, to ignore learning how to make temporary employment work in your best interests is to go the way of the dinosaur. The species that adapts survives.

Executive Temp is intended to be more than just a survival guide. I hope it is the source book that helps you put a personal stamp on success, the one that imparts the necessary insider information for you to succeed and become one of the "haves."

It is crucial to take charge of your career by moving to an entrepreneurial mind-set, to focus on what is best for *your* security, *your* skill sets, *your* freedom, *your* happiness, *your* definition of success. Savvy career tacticians will accept the reality of change, retooling and reengineering their strategies accordingly to adapt to a changed job market.

To take a small liberty with an old Chinese proverb . . . "Give people fish and you feed them for the day. Teach them how to fish and you feed them for a lifetime."

Behold! *Executive Temp . . . The Compleat Angler.*

1 *The Entrepreneurial Mind-Set*

Flexible staffing is in; that is a fact. Your present job may last a month or a year, but it will last only as long as there is a need for your service (as will you). What kind of label do you intend to put on the services you may furnish to companies, for however long they are needed? Will you consult? Will you manage projects? Will you engage in migratory management? However we choose to describe it, we are all temporary in this life. What's in a name?

In the Introduction I refer to "successful" temporaries who manage to get the best hourly rates and the choice assignments working through agencies. I'm referring to those who treat their contingent employment as a business that they manage. They are in charge. They are flexible enough to change direction quickly if a better opportunity presents itself. They do not think of themselves as agency employees, but rather as business colleagues of the agencies and their clients. They adapt to the new remuneration and never forget that their *time is money*. They have a plan and are usually working on some aspect of it during each assignment; small business owners wear many hats. So how does this translate into an entrepreneurial mind-set?

Let me tell you a story. A few years ago, I accepted a temporary agency assignment working for the division head of a sales and marketing subsidiary. The first week on the job I found out what the VP *really* wanted "the temp" to do: solve the problems of the company's day-to-day administration and support, both immediately and for the long term, by securing additional temporary help (they were under a hiring freeze). To accomplish this, I determined I must hire three word processors, proficient and talented enough to furnish daily support to a sales staff of thirty and willing to make an eighteen-month commitment to the assignment. Along with that, I would need to set up a word-processing center, also staffed with talented and self-directed temps who could work with minimal supervision for two to three shifts per day as needed, depending on the work load. Since I wasn't interested in coming on board permanently (more irony, another job offer) I had to find and train a permanent replacement for myself, someone who could run the day-to-day operation when I left. I told the agency that my assignment had turned into a real job and that to do it, I wanted real money. So, I invoiced the client directly at my normal "consulting" rate and stayed on site for eight months organizing, hiring, training staff, and fine-tuning the operation. The agency agreed not to charge the client a fee for my services, while I in turn agreed to hire temps from the agency whenever feasible, but only if they met my standards.

What kind of a temp was I? An administrative assistant? A consultant? A project manager? A portable manager? In doing what needed to be done, I was all of the above and more. At some point, no doubt, a business school professor will coin a convoluted phrase to describe this phenomenon—a multifaceted versatility manager, or other such term. Until such time as the nomenclature is settled, let's look at one of the more common terms that is presently used for interim and project work, *consulting*.

A Rose is a Rose is a . . . ?

Many interim management workers refer to themselves as *consultants* rather than temps for reasons of prestige and ego. How is a consultant different from a temp? In focus, my friend, and attitude. An old joke about doctors comes to mind. Question: How is a doctor different from God? Answer: God doesn't act like a doctor.

Generally, consultants are brought in to advise. They recommend procedural innovations or determine work that needs to be done, but they are not there to execute the changes. They are hired for their strategic thinking and expertise, often concentrating on how to automate tasks and processes in order to cut costs and jobs. If they are not independent operators, their activities are managed by a consulting firm.

> *Consultants . . . raise to an art form the dissemination of biased information. Their handling of collected data invariably has two results. They find a way to have the finished report coincide with the opinion of the person who hired them. Secondarily, they usually find a way to make the final report become an entree to their being asked back for more consultations.*

This definition comes from Joseph S. Casciato's and Robert M. Vass's book *Infomaniacs—A Brown Paper Bag View of Information Interaction in Corporate*

America. Maybe it's a little cynical, but there is more than an element of truth to it.

On the other hand, *interim employees* (under multifarious labels), are usually brought in to do a specific job. They are experienced line managers performing task-oriented rather than advisory work on site, and their daily activities are managed by the company whose work they are doing. An interim worker completes a project or manages a department for a period of time. But the line between interim workers and consultants blurs in usage as everyone becomes more independent and entrepreneurial. A consultant may begin the project advising but end it by executing the work on an interim basis until "the right person" can be found and trained to maintain the changes proposed, then effected.

In this book I use the terms *temporary, contingent,* and *interim* interchangeably and refer to those who do such work as *temporaries.* The easiest and quickest way to get immediate work is to register with a temporary employment company, commonly called a *temporary staffing service* or a *temporary agency.* These companies employ people who work as temporaries on interim assignment at the client's site. As employers offering these services, these agencies are subject to the same state regulation as other companies regarding unemployment insurance, disability insurance, and workers' compensation. Their employees (temporaries) are therefore covered under state regulations and, as such, are entitled to plan benefits.

Entrepreneur is another word with a meaning that blurs as it stretches to cover disparate activities. Most people think of entrepreneurs as creative, independent individuals, producing new products or services that grow into business empires—a Tom's of Maine, or a Ben and Jerry's. However, when all of the insider trading scandals hit the news a few years ago, the press began using the term to describe rapacious and greedy (albeit enterprising) arbitragers, several of whom ended up in prison for their illegal activities.

Corporations got into the act too. Hoping to encourage original thinking from their troops, instead of the usual "follow the leader" mentality, they bestowed the entrepreneur mantle on employees who found an easier method to accomplish the mundane, or to save the company money. The meaning stretched to include managers running the little "start-up businesses" (hardly risk-fraught, existing as they did within the framework, and under the protection, of giant companies), for which a corporate variation was coined, "intrapreneuring."

I had better explain what *I* mean by the phrase *entrepreneurial mind-set.* I use it in the sense of taking a dynamic, business approach to temporary work, one that includes eight distinguishing characteristics:

1. Loyalty and commitment to *their business* and to the *quality* of the work or service they produce. Moving in and out of interim work successfully necessitates letting go of the illusion that secure jobs exist. As pointed out earlier, the job (and you) will last only as long as there is a need for the service you provide, whether that period is two weeks or two years. The biggest asset of temporary workers to a company is that they are expendable. *You* are your new business.

All jobs are portable. But then, so are the people who perform them, and the portfolio of experience and skills they use to do so. Gone are the days when employees' careers were dependent on the companies employing them. So much has been written about the broken social contract and betrayal of loyalty between corporations and employees that there is no need for me to drone on about it here. Suffice it to say that no one will look out for your employment or career except you, as president of your "career business."

Whether you call it enlightened self-interest or looking out for number one, this reality requires a change of focus.

2. Goals and a plan/strategy to reach them. Success neither takes place in a vacuum nor happens by accident. Enterprising temporaries have goals, as well as an organized approach to achieving them safely and with relative ease. Why choose to travel the highway that goes through a swamp or necessitates white water rafting to reach a destination? A plan means you have taken the time to think through and inform yourself of some of the risks—and weigh them—before flinging yourself into space.

3. An organized approach to executing the plan successfully. "The journey of a thousand miles begins with a single step," goes the Chinese proverb. Putting any plan into action means breaking it into a series of steps that can be executed in a logical sequence. There must be an expectation of success, or why bother committing to the plan at all.

A Goal, a Strategy, an Organized Approach . . . in Action

Matthew Schiffgens and I shared adjacent cubicle space at the corporate offices of an HMO. My assignment was temporary; he was the new "permanent" government relations associate, fresh out of graduate school. Matthew had supported himself and financed his education through temporary work, securing an assignment through a friend in the national advertising department of a brokerage house, filling in for an employee on a month's leave of absence. The department wanted him to stay on when the assignment ended, so they worked with him to arrange a flexible schedule. He worked for the company three days a week and crowded his classes into two days a week. During the three and a half years he temped there, his schedule was flexible enough to include a tour of Costa Rica. He also took a month off for his wedding and honeymoon.

Enterprising Matthew had a goal and an organized approach to reach it. It never occurred to him that such a plan might be unsuccessful. He has fond memories of his temp years.

4. Fiscal responsibility. Time is money. Temporaries calculate the fees they charge for their knowledge, skill, and experience by the hour. The successful temps maintain a constant awareness of the correlation of their time to remuneration. When employees receive an annual salary, the economic risks of the enterprise are borne by the company. Temporaries assume the economic risk for their business ventures, and that encompasses *knowing what their services are worth and receiving parity*. Temporaries cannot price their services realistically or competitively without a knowledge of niche markets and rates. Price too high, you don't get the work; too low and your services are not respected. Fiscal responsibility includes prudently managing the flexible income that goes hand in hand with flexible staffing, for times of less work, no work, or no desire to work.

5. Open-mindedness and flexibility. Enterprising temporaries are flexible. They will modify their plan to reach a goal, if doing that makes more sense, or they will go after better opportunities overlooked initially. Their curiosity and open-mindedness allows them to explore unusual options. For some people, just considering temporary work through an agency for the first time is an exotic first step.

Open-Mindedness and Flexibility . . . in Action

Some of you may remember Andrew Kasaija from *Temp by Choice*. He is the systems consultant who used temporary employment to supplement "down time" between projects. When I next caught up with him, I found to my surprise, that he had taken a "permanent" job with a temporary help company. The new corporate thrust into outsourcing departments had expanded the agency's business to the point that they wanted to bring him and several other "stars" onto their staff full-time for longer projects. They kept throwing money and benefits at him until, as he said, "It would have been dumb to continue turning them down." Andrew changed his plan because it made sense to do so at that time in his life. His open-mindedness allowed him to explore another option and a more lucrative opportunity. Three years later, the job no longer suited his needs. Not surprisingly, Andrew left to form his own consulting company.

6. Awareness that employment continuity relates directly to skills growth. This is a self-directed career path. If time is money, then employment continuity necessitates skill growth. Each project or assignment should be assessed according to three criteria: Whether it (1) broadens or deepens present skills or experience, (2) whether it has the potential to develop new skills, and (3) whether it increases the ability to secure another project. Broadening a skill base increases the value of a career skills portfolio. Former successes may have been measured by status or rank, but the new defining criteria are substantive accomplishments. Entrepreneurial temporaries have a talent for recognizing opportunity and creating their own jobs. On the job, they have a commitment to the substance of the work itself, how it showcases their talent as a "quick study," and what they will learn from it. They focus on a project, assimilate the knowledge, complete the assignment, and move on.

7. Network alliances. Networking is the informal method by which information and knowledge are acquired and passed along. Effective networking is a way to seek out new assignments, increase a circle of influence, develop client relationships and new sources, and receive peer feedback. "Information Society" is a 1990's catch phrase; take it to heart by developing a commitment to life-long learning for both your specialty and your generalist skills. The better you network, the less likely you will be to reinvent the wheel.

8. Communication skills and the ability to market yourself. Never have communication skills been more important. Good ones are crucial, both to market what you do to the people you want to do it for, and to exploit your market niche.

The ability to make decisions is implicit in all of this.

Characteristics of Entrepreneurial Temps

1. Loyalty and commitment to *their business* and to the *quality* of the work or service they produce.
2. Goals and a plan/strategy to reach them.
3. An organized approach to successfully execute the plan.
4. Fiscal responsibility.

5. Open-mindedness and flexibility.
6. Awareness that employment continuity relates directly to skills growth.
7. Network alliances.
8. Communication skills and the ability to market their skills and services.

"Climate" Control

The entrepreneurial mind-set will take you only so far. It works best in tandem with a broad knowledge of which skills are transferable to all industries, and an awareness of both the trouble signs that may lead to reduced needs for particular services and the signals that an industry is shrinking. I call this combination of skills climate control. Recognizing the current catch phrases is protection against being caught unawares. Understanding what the trends and their offshoots mean to your work environment enables you to use them to your advantage. The purpose is to keep your career buoyant—and keep you calling the shots in your life.

Catch Phrases

Job outsourcing is paying another company to produce goods and provide services that used to be done in house. The rationale behind it is to get rid of all the extraneous functions, downsizing to the core of what a company does best and subcontracting all the rest to companies for whom such a function is what *they* do best. Sometimes a function will be outsourced until such time as the technology becomes available to automate or "de-skill" it. After further cost cutting, it is then brought back into the company.

Artificial intelligence, primarily known for its use in robotics, is changing how employees are taught to do a job. As computer programs increase in sophistication, becoming more intuitive as well as more interactive, they are replacing people trainers in the training function. Why employ trainers who need services, benefits, and salaries when an interactive program can do the work? If this works so well in one area, why won't it work well in another? Watch how it spreads.

Telecommuting brings to mind an employee working from home or at another location away from the workplace. Of course, if people can telecommute, so can jobs and functions. While it would depend on the product or service, picture this: main headquarters in Dayton, customer service in Atlanta . . . or another country. For instance, in January 1998 Oxford Health Plan opened a claims processing center in Ireland to handle insurance claims during the hours when its U.S., processing facilities are closed. It employs five hundred people, and once it reaches operating capacity, it will process claims around the clock. (And the executives will get to take trips to Ireland to visit it.)

Irreducible core is the term used to describe whatever is left after de-skilling, automation, outsourcing, and exporting.

Catch Phrases

Job outsourcing Paying another company to produce goods and provide services that used to be done in house.
Artificial intelligence No longer used solely for robotics, is becoming more intuitive as well as interactive, and now replacing people in training functions.
Telecommuting Working from home, or at a different location.
Irreducible core Whatever is left after de-skilling, automation, outsourcing, and exporting.

"You're fired!" is a passé phrase from another era. From the people who brought you "intrapreneuring" comes a list of euphemisms for the termination event. The following were quoted in *Executive Recruiter News:* rightsizing, force reduction, work force adjustment, indefinite idling, redundancy elimination, involuntary separation, skill-mix adjustment, work force imbalance correction, chemistry change, negotiated departure, redeployment, destaffing, degrowing, dehired, dismissal, axed, canned, let go, deselected, decruited, excessed, transitioned, vocational relocation, release, selective separation, coerced transition, executive/management culling, personnel surplus reduction, career assessment and reemployment, fumigation, early retirement, saves, force management program, people action, drowning the kittens, dumbsizing, laid off, reduced-inforce, rightsized, smartsized, outsourced, bought out. Just when I thought I had heard everything, along came William Lutz, author of *The New Doublespeak* and the following outrageous examples: Procter & Gamble did not fire 14,000 workers; they were "strengthening global effectiveness." Bell Labs explained that 140 employees were "involuntarily separated from the payroll." General Motors of Canada engaged in a "lean concept of synchronous organizational structures." But the most bizarre example came from Stouffer Foods, whose fired workers were offered "schedule adjustments that allowed them the opportunity to work zero hours for no money."

Offshoots and Mini-Trends

Vendor on Premises means temporary agency personnel on location at the company to provide and manage the employees for entire departments, such as mail or security. In some cases, one vendor or agency, the Vendor on Premises, will be in charge of securing all temporaries from approved agencies/vendors and supervising the temporary help for the entire company.

Importing specialized workers to fill technical jobs, as AT&T did in early 1996. The same week it announced it was cutting 40,000 jobs, AT&T filed an application with the U.S. Department of Labor for sixteen immigrant visas to hire electrical engineers, computer engineers, software developers, programmers, and a statistician for its Bell Laboratories in New Jersey. Under a specialized H-1B visa program, that allows companies to bring in overseas workers for up to six years, companies do not have to test the U.S. market to see if any downsized workers are available to fill the openings. (The 65,000 worker quota was exhausted by the end of 1997. Legislation to increase the quota has already passed the Senate and is expected to pass the House.) In this instance there were, given the large number of technical workers downsized from the Defense Department and high-tech companies. As you may have surmised, however, imported workers come in at considerably lower salaries.

Tele-operating: A Technology Fable for Our Time

In the old days, workers operated machines with their hands. They stuck stuff in, yanked it out, pulled levers, turned knobs, and so forth. Later on, machines were operated from control panels, numerically controlled lathes, and automated processes. Today furnaces and machines are operated from central rooms looking down on the flumes and rollers below with workers toiling at keyboards and terminal screens. If machine controls can be separated from the machine by a hundred feet, they can be separated by a hundred miles. Or a thousand miles. Or ten thousand miles. Tele-operating simply means remotely controlling a machine from any distance. Rather than move the jobs to another country and worry about political instability or shipping costs, "tele-operate." Put the plants in New York close to market over an interstate highway system, and put the workers in Nairobi. All that is needed are some cheap terminals, a telecommunications satellite, and low-wage workers.

Bruce Hartford, *Solidarity*

Signs of Cut-backs/Layoffs Coming

Knowing the warning signs of impending cutbacks is just as necessary on an interim assignment as it is in a "permanent" job. Unless you have a contract that strictly defines how the project is terminated, you can have it canceled out from under you with little or no notice. Here are some of the danger signals:

1. The company appears oblivious to sweeping changes in the industry, or in its area of industry dominance, and goes about business as usual.

2. Your division or department conducts business as usual while cutbacks are going on around it, both above and below.

3. There is little work; the challenging work—and critical information— are going elsewhere. There are mysterious "suits" and consultants around, and rumors of mergers or leveraged buyouts abound.

4. You and/or the division are remote from the customers. The company's hiring freezes and early retirement incentives have come and gone, and there has been a formal announcement that "the layoffs are over." Cutbacks will surely follow.

5. Departments that are early targets for cutback, automation, and outsourcing include advertising, public relations, human resources, support services, and research and development. The good news is that public relations, sales, marketing, and accounting skills are readily transferable to other industries.

Career Buoyancy

The first step in making changes is to understand the issues involved in order to know what you have to change. Twelve years ago I was a technical trainer teaching people about the "new" technology—computers and software. More people were fearful of looking stupid while trying to learn than they were of the technology itself. It was so unfamiliar, it had such an unusual vocabulary surrounding it, and technicians often made it appear arcane and mysterious. Of course there were some, both male and female, who swore that their hands would never touch a keyboard.

I used to tell classes the following:

Learn how to use the technology. It can make your job easier if you know it well. I can assure you these computers will be here next year and the year after. If you do not learn how to use them to your advantage, you are the ones who won't be here. There is nothing hard about what I am going to teach you today, just unfamiliar. Once I show you its secrets, you'll see how simple this stuff is. In fact, by the time we break for lunch, I promise that each of you will have produced a simple spreadsheet without my help, by following some written instructions.

I never had one class fail to complete the spreadsheet before lunch.

The fear with which many approached the new way of doing business reminds me in some respects of what is happening today. To understand the issues, the new vocabulary of catch phrases, is a good first step. Like the computers, this job market will be around for a while and will continue to change the old ways of planning a career. None of it is hard, just different.

A Fable for Our Time: The Fairly Intelligent Fly

A large spider in an old house built a beautiful web in which to catch flies. Every time a fly landed on the web and was entangled in it, the spider devoured him quickly, so that the next fly who came along would think the web was a safe and quiet place in which to rest. One day a fairly intelligent fly buzzed around above the web so long without landing that the spider appeared and said, "Come on down." But the fly was too clever for him and said, "I never land where I don't see other flies, and I don't see any other flies in your house." So he flew away until he came to a place where there were a great many other flies. He was about to settle down among them when a bee buzzed up and said, "Hold it, stupid, that's flypaper. All those flies are trapped." "Don't be silly," said the fly, "they're dancing." So he settled down and became stuck to the flypaper with all the other flies.

Moral: There is no safety in numbers, nor in anything else.

James Thurber, *Fables for Our Time*

FURTHER READING

Job Shift, William Bridges, Addison-Wesley Publishing Company, 1994.
Multipreneuring, Tom Gorman, Simon & Schuster, 1996.
The New Rules, John P. Kotter, Simon & Schuster, 1995.
We Are All Self-Employed, Cliff Hakim, Berret-Kowhler Publishers, Inc., 1994.

2 *The Vision and the Plan*

O ne hundred percent of the workforce is temporary," says William Bridges, author of *Job Shift*, and "it is temporary for two reasons." He considers the "job"—and the conditions that created it—waning social artifacts. He maintains that all of the work arrangements presently in place have been created to meet productivity needs in an immediate but *changing* situation and are, themselves, temporary.

Even if your ultimate goal is a successful and fulfilling corporate career (such as may still exist for a while), you must not overlook the strong possibility that right along with that particular career, you will engage in periods of project work, interim agency assignments, and/or consulting. Look at it this way. If you were a person who had married eight or nine times, you would still be considered a monogamist, albeit a serial one. During your career, you may work for eight, nine, or more companies. For those periods of "permanent" work, think of yourself as a serial or sequential career professional.

As early as the mid-1990s, there were reports in the business press of a confidential Bank of America memo estimating that within a short time, only 19 percent of the bank's employees would be working full-time. In August 1998, the Human Resource Institute at Eckerd College in St. Petersburg, Florida, reported that only 61 percent of the companies they had surveyed expected more than three quarters of their work force to consist of full-time, regular employees in the next decade—down 84 percent from 1998. Corporations are devising blueprints for the eventuality of a greatly reduced core of permanent workers, augmented by professional temporaries. Shouldn't you be preparing for it as well?

If this chapter has a goal, it is to impress on you the necessity of using vision, purpose, and your own blueprint to set the course for your business undertakings. It has a series of exercises to help you prepare a realistic business plan for these ventures. The more you analyze, the more information you are able to gather, and the better your chances are for success, not just survival. Unless, of course, you go to the opposite extreme where analysis becomes paralysis—"No time to work on the business, I'm too busy analyzing."

"Look reality in the eye and it won't take you by surprise," say Paul and Sarah Edwards in *Finding Your Perfect Work*. "You can grab hold of what you can see and shape it into what you would make of it."

Throughout the book I will use the term "career business" to cover the phenomenon of the multiplicity of business ventures that constitute a career in the tail-end of the nineties. As we march toward the millennium, most of us will be paying our bills with money earned from a combination of self-employment, periods of full-time employment with a company, contract work, and interim work through temporary help companies.

In 1997 it was estimated that there were over 14 million self-employed people in the U.S. and that the number was growing at the rate of 1,500 per day. In the future, most of us must create our own livelihoods based on our personal choices about the kind of life we want to live. As you may already know, small businesses have dismal success rates. Every year, over a million are started, 40 percent of which will have failed by the end of the first year. Within five years, more than 80 percent will bite the dust, and 80 percent of the 20 percent that survive the first five years will fail in the next five.

First, the Vision

Suppose your career focus is professional advancement and recognition in a specialty. You must ask yourself to what end? Do you want to be the preeminent U.S. or world expert in your field? Or would you rather be a highly regarded local expert? Will you use your expertise in a one-person consulting practice? Or will you form a consulting company that will grow to rival the consulting greats? Think about it. To succeed in this "new world order" you should be specific about your goals. Don't limit your aspirations. What is it that you are *really* trying to do? Your vision could and should be huge, but can you describe it clearly and concisely? How do your talent and experience relate to it? Do you have a vision for your career business? What is it? Only you can answer that question.

Take a look at the whole picture. If you were telling your "vision" as a story, where would you want to be at the end of the story?

Terri Lonier, author of *Working Solo* and a nationally recognized expert on small business and entrepreneurship, says this about vision:

I encourage solo entrepreneurs to take time to create a BIG vision. It gives you a context for your efforts, and keeps you striving for bigger goals. If your vision is only 25 percent of a circle, and you get half of it, then you've ended up with a pretty slim achievement. But if your vision is 100 percent of a circle and you get half of it—well, that's significant. In fact, half of the big vision is DOUBLE the entire smaller vision. So I always encourage people to stretch their thinking.

Then the Goals

Your challenge is to figure out not only how the various facets of your career business will fit into a changed business community and workplace, but also how they fit into your hopes and dreams. At whatever point the two are compatible is the point you will be ready to set goals and develop a plan. Goals should be specific and measurable. They must also be practical, workable, and attainable. Have them identify *what* you are after, not how you are trying to get there.

Before you can successfully launch an enterprise, you must be able to describe what it is, what its present and future markets are, and what differentiates it from similar undertakings. It's not enough that your business pleases you; it must please others. And it doesn't matter that you have come up with a great idea. Unless you specifically define *what you want to do* and *how you intend to go about doing it,* your "business," your "consulting service," your "career strategy" will remain a bunch of ideas rattling around in your head. That is why I suggest writing down your answers to the questions that follow.

Here is an exercise to assess the compatibility of your business life with your personal life and to sort out the priorities of both. You are going to ask yourself *who? what? where? when? how?* and *why?* See where the inconsistencies and incompatibilities show up. Please write down the answers. Get a pencil and paper now; don't put it off. Scribble answers as well as related thoughts that pop into your head. You can always refine your ideas and edit them later. Table 2.1 offers one set of possible answers.

Table 2.1 **Setting Goals**	
What do I want to be in the business world?	What do I want to be in my personal life?
Own boss doing work I love	*A loving mother, a caring friend*
To whom do I want to be it in the business world?	To whom do I want to be it in my personal life?
All the naysayers who said it can't be done	*My children and friends*
When do I want to do it in the business world?	When do I want to do it in my personal life?
By the time I am forty	*Now*
Where do I want to do it in the business world?	Where do I want to do it in my personal life?
Manhattan	*A quiet farm upstate in New York*
How do I want to do it in the business world?	How do I want to do it in my personal life?
Ethically and compassionately	*Without marriage*
What is my reward in the business world?	What is my reward in my personal life?
Respect, money	*Respect, love*
How do I define success in the business world?	How do I define success in my personal life?
Respect, money	*Respect, love*
What must I give up for success in the business world?	What must I give up for success in my personal life?
Home life, farm in upstate New York	*Conventional "respectability," Manhattan*
Why do I want to do it in the business world?	Why do I want to do it in my personal life?
Control own destiny	*Love and continuity*

This entrepreneur needs to reconcile some conflicts. The priorities are not mutually exclusive, but any plan will need to encompass both personal and business priorities if there is to be reconciliation and balance.

Job Titles and Functions for the Career Business

Many self-employed professionals get started because they excelled in their specialty and believed they could be more successful on their own than as an employee. Don't confuse being a good technician with being an entrepreneur or an entrepreneurial temporary. Good technicians need only do the job well to succeed. Self-employment adds a whole new set of responsibilities.

A buoyant career must be thought of as a business, and you must be a businessperson to succeed at it. In other words, along with being the president of your own business, you are its manager and administrator too. However minuscule a one-person shop may seem at times, a variety of functions are needed to run it.

- accounting and related record keeping
- cost estimating and pricing
- scheduling and time management
- financial management
- marketing and sales

If you examine the functions needed to run a one-person shop and use as a frame of reference the old and familiar corporate organization chart, I think you will be surprised to find the number of roles that one individual fills and the scope of these roles in making a business work. The layers of management alone will also make you wonder how anything gets done in a large corporation.

Let's take a look first at some of the strategic functions. Imagine yourself in each of the roles. *As President,* you are responsible for the overall achievement of the strategic objective, your vision. *As Vice President, Strategic Planning,* you are instrumental in developing and fine-tuning the strategic plan. Filling the role of *Chief Operating Officer,* you are accountable for keeping clients and/or agencies happy by delivering to them what has been promised by your Marketing Department. In your *Vice President of Marketing* role, you must discover new clients and agencies, as well as find innovative ways to provide them with what they require, easily and at competitive prices. *In your CFO persona,* you achieve the profitability standards, secure needed capital at the best rates, and support the Operations and Marketing functions in fulfilling their accountabilities. These are your *strategic* functions in developing the business.

Wait, there's more. Someone has to do the actual work. That was working *on* the business. There is work to do *in* the business. *You are the Sales Manager,* selling your portfolio of skills, and the *Marketing Research Manager,* figuring out which staffing services and clients to sell them to. You report to the Vice President of Marketing, who is busily figuring out your overall marketing strategy. You are a *Production Manager* and a *Service Manager* reporting to the Vice President of Operations. You are the *Accounts Receivable Manager* and the *Accounts*

Payable Manager reporting to the Vice President of Finance, who reports to the CFO. You are a busy person. If you want to do further reading along these lines, take a look at *The E-Myth,* by Michael E. Gerber. He looks at the myth of entrepreneurship and its link to knowing how to run a business, as opposed to being skilled in one's area of expertise.

Again, use an organization chart to lay out your business as you envision each function, listing all of the tasks related to the functions. After you have done that, flag any tasks that can be organized in some way, either immediately or further down the road, to delegate to another person less costly than your valuable self. This will free up more precious time to work *on your business*—to do the necessary strategic work that often gets neglected because you are too busy working *in* the business. In other words, you should search for ways to replace yourself in the mundane administrative and/or clerical busy work. It is hard to make a lot of money when you are the entire labor force. If, for financial reasons, you are unable to hire help, another strategy is to take temporary assignments that are either undemanding or have a lot of downtime and get both the client's work and your work done on the job. I explain how to do this in detail in Chapter 5.

Plan from the beginning that as soon as it is feasible, you will funnel clerical tasks to a temporary who works for a lower rate of pay. Identify the administrative jobs that take up the bulk of your time and energy, and either find ways to streamline them or hire them out. Don't try to do things that others can do better and more cost-effectively. Focus your energies on your business specialty and pay others to do legal, tax, accounting, and other specialized tasks. To keep up with technology, establish a relationship with a computer consultant. You want to spend *your* time clocking the maximum number of billable hours.

In a successful and growing business, your time becomes worth more than many of the things you spend it on. Look to business associates you can barter with or purchase from and explore cost-sharing opportunities in which you share personnel, equipment, or services. **Two of the most common entrepreneurial time wasters are trying to do everything yourself and overworking.**

You don't have to settle for a difficult, muddled, or inefficient way of working, though. For instance, if you could apply the time you spend balancing a checkbook, writing checks, and stuffing and stamping envelopes to doing more business, you should do so. One solution might be electronic bill paying. There is something to be said for the way electronic payment conveys the image of a progressive small business owner who is on the cutting edge of financial management. The combination of computerized money management and electronic bill fulfillment is worthy of consideration. If this service is of interest to you, call the customer service desk of your bank to see if it serves your needs in this area. Perhaps you can get feedback from clients who are already using this method. There are several software packages for this purpose. You will want to investigate which ones are the most user-friendly.

Develop a Plan of Action

Here are some general guidelines for your plan of action. It must reflect reality and be flexible enough to adapt as circumstances change. The plan should alert you to any gaps in your skills and knowledge that might impede you from carrying it out. It should have specific steps to complete. And finally, you must be able to communicate the results of your planning to others who will assist you in its implementation. It is essential that whatever system you use to obtain information, whether tracking expenses or managing projects, is accurate, timely, and effective for your purposes.

Bear in mind that even the best-laid business plans cannot factor in the project that goes awry because the client undergoes yet another reorganization and you must sell it to the new cast of characters; or the project that is canceled because the senior decision maker changes his or her mind. Be prepared for some setbacks, but don't let them discourage you. It happens to everyone. Prudent entrepreneurs protect their backsides with alternative plans.

Now you are ready to write out the answers to more questions. As you continue to get the ideas and plans out of your head and onto paper, keep your answers highly specific to your venture. Specify the products or services to be developed and marketed, and note where and how these things will be done. To whom will you sell them, and how do you expect to reach potential clients? Don't use generalizations, not even one. Be rigidly factual and practical.

If you are continuing in your existing line of work, look to your competition and your former place of employment. The image you convey may be different, but it must be on a par with what your clients expect in commercial settings.

The Preliminary Plan

The preliminary plan is an exercise to make clear in *your* mind how you might want to proceed. It has some of the same questions as a formal business plan, but it is less detailed. The idea of writing a formal plan all too often leads to paralysis. If you start small with this preliminary plan, all of the elements can be expanded at some future date. In the meantime, you will be refining and clarifying ideas into a plan of action that will serve you well.

1. What exactly are you trying to do with your portfolio of skills? Suppose you are presenting yourself to general and specialty agencies for project work. If you cannot describe your portfolio in twenty-five words or less, how will you publicize or advertise it as a business venture, or even talk about it to other people?

2. If yours is a business idea, why do you think it will sell? Is it original, a new concept, or a combination or adaptation? How do you want it to be perceived by buyers or clients? High end? Mass appeal? Any particular shade in between?

3. What are the benefits or the advantages of your product or service? Have you thought about what the resistance will be and how you will overcome it? Are you a resource or a liability to your service? Why?

4. Is it something people want or need? If it is something not needed, why will they want to buy it anyway? Will you have to create a need through promotion and advertising?

5. Who are your ideal customers? How will you connect with these potential customers? (Through trade or consumer periodicals, organizations, trade shows, directories, mailing lists, networks?)

6. How long will it take you to get up and running?

7. Who is your direct competition, and why are you a better choice? Distinguish your service or product from your indirect competition as well.

8. How you will beat the competition? Better design? Quality service?

What Form Will Your Business Venture Take?

As you engage in a variety of income-producing activities, you will probably use a business form as an umbrella to cover your business enterprises. The most frequently used configurations for small businesses are sole proprietorships, partnerships, limited partnerships, subchapter "S" corporations, and limited liability companies (LLCs).

I have been a sole proprietor for the past twelve years. I became one because it was easy, but I have remained one because it seems to be a good umbrella for my several business ventures.

If you decide to be a sole proprietor, get a DBA ("doing business as") certificate, obtainable in county offices for a modest sum in most places. The range is $10 to $50, except in New York City, where—naturally—it costs $130. Basically, the DBA registers your business entity and name as a sole proprietorship. It makes your business records and income discernible from your personal ones for tax purposes. The other necessity is having a separate checking account for your business expenses. It doesn't have to be a commercial account, just separate. After you have been in business for a while, apply for a credit card in your business name to use for the business expenses. Further down the road, you might want to get a tax ID as well.

There are many books that go into great detail about the benefits and disadvantages of each configuration. A good one in this category is the Nolo book, *Wage Slave No More: The Independent Contractor's Legal Guide,* by attorney Stephen Fishman. It has a chapter devoted to business forms that includes detailed pros and cons for each designation. Your tax adviser and/or attorney will also have opinions about the relative merits of each in your case. I urge you to research the subject thoroughly before making a decision. If the selection is something you plan ahead of time, you will lay the foundation for an effective structure, rather than falling haphazardly into one. The main forms, along with a brief description of each, are shown in Table 2.2.

The Business Plan

The best advice I can give you is to take the time to do a business plan; you will never regret it. A formal plan provides a structure for how you communicate your ideas to the business community. It furnishes the framework on which to build your business, the means to manage it, and the yardstick to measure your progress. It will help you evaluate changes in your industry, your market, and yourself. Any of the resources listed in Appendix A under *Business Plans* will take you through the process step by step.

Mistakes

If you read enough business books, you will see that most of them have similar lists of common business mistakes. There is a reason for this: People keep making the same mistakes. People still think that they can turn their hobby into a business just because they love it and do it well. There are those who believe that some sort of cosmic alchemy will take place whereby the needed money and clients will magically appear. You can be an expert at what

---

Table 2.2 **Business Forms**

Sole Proprietorship–One owner, not a legal entity

Advantages: Low start-up costs, freedom from most regulation, owner in direct control, tax advantages, profits solely to owner.

Disadvantages: Unlimited liability for all obligations and liabilities of business, difficulty of raising capital, difficulty of creating value that can be sold.

Partnership–(general and limited)–Two or more people doing business together

Advantages: Ease of formation, low start-up costs, possibility of additional sources of venture capital, tax advantages, limited outside regulation.

Disadvantages: Unlimited liability for general partners (limited partners are liable only to amount of their capital contributions), divided authority, difficulty of raising additional capital, difficulty of transferring interests.

The Corporation is a legal form organized to conduct business. It has a legal existence distinct from its owners. Two form variations popular with small businesses are the Sub S and the LLC, described below.

  Corporation Sub S–*Advantages:* Liability limited to amount of capital contribution, tax advantages, specialized management, transferable ownership, perpetual life, very suitable for growth (C corp).

Disadvantages: Most closely regulated, expensive to organize and run, harder to adjust interests in profits and losses, can have only one class of stock but can have differences in voting rights of common stock, limited to thirty-five (individual) shareholders.

  Limited Liability Company (LLC)–*Advantages:* Liability protection of a corporation without the double taxation of a C corporation.

Disadvantages: Not available in all states. Some jurisdictions tax LLCs twice. IRS guidelines are ambiguous. Considered risky due to lack of case law and tax rules on record.

---

you do, but a real amateur at marketing it. Or you can sell all day long, but if you don't have a legitimate product or service to deliver, it won't matter. Here is Terri Lonier's story of her journey through the process.

> *My first solo business was as a ceramic potter and sculptor in Chicago in 1978. I had graduated with a master's degree in ceramic art, and after grad school I taught for several years at colleges and universities in the South and Midwest. But academia was not for me. I never quite fit in with the politics, and I was too young and naive to figure out how to play the academic game. So I moved to Chicago and set up a pottery business in a group studio, called Lill Street Studios, with about sixteen other potters and sculptors. After about a year, the studio wanted to have some*

visiting artists come in. I had made lots of friends with ceramic artists over the years, and invited them to come to the studio, and promoted the seminars, and the program was launched to great success. That process made me realize that I was more talented at program development and organizing than I was at making porcelain pots. This type of realization is one that many solo entrepreneurs face. Their first business passion shifts after they confront daily business challenges. They realize that just because they THOUGHT their business idea was a good one doesn't mean it automatically translates into a business that can sustain them emotionally or financially.

Despite warnings about downsizing becoming "dumbsizing," corporations have continued to make hasty, across-the-board cuts that come back to haunt them on the bottom line. Their mistakes show up in their public relations, in strained relationships with customers and suppliers, and in demoralized employees. The replacements who are hired arrive knowing little about the company and soon repeat their predecessors' mistakes.

I call this the "those ignorant of history are doomed to repeat it" syndrome. Corporate mistakes open up more opportunity for your career business pursuits to succeed. Read the "history lesson" of mistakes common to most small business failures, and make sure *you* don't repeat the errors of your predecessors.

Mistakes common to most small business failures

- lack of vision
- poor planning and management
- insufficient money to fund and run business
- trying to do everything yourself
- too much technical concentration and not enough attention to business
- poor marketing and selling
- poor record keeping
- lack of money management
- lack of flexibility
- failure to keep up with trends, technology, etc.
- inability to analyze needs of clients
- underestimating competition, overestimating ability to deal with it

---

Here are a few personality traits common to "lapsed" entrepreneurs:

Personality traits common to failed entrepreneurs

- poor interpersonal skills
- refusal to accept criticism
- refusal to accept responsibility
- procrastination

Preventive Medicine

Without being pessimistic, expect things to go wrong and have alternatives ready to be implemented if needed.

Have a plan and follow it. You are traveling in unfamiliar territory. You wouldn't begin a lengthy automobile journey without consulting a road map. The business plan is your road map.

You will learn from your mistakes. Just make sure that they are $50 mistakes rather than $5,000 mistakes. Keep expenditures to a minimum the first year.

☐ Delay any expenditures as long as possible. For instance, if you don't get substantial discounts for prompt payment, take thirty to forty-five days to pay your bills.

☐ Don't start believing your own publicity and become a pompous ass. You are never too important to do a job, even if the client isn't as prestigious as you would like.

☐ Don't turn down jobs you can make a profit on just because they are small and you have hopes of landing bigger ones. A job in hand is worth more than five hot prospects that may never come to fruition.

☐ Don't discount your rates unless there is a compelling reason. You are worth what you cost, and you have mastered a spiel to educate your clients why this is so.

☐ Do ask clients to sign a simple agreement with you, and ask for part of the money up front. Don't rely on promises; get it in writing.

☐ Don't pirate clients from your temporary employment agencies. Follow the contract to both letter and spirit of the law.

☐ Treat every coworker on projects or temporary jobs as though he or she is a future client. Be nice to people who have been fired. You never know where they will end up.

◻ Make every effort to understand each company's needs and find ways to meet them. If you're not clear about goals, ask. Companies are very fickle these days, and priorities can shift suddenly.

◻ Stay up to the minute. Take advantage of every chance to develop new skills or improve old ones, especially participating in in-house training programs.

◻ Stay abreast of local economic trends by getting on the mailing list of your regional business development center. These centers are found on many college campuses. For the one nearest to you, call the Small Business Administration's hotline: 800-U-ASK-SBA (800-827-5722).

◻ Keep up with news of your industry by joining a trade group, reading professional journals, and talking with everyone you meet in the field. Build and maintain your network of associates and friends.

◻ *Know your value in the marketplace!*

Keeping Track of Your Plan

How do you keep track of all this planning? The important thing is to develop a system that works for you. If you buy project planning software, you must take the time to learn how to use it. You might experiment by using a calendar or a time line to chart your progress on projects. Do, however, define the scope of each project by setting start and end dates. Then break it down into bite-sized chunks:

1. Develop a task list.

2. Establish links between the tasks.

3. Give each task a timetable.

4. Assign the appropriate resource (people or material) to each task.

5. Review the day-to-day items, if not daily, then at least weekly.

6. Review the big picture monthly.

7. Update the plan as needed.

Ease the Transition with Moonlighting

Many people start their businesses while still employed full-time. They do so to test the new business' viability before committing to it. The term for it, of course, is "moonlighting." With a little forethought, any number of new business tasks can be taken care of from full-time employment. You can use full-time employment strategically to accomplish more important goals. Here are a few suggestions:

1. Expand your present credit lines or apply for cards you don't have while you are still employed full-time. It is not as easy to do so once you are self-employed.

2. Find out which professional and support organizations exist for your specialty and begin to attend meetings. Look into the local chamber of commerce or other business networking organizations. When you become self-employed, the nature of your former business friendships will change. Your life will be quite different from that of current friends who work mainly for one company. It is important to begin making the acquaintance of other entrepreneurs like yourself.

3. Join professional organizations, at company expense, whose memberships will benefit you and will still be good when you leave. Take pertinent company or company-reimbursed training courses whenever possible.

4. Subscribe to periodicals at company expense where appropriate. Make use of corporate libraries to research your industry and markets.

5. Use up remaining personal days, sick time. Schedule elective surgery or medical procedures you may have put off. Have any problems taken care of while you are still on salary.

6. Decide which your business will be: sole proprietorship, partnership, corporation, S corporation, LLC. Do the research, make the decision.

7. Take care of any registrations, name searches, published notifications, or paperwork connected with your choice of name and business entity.

8. Consult with your tax person or financial adviser about how your deductions will change when you have multiple business pursuits. Devise a system to log your tax receipts.

9. Choose a name for your umbrella entity. You will be surprised how much time and thought this entails.

10. Take care of paperwork for licenses and/or permits if your business calls for it.

11. Talk to your insurance adviser about any changes you may need to make in your policies and what the costs may be. Start looking into medical and disability coverage.

12. Research which free publications will be helpful to your endeavors and send away for them. Ditto regarding time on the Internet visiting sites with helpful information.

13. Think about office space and supplies:

    a. If you expect to lease space, start looking at potential areas and sites as well as making contacts.

    b. If you plan to work at home, get graph paper and use paper scale models to sketch room and furniture arrangements, or start moving furniture around to give yourself space.

    c. Buy whatever items you don't have—desk, chair, file cabinet, computer, printer, office supplies—a little at a time.

14. Query the local zoning board or building department (anonymously) about community residential or zoning regulations that apply to home offices.

15. Select stationery and business cards once you have chosen a name. Don't overlook doing them yourself on the computer. Check Appendix A under *Business Cards, Letterhead, Forms* for catalogues of products and under *Brochures and Mailing Pieces* for help with layout and design.

16. Start an ongoing list of all business friends and contacts to notify that you are in business.

17. Talk to people who are in business for themselves, preferably a similar business to the one you're planning: What were some of their problems, their surprises? What did they wish they had done first? What would they have done differently? What advice would they give you?

18. Set deadlines and target dates. Keep a log of what you have accomplished. Otherwise, you will lose track of how much you have achieved, thinking only the more you do, the more you have to do.

An Organized Approach to Temporary Assignments

While the strategic use of temporaries is nothing new, the idea of enterprising entrepreneurs working as temps periodically to use the system to their advantage may take some getting used to. This decade of downsizing has increased the number of "temporary" business opportunities right along with swelling the number of temp jobs.

The most effective way to find temporary assignments is to work through temporary staffing services (your "talent bookers") to bring the jobs and business opportunities to you. However, entrepreneurs who engage in temporary employment *without a plan* and solely to earn extra money *are missing the point.* Yes, temping is a way to immediately increase cash flow during lean times, but with a little planning, it can be a strategic tool to accomplish much more important goals. Here are a few ways you can use temp assignments to benefit your business:

□ Gain insider information to determine the best way to pitch your services or products to an industry or a particular company. Over the course of an assignment it may be possible to find out what a company's major products and services are, as well as who their customers are. You will certainly get a feel for how they are viewed by *their* customers. Learn who selects their vendors; how these decisions are reached; and how long the process takes.

□ Discover companies unknown to you in new geographical areas. Agencies tend to specialize in certain industries, and they employ sales teams to canvass for clients. For instance, if you register with at least four agencies, they will each have different clients. Their clients have clients, and you have the potential to increase your knowledge base by at least a factor of four.

□ Evaluate business equipment, office products, hardware, and popular software as they are used on a daily basis. I was able to postpone the purchase of my first laser printer for almost two years because I consistently worked as a temporary and had convenient access to them. Although cost was definitely a large consideration for me then, when I finally made my purchase, I knew from my work as a temp which printers I didn't want at *any* price.

□ Uncover innovative approaches and fresh opportunities in the process of investigating new industries/companies. If you keep an open mind and are flexible, a different opportunity or unusual direction may be much more lucrative than the ones on your plan.

□ Consider this potential benefit as well. Work rarely flows in a steady stream. Along with high-volume peaks, there are valleys of little or no work, or downtime. Downtime is a good time to accomplish your own work—research, correspondence, telephone calls, catch up on your business reading—while receiving an hourly stipend. When there is no assignment work, you are not expected to sit idly staring into space. It is actually to your benefit to look industrious. It also reinforces the need for your services—temporarily, of course.

Business Benefits of Temp Assignments

1. Gain insider information.
2. Discover new companies, new opportunities.
3. Evaluate business equipment, office products, popular software and hardware.
4. Uncover innovative approaches to business problems.
5. Use downtime to accomplish your own agenda.

Ethics and Legalities

This is not to imply that your temporary assignments are sources for poaching agency clients. While you cannot solicit business on the job, companies will solicit you. "What do you *really* do?" is a common question, and when asked, you tell. At the end of the assignment, leaving behind a business card or a brochure is certainly acceptable. The agency timesheet states the terms of the contract between you, the agency, and the client. Usually you cannot work independently for a client for a period of thirty days to six months without the client being liable to pay a fee to the agency. If you are offered a project while on the job, you can negotiate a release from the agency in order to accept it. *Everything is negotiable.*

Chapter 3 is all about finding the best agencies for your needs and how to register with them expeditiously. There is, however, one final task before you open your doors, so to speak, a checklist to consult. Think of this final checklist as a template to get you started on the right foot. Add or subtract items as necessary.

Final Checklist

1. Do you need a license for any of your business ventures?

2. Have you taken care of the paperwork for your business entity (DBA certificate, corporation, etc.)?

3. Do you need to collect and pay sales taxes on your services?

4. Does your home office conform to the local zoning ordinances?

5. Do you have a standard contract or boilerplate letter of agreement for people to sign when they engage your services?

6. Do you have business stationery and cards?

7. Have you spoken to your tax adviser about deductions? Do you have a process in place to save receipts methodically rather than tossing them in a box or a bin?

8. Do you have a separate checking account for business?

9. If a federal tax identification number is appropriate for your business, have you sent off the paperwork?

10. Do you have disability coverage and, at the very least, catastrophic medical coverage?

11. Does your homeowner's or renter's policy cover the liability for your business ventures?

12. Does your automobile insurance cover you for business?

We're a people who believe in planning, scheduling, organizing and controlling everything. Sometimes you have to give that up and go with the flow. Think about the weather. When a blizzard blows in and shuts down roads, there's nothing to do but wait it out. No matter what you do, you can't stop the snow from falling or the wind from blowing. You can, however, keep the pantry stocked so you don't starve before the storm breaks. The moral of this story is to plan ahead and go with the flow.

—Dixie Darr, Editor/Publisher *The Accidental Entrepreneur*

FURTHER READING

The Business Planning Guide: Creating A Plan for Success in Your Own Business, David H. Bangs, Jr., Upstart Publishing Company, Inc., 7th edition, 1995. Includes examples, forms, and worksheets. A diskette with plan templates is available separately.

The Complete Book of Business Plans, Joseph A. Covello and Brian J. Hazelgren, Sourcebooks, 1997.

The E-Myth Revisited, Michael E. Gerber, HarperBusiness, 1995.

Great Idea! Now What? Howard Bronson and Peter Lange, Sourcebooks, Inc. 1995.

How to Write a Business Plan, Mike McKeever, Nolo Press, 4th edition, 1997. Contains how to write a business plan for a new or an expanding business as well as a streamlined method for writing a plan in one day.

3 *Jump-Start with Agency Work*

*I*t takes time—that nonspatial continuum we all have so little of—to develop useful business relationships. It also takes time to build a stable, income-producing client list. There is a shortcut, however. You can do interim work through temporary employment companies and have the potential to accomplish several things simultaneously. The *least* benefit you will gain is earning extra income while expanding your circle of business contacts.

As we saw in the last chapter, there are any number of ways to use temporary work strategically to reach your goals. And if you are worried that you won't find a temporary help agency with assignments or projects in your area of expertise, there is probably one or more of them for just about any specialty you can think of. For instance, Kennedy Publications lists the following industry categories for their *Directory of Executive Temporary Placement Firms,* meaning that the firms listed in the directory supply temporary workers in the following industries:

Administrative services	Human resource management
Aerospace	Information technology
Agriculture/forestry/fishing/mining	Insurance/risk management
Architects	Lawyers
Biotech/genetic engineering	Management consultants
Communications	Manufacturing
Construction	Packaging
Energy/utilities	Pharmaceutical
Engineers	Real estate
Environmental services	Research and development
Finance and accounting	Retail trade
Fund raisers	Sales and marketing

General management	Scientists
Government/public administration	Technicians
Healthcare, physicians	Transportation services
High tech/electronics	Wholesale trade

The correct terminology for the place where one seeks interim jobs, in the strictest sense, is a "temporary staffing service," or "temporary help company." The term "agency" is commonly used in many areas of the United States, including New York, where I work. I use *staffing service, agency, temporary help agency,* and *temporary help company* interchangeably in this book.

Temporaries working through agencies for one of their clients are on the agency payroll and are considered their employees, performing W-2 work as opposed to 1099 employment.

"Business colleague" is the appropriate term for the relationship between professional temporaries, who manage their temporary work as one of several businesses, and the temporary employment companies using their services. In these instances, agencies function in a manner closely akin to bookers; they "sell" a temporary's talent and expertise by the hour, taking a "commission" (a portion of the hourly rate charged to clients) for doing so. Unlike professional bookers, however, agencies do not actively market an individual temporary's services. Professional temporaries use several "booking" agencies, but the temporaries themselves are the managers of these multiple relationships.

General Tips for Finding Temporary Help Agencies

I have not included lists of temporary help companies in this book, because names and addresses change, and agencies go in and out of business, or merge with other companies. To find suitable agencies in your community, start by making a trip to the library. Libraries have directories, both of professional associations and of temporary help companies, that are updated yearly. In addition, many libraries have CD-ROM databases that list agencies by location and furnish comprehensive information about their business activities.

Read the classified ads in the daily newspapers, especially the weekend editions. Agencies advertise for the skills they need. Take a look at the specialty newspapers that market to a particular profession. If you live where there is one geared to performers, temporary help companies probably advertise heavily in it. Performers are great users of agencies for their "day jobs." Again, your local library is a good place to do this. Librarians can steer you to sources you may not know about.

Use your Internet browser to search under "temporary employment agencies" or in areas of specialization.

Check out the Web site for the Contract Employee's Handbook (http://www.cehandbook.com). It lists "full disclosure" agencies that will freely and openly disclose to you the *billing* rate for the assignment. In addition, it lists "pass through" agencies, those that charge a minimal fee to process the paperwork of client companies requiring the use of an agency or "employer of record."

The Yellow Pages lists agencies under "Employment Contractors: Temporary Help" and includes information about them through their advertisements.

Often, temporary employment companies congregate in one or two office buildings, conveniently located for many of the clients they serve. Finding out where the clusters are allows you to make more efficient use of your time when you register, and later on when you are delivering timesheets or picking up paychecks.

Professional membership organizations may be a good source for referrals to specialty agencies. Some organizations maintain employment hotlines and job banks. If you are unsure that your qualifications are adequate for a particular specialty, consider talking to one or two of these agencies and having them assess your skills. You will learn if there are gaps in knowledge or proficiency that you need to correct, and you may get a feel for what kind of work is available for you to go after as an independent contractor.

Finding a Staffing Service

1. Library: directories, CD-ROM databases
2. Newspapers: weekend editions
3. Specialty newspapers
4. Internet browser
5. Yellow Pages
6. Membership organizations
7. Agency clusters

Check out these annually updated directories:

National Trade and Professional Associations in the United States, Columbia Books.

Directory of Temporary Firms, Kennedy Publications.

Directory of Executive Temporary Placement Firms, Kennedy Publications.

Finding the Right Agency for a Specific Need

The most effective way to find agencies to serve your needs is to have a clear understanding of what your purpose is ahead of time. If your intent is to bring in extra money *and* (there should always be an *and*) expand your specialty knowledge base, you will want to explore opportunities with agencies supplying professionals in your field.

Suppose that you recently did a promotional mailing and now need to complete a number of follow-up calls to line up future projects, *and* have some money coming into the coffers while doing so. In this instance you might want to investigate working at an undemanding job that gives you a lot of downtime to get your own work done.

Table 3.1 **Determining Needs and Strategies**

Need	Strategy
Money now!!!	Register with general agencies. Seriously consider any job where you are overqualified. If you're a financial wizard, do financial grunt work as an entry-level analyst for a few days. Administrative assistants and secretaries are always in demand, and often these jobs allow for some flexibility to get your own work done.
A job with a particular company, or insider information about it.	Call the Human Resources Department of the company. Ask for the names of the agencies they use. Sign up at the agencies. Tell your counselor of your particular interest in working at the company.
Information about a particular industry.	Research which agencies serve the industry and register with a few of them. Tell their work coordinators you wish to work in the industry.
And so forth . . .	

Registration Planning

Registration with temporary help companies that specialize in management or executive positions often requires the same protocol you use to deal with executive search firms; that is, you may write to them and enclose your resume (which they may or may not acknowledge), but you should not call or drop by.

After reading over your material, if they are interested either in meeting you or speaking with you, they will call. But who knows which agency has which procedure? Call for information first before sending a letter.

Note: Neither overlook nor discount general agencies as a source of opportunity. They have long-term relationships with clients and can get a specialized rate for you.

For general agencies, use your normal resume; being "overqualified" helps more than it hinders. If you decide to redo your present resume, you might want to emphasize your administrative skills, add your knowledge of computers and software packages, if appropriate. Whether your goal is a permanent job, a career change to a new industry, or pitching your portfolio of skills to a number of sources, develop an all-purpose resume that highlights special skills and one or more specialty resumes. Do this in conjunction with putting together a portfolio of work. Check out *Portfolio Power* by Martin Kimeldorf (Peterson's, 1997). It's an excellent step-by-step guide that helps you to create professional portfolios on paper or electronically, and then shows how to use them to your best advantage. It has a comprehensive section for ex-military personnel.

Once you figure out how you want your resumes to look, here are four sure-fire ways to look like a pro when you register. These tips also expedite the registration process.

1. Compile a "personal data fact sheet" (Figure 3.1) of the answers to commonly asked questions, such as where you went to school, your military service record, and references. Frank Joerss designed the one included here. He said he was able to use it in lieu of filling out an application from about 85 percent of the time. At the very least, have the answers to these questions scribbled down for reference.

2. If you have worked as a temporary before and are expanding your agency base, take the time to prepare a list of the firms you have worked for, to whom you reported, and in what capacity. When the agency counselors interview you and ask what companies you have worked for, you can hand them a professional-looking information sheet, like the example shown in Figure 3.2.

3. Develop an effective portfolio of work samples for each of your marketable skills. Put together a few selections from your desktop publishing prowess, some elaborate charts, a market survey you conducted (delete any proprietary or confidential information), that can be shown to an interviewer, or left behind to showcase your talent. Choose examples that you can make interesting comments about, such as why it is important, what it represents, the challenges you overcame, and the skills you used.

Figure 3.1 **Personal Data Fact Sheet**

This fact sheet is being submitted along with my resume in lieu of any standard employment application required.

NAME:	Karolyn Devin
ADDRESS:	1188 Lemon Avenue, La Mesa, CA 94102
TELEPHONE:	(619) 948-5773
SOCIAL SECURITY:	503-80-6034

CITIZEN OF U.S.?	Yes	**EVER BEEN CONVICTED OF A CRIME**	No
UNDER AGE 18?	No	**MILITARY SERVICE?**	None

EDUCATION

NAME OF SCHOOL	ADDRESS	DEGREE	MAJOR STUDY
San Diego State University	San Diego, CA	B.A.	Elementary Education

COMPUTERS/SOFTWARE DOS and Windows Environment

Word Processing	**Spreadsheets**	**Databases**
WordPerfect	Lotus 1-2-3	R-Base
Microsoft Word	EXCEL	

EMPLOYMENT HISTORY (For responsibilities, please see resume.)

1. Shaw Children's Wear	From:	1997–present
121 Olive Terrace	Job title:	Administrator
Lemon Grove, CA	Reported to:	Edna Shaw
(619) 946-3507	Reason for leaving:	Graduated from college

REFERENCES

1. Dr. Connie Daglas, Faculty Adviser	(619) 867-5145
2. Dr. Gail Holden, Professor of Oceanography	(619) 667-0123

So Many Agencies, So Little Time . . .

Registering with multiple agencies is especially important in any economy. No one temporary help company will keep you busy at jobs you want to do, as often as you want to do them, even in the best of times. To register with one agency only limits your opportunities considerably. Also, you have all the problems of a single employer with few of the benefits. The example I use in my seminars is to consider each agency as an opportunity to meet and observe the work environment of thirty new and different clients. Think of how much you expand your horizons every time you add a new agency to your "stable." One agency equals thirty contacts, two agencies equal sixty, and three agencies give you ninety new ways to expand your knowledge base. You can increase your opportunity potential threefold with only a little more effort on your part.

Standard Registration Procedure

Don't underestimate the importance of your appearance in securing assignments. Look your most conservative and corporate anytime you are dealing with agencies. It will result in your being considered for the better jobs.

Figure 3.2 **Partial List of Temporary Assignments**
Executive/Administrative Assistant

Investment/Brokerage/Banking
PaineWebber
Goldman Sachs
Donaldson Lufkin & Jenrette
Merrill Lynch
American Express
Prudential Securities
Smith Barney
NYNEX Credit Corp. *(president)*
Morgan Stanley & Co.
Chemical
ABN Amro
Swiss Bank
Creditanstalt Bankverein

Insurance
MetLife
Marsh & McLennan
American Royal Re *(president)*
Prudential
Mutual of America
MONY
Manhattan Life *(head of marketing)*

Law Firms
Shearman & Sterling
Bachner Tally Polevoy & Misher
Simpson Thacher & Bartlett
Reid & Priest
Proskaur Rose

General
Deloitte & Touche *(head of HR)*
Sunbow Productions *(president)*
Commonwealth Fund
Jerrold Corp. *(regional VP, sales)*
New World Coffee *(president)*
Hill & Knowlton
Health Insurance Plan of Greater NY

Publishing
K-III Magazines *(president)*
K-III Communications *(head of HR)*
John Wiley & Sons *(president)*
PC Magazine (CFO)
Glamour Magazine
People Magazine
Quebecor Printers

To begin, select five agencies for registration—four to work with and one to practice on if you need it. If you plan it well, you can register with three in one day, so choose agencies that are located close to each other, if possible.

Take with you:

1. Several copies of your resume and personal data fact sheet.
2. *Two* acceptable forms of identification to show proof of citizenship for the I-9 form. For U.S. citizenship, agencies will accept *two* of the following: a driver's license, a social security card, a birth certificate, or a passport.
3. Your list of references, with addresses and telephone numbers. If another temporary referred you to an agency, have her/his name handy—and mention it. Better yet, ask the person to make an "introductory" telephone call on your behalf.
4. Your portfolio of work samples.

You don't necessarily need to schedule an appointment to register with agencies that staff for general office services. My preference is to skip the appointment and keep my schedule flexible. However, it is wise to inquire ahead of time what the hours are for interviewing or testing (some may do it only between the hours of 10:00 A.M. and 4:00 P.M.), and which day is payday. Paydays are hectic; temporaries employed by that agency will be coming in to pick up paychecks. Avoid registering on paydays unless you want to take a look at the other temporaries. Just observing the way they are dressed will give you an idea of the nature of their assignments and the kind of placements the agency makes.

The temporary help company's receptionist will hand you forms to complete. Many times it is the receptionist who will administer, or at least oversee, any tests that you take. Next comes the interview by a counselor (work or service coordinator is another name). Counselors are staff employees who assign temporaries to the job orders received by agencies. If you have no keyboard or computer skills, do what it takes to acquire them through an adult education course or a vocational school as soon as possible. Until then, even if you are not interested in secretarial or administrative work, the majority of coordinators at general agencies will still insist on a typing test. You will be more marketable if you take one. Light typing may be part of a research job or a customer service spot (labels, envelopes, short memo) that would pay a higher rate and may lead to other opportunities within a client company.

Most general agencies administer grammar, vocabulary, and spelling tests. Some give a simple arithmetic test. See the sample tests at the end of the chapter (Figures 3.4–3.9).

For those people with computer skills, almost all agencies will test you on at least one of the software packages you claim to know. More and more agencies are using "hands-on" tests. A popular series is "Quiz." Most agencies furnish reference templates as well.

Representative questions for windows, word-processing and spreadsheet tests are listed at the end of the chapter. If you can perform the functions listed on these tests, you will have no trouble passing any of them.

If you are a beginning computer user, or if you are taking a test on a software package that is somewhat new to you, you can purchase templates and reference products at software stores. These products pack easily and are portable for use during testing as well as on the job.

Word processors: Take a "fast longhand" test on the Dictaphone for increased marketability and more money. The objective is to be considered for as broad a range of jobs as possible. You can probably scribble the immortal rambling of the dinosaur who still dictates at thirty words per minute. (Transcribe immediately afterwards while your memory is fresh and you can decipher the scribbles.)

Practice If You Need To!

If interviewing and testing throw you into a panic, practice on an agency you don't care about, even if it means traveling to an adjacent town to do so. Subsequent interviews will only get better. The object of this exercise is to get some practice playing the interview game; anything else is frosting on the cake.

Questions to Ask Agencies When You Register

No one agency will be perfect for all of your needs, but several may complement each other and serve you well. You can get a good feel for which ones will be best by asking the right questions during the registration. The questions that follow will help newcomers to temporary employment iron out some of wrinkles of the adjustment period, but you will want to come up with a few that are specific to your interests. None of these questions is impertinent or out of line. If the interviewer is evasive or reluctant to answer, you might want to reconsider working for that particular staffing service.

1. What are the agency's business hours? Do they use an answering service after hours? . . . an answering machine? How frequently are their messages checked? Do they use call forwarding to an agency employee?
   This information is especially important when you must reach them in an emergency. Rare is the life without an occasional emergency; almost as rare is the emergency that occurs during normal business hours.

2. When must timesheets be in? What day of the week is payday? Is the check from a local bank? Are there convenient check-cashing arrangements? Are they open late on payday? Find out whether timesheets can be faxed, hours called in, paychecks delivered.
   If the agency closes daily at 5:30 P.M., without exception, what kind of arrangements will they make for you to get your paycheck if you don't finish working until 6:00 P.M.? If your assignment is located at some distance from the agency, will they let you call in your hours or fax the timesheet to them? When agencies have a large number of temps at one location, they will often deliver the paychecks.

3. What are some of the industries the agency serves? Who are some of their client companies?
   If you have an intense dislike of attorneys, and law firms make up 90 percent of their client base, this may not be the right agency for you.

4. What is the range of pay rates for different shifts? (first shift: 9:00 A.M. to 5:00 P.M., second shift: 5:30 P.M. to midnight, third shift: midnight to 8:00 A.M.). At what point does the staffing service give merit or seniority increases in hourly rates, In a month? A year? Never? What are their weekend and holiday rates?

Do they give you straight answers to these questions? Make notes on any information you get regarding their rates and the frequency of their increases.

5. Ask the counselor to explain the agency's overtime policy, late shift, and weekend differential rates.

A full explanation of overtime pay can be found in Chapter 4, page 61. The purpose of asking the question is to alert you to potential future problems so that you can either prevent them or deal with them at the time they occur. If you find the counselor gives you erroneous information here, this is neither the time nor place to get into an argument about it.

6. Does the agency have medical or dental benefits?

Most agencies have descriptive brochures about their plans. Don't be surprised to find so many restrictions that the benefits are virtually useless to you (i.e., no breaks in employment, or a required number of monthly hours).

7. Does the agency offer vacations? Training?

Vacations: The restrictions are similar to medical and dental benefits. *Cross training:* Having a place to learn and practice a new software package or swap information with another temp is invaluable. Some agencies will even pay a trainer to teach temps they feel are worth the investment. However, don't be manipulated into accepting a lower pay rate as a way of "showing gratitude" for the extra training.

8. Does the agency have referral bonuses?

Refer colleagues and get anywhere from $25 to $100 when they work fifty to one hundred hours for the agency.

9. Does the agency have a temp lounge or some place where you can stand by waiting for work? May you use their telephone when you stand by? (It is critical to stay in touch with your other agencies for potential opportunities.)

10. What is the agency's policy if you accept a permanent job from a client? Temporary staffing services are prohibited by law from charging a permanent placement fee. Instead, they are permitted "liquidated damages" equal to a percentage of the annual salary of the person placed. Another case of a rose by another name. Most agencies call it a "finder's fee." Usually the terms of their contract with you and clients are spelled out on the back of the timesheets. Everything is negotiable. Waiving finder's fees from a good client is not unusual.

11. Is the agency a member of the National Association of Temporary Staffing Services (NATSS) or a similar state association?
NATSS is a national trade association that furnishes legal, legislative, and regulatory information to its members. Its members subscribe to a code of ethics. While it implies a certain level of professionalism, it's no guarantee of a good service. If the agency is not a member of any association, you might inquire why.

12. Ask counselors interviewing you how long they have been with the agency and what they like best about working there.
As a whole, the industry has a lot of turnover. Answers to these questions will give you some idea of the counselor's depth (or dearth) of industry or agency knowledge.

Questions Agencies Will Ask You

Besides the usual interview questions about present skills and former employment, agencies may ask the questions listed below.

1. Why do you want to do temporary work? If you have never worked as a temporary before, the interviewer is going to ask you that at one point or another. Give some thought to your answer and make sure it serves you well. Agencies have no incentive to invest time or effort placing people who only want to work a short time. Job seekers looking for full-time work might consider stressing their willingness to investigate a variety of opportunities and their lack of urgency to make a final decision.

2. Do you have any scheduling restrictions? If you have the flexibility to work hours other than nine to five, such as evenings or weekends, it makes you more marketable. Don't tell the interviewer, "I can work from 10:00 A.M. until 2:30 P.M. weekdays. I must be home when my children get out of school." It is better to arrange for after-school care one or two days a week if needed and say you can work 9:00 A.M. to 5 P.M. on those days, whichever ones they are.

3. What type of work are you looking for? Is there any kind of work you won't do? Keep an open mind; it makes you more marketable. You really can't judge the work until you get on the job.

4. What hourly rate are you looking for? What is the lowest you will accept? Do your homework ahead of time. Research what your skills are worth in the marketplace, and what range of hourly rate you may be offered for them. I recommend that you consider accepting a lower rate on the first assignment (provided it is a short one) in order to establish yourself with the agency. If you haven't worked as a temporary before, think of it as a subsidized apprenticeship. You can always negotiate a higher rate once you are established with the service.

5. What form of transportation will you use? Don't share information about your elaborate arrangements to get to the train station or to borrow a car. Your mission here is to allay any fears a counselor may have about your arriving on time.

Timesheets

If you have always received an annual salary, keeping track of hours takes a little getting used to. Most agencies use some form of timesheet to keep an accounting of your hours for their payroll. It is often a $3'' \times 8.5''$ quadruplicate form that must be filled out by you and signed by your supervisor. There is a place for the date/day of week, time started, time finished, meal breaks, and total hours. The copies serve as receipts for you and the client. There is nothing complicated about it. Most agencies make the timesheet/payroll process easy for their temporaries by letting the temps call in or fax their hours on Friday and then dropping off a signed timesheet when they pick up their checks.

If you aren't treated well during registration, take heed. The agency is probably putting its best foot forward to interest you in working for them. This is the courtship stage. This is as good as it gets. While you can't judge an agency by its office decor—some are tacky at best—you certainly can judge by the behavior of its personnel. There is never a good enough reason to work for rude or patronizing people except, perhaps, briefly in an emergency situation.

Over the years I have had a few agencies proudly tell me (in my capacity both as an applicant and as a client) that they give morning wake-up calls to their temps. This tells *me* the agency employs people they don't trust enough to get themselves out of bed in the morning. Thanks, but no thanks.

Be Persistent

Most people new to temporary employment register with one or two agencies and then sit back and wait for the telephone to ring. A common complaint is, "I was never called for any work."

You must call and give the work coordinators your availability—daily—until you are working. (An exception to this would be if during the interview you and the counselor agreed on doing it another way.) Once you are working, call to let them know your work telephone number and when you will be available again. These are quick calls. For instance, on Monday morning:

"Hi, this is Frieda Lewin. I'm looking for work for today and the rest of the week. I can be reached at home, 633-8712."

If you don't get work, or you only get work for that one day, call again in the afternoon.

"Hi, this is Frieda Lewin again. I'm still looking for work for tomorrow and the rest of the week. Call me if you get something. My number is. . . ."

This is how you get started.

Discussing Potential Assignments: General Guidelines

Here are guidelines to keep in mind when you receive the first call to discuss an assignment.

1. Keep an open mind and try to accept most assignments. While the job description may not thrill you, it may also not be accurate. Ask specifically what kind of work the job entails, and for what percentage of the time. (The conversation might go something like this: "Updating spreadsheets? That sounds pretty much like data entry to me. Will I be doing this part of the day, all day? What else will I do? Do they want any charts or graphs?") If counselors do not have answers to your questions, they can call the client to find out. It is in everyone's best interests to place the right temporary in the job. Remember that each contact helps to build your image and reputation, whether you are working through an agency or on your own. Don't immediately reject an assignment that doesn't fit well into your plan. Your original concept, no matter how brilliant on paper, will almost certainly change once it is exposed to the test of the real world. So test opportunistically, and get paid while you hone your services accordingly.

2. Declining assignments. If you find after talking that the assignment is not worth a try, tell the counselor, "I don't think I'm the right person for this job, but thanks for thinking of me. Keep me in mind for something else." Counselors are well aware that neither jobs nor temporaries come in "one size fits all."

3. Settle the rate. Usually pay is not discussed until it is determined that you are able to do the job and want to do it. When you are first starting out, I advise you to take what is offered (unless the offer is ludicrous). You need to "prove yourself" to the agency. Once you have shown what you can do on an assignment, then negotiate a better rate.

4. Counteroffer. Suppose your usual rate is $30 but the counselor says, "I can pay $25 an hour for this spot." You can counteroffer with, "Why don't we meet halfway? Can you pay $27.50?" There is no reason that you should bear the entire rate cut, and you are offering to meet halfway. Ask what the billing rate is. Agencies are well aware that a low rate doesn't always buy value. Their reputation and continued business with the client depends on how often they send a person who performs well on the job. Often that means they will take a smaller percentage of the fee.

5. The client wants to interview you. If the assignment is a long-term one, I believe it is in your best interest to meet the people and to take a look at the work environment. You will get a better feel for whether or not to commit for a significant period of time. I do not interview for assignments shorter than one month. For longer projects, I will interview if the appointment is scheduled before or after business hours. I do not take tests for any assignment. Companies requiring interviews or testing for short assignments are duplicating the agency's work and wasting the temporary's time. If I wanted to engage in those unpaid activities, I would spend my time applying for permanent jobs. Your time is worth money; don't forget it.

Special needs: Physical limitations need to be mentioned. Someone with a broken foot and limited mobility would inquire about building access and stairs. Nonsmokers need to know if they will be in a smoke-free environment. Smokers may want to wait until they are on the job to ask about the company's policy on where they can smoke (at their desk, in a lounge, outside the building) in case the staffing service is not "smoker-friendly." I am told this can sometimes be a problem.

Design an easy form to record job information. It serves both as a reminder to get complete information and as a record of the assignment. The one I use (Figure 3.3) is easy to carry in a pocket or bag for quick reference.

Specific Questions to Ask Before Taking an Assignment

1. Verify the hourly rate and make a note of it.
2. What is the assignment length? What are the daily hours? Is overtime expected?
3. What is the company name and address (including floor)? What is the name of the person you report to?
4. How do you get there? Get the names of cross streets and public transportation information if needed. What about parking? Is it free? Will the client or company pay for it? Are there affordable and convenient places to park, if you must pay?

Knowledge Is Power

The media seem to focus primarily on the negative elements of temporary work and to portray all contingent workers as victims. Novices can be exploited, but knowledge is power. Temping well is a skill to be learned, just as testing well on exams is a skill good students learn. It is difficult to exploit enlightened people. To that end, here are a couple of laws you should know about.

The Fair Labor Standards Act: Minimum Wage and Overtime. This is a federal law. It states that employees paid hourly are entitled to the applicable minimum wage and to time and a half (premium pay) for every hour worked over forty in one week. This includes job-titles that would ordinarily be considered exempt on a full-time basis (accounting, technical training, etc.). In other words, employees who are paid an hourly wage must be paid overtime.

A common misconception among agency temporaries is that they must put in their forty hours at one client company to qualify for overtime. That is not the case. Under state law they are considered employees of the temporary help company. *Temporaries qualify for overtime as long as they work for one agency over forty hours, even if they work for a different client every day of the week.* Because the temporary help company is considered the employer, it has an obligation to inform its client that the temporary in question will be billed out at a higher rate after forty hours. *Even if the agency is unwilling to charge its client the higher rate, it is still legally obligated to pay time and a half to the temporary.*

Figure 3.3

Assignment Form

Company _____

Address _____   Floor _____

Ask For _____

Agency _____   Rate _____

How Long _____   Hours _____

Software _____

Duties _____

Directions _____

Tax Reform Act of 1986: Pension and Health Benefits. If temps perform "substantial services" (1,500 hours a year) to a company and make up more than 5 percent of its total "lower-paid" work force, the company may have to provide the same health and pension benefits to them as it does for its permanent employees, or pay taxes on their plan contributions. The total of 1,500 hours is between eight and nine months (using 40 hours of work per week). The law applies to temporary staffing services and their clients. There is more information on this in Appendix C.

Assessing the Company for Future Projects

Before going on any assignment, think of ways it might benefit you and what you can learn there—in other words, how can you increase the scope of your knowledge or expertise? Look for opportunities to develop new skills. Will any of this enhance your ability to secure another assignment? Sharpen your observation skills by watching the interaction of employees with one another and consider what that tells you about the company.

Observations on the Job

1. How do the people relate to each other? Do they work alone or in groups? Is there an air of frenzy and confusion? Are employees relaxed and casual? Stiff and formal? Quiet and fearful? Are they pulled out of the bathroom to take calls from honchos?

2. Are there minorities and women in upper management? Their numbers and placement tell you about the salary structure and advancement opportunities in the company. What type of employee is most valued? MBAs? College grads? Up-through-the-ranks? Docile? Feisty? Is there a lot of turnover? Does the company have mostly new, temporary employees in support and administrative positions? If so, why?

3. What are some of their success stories? What does that tell you about the company's definition of success? What are some of their war stories? "Funny" stories? In one company I worked for, the management personnel thought it was funny to fly a job candidate in for an interview, have the key people be too busy to see him or her, fly the candidate out again, and then reschedule another trip. Not my kind of company, how about you?

Research on the Job

1. Is the company publicly owned? Privately owned? Large conglomerate? What is its relationship to the parent company? What are the company's major products and services? Who are their customers?

2. What has been the growth pattern over the past decade? How may employees have been laid off? How is the morale of the remaining core employees? Does the company have a recent history of downsizing? Locally, nationally, internationally? Is there an overall or selective hiring freeze? Have the hiring freezes been sporadic? Has the company ever stated that the organizational changes were complete and then carried out others that closed locations or facilities? Are there recent unexplained top management departures?

3. What's the stock price doing? What kind of comments does the company get in the financial, trade, and local presses? Has the organization lost market share in any of its key products or services in the last two years?

4. Have there been recent cutbacks in executive training and development?

5. Does the organization have a reputation for secrecy concerning future plans?

Future Considerations

Anytime you can broaden your array of skills, it increases the value of your skills portfolio. As Anne Miller says, "There's no such thing as bad knowledge." Anne is a successful presentation and sales skills training professional who used to joke about being "the Career Change Queen." She used permanent jobs to gain the knowledge and credentials she needed to eventually go into business for herself.

Anne started out as a high school English teacher. After a few years, she decided to leave teaching for publishing (an M.A. in English, honors grad, perfect fit, right?). Wrong. When she couldn't find a job in publishing, she took an interim secretarial job at Smith Barney. She hated it, but she learned about the securities business. Within a year, she parlayed that knowledge into a better spot, assisting a trader on a trading desk. She hated that job too, but was able to learn about selling and trading on the New York Stock Exchange. She took this knowledge of "buyers and sellers" to land a job at *Institutional Investor* magazine, this time as an ad director, selling ad space. A family tragedy, the sudden death of her father, made her confront not only her own mortality but what she was doing with her life. From that point forward, Anne began to take her career seriously. During her attendance at a sales training seminar, she suddenly realized she could "do it better." That led to another job change: selling training packages for a sales training company. One year later she left to set up the New York branch of a presentation skills company. She ran that company for three years before leaving to go into her own business: teaching presentation and sales skills training seminars. That was sixteen years ago.

Anne collected her knowledge and used it to her advantage intuitively. There is no reason you can't follow in her footsteps—with a little planning.

Assignment Selection: Questions to Ask Yourself

1. Are there related fields worth gaining experience in that would enhance your present career?
2. Are there companies or industries where you could pick up useful information, helpful contacts, or applicable skills?
3. What kinds of temporary jobs can you secure to start collecting the information, skills, and contacts?

This is your reminder to assess every project or assignment according to three criteria:

1. Does it broaden or deepen your skills and/or experience?

2. Does it have the potential for you to develop new skills?

3. Will it increase your ability to secure another project?

Be on the lookout for opportunities. Watch for ways to create your own jobs.

Sample Tests

Figure 3.4 **Spelling Test**

Please circle the correct spelling.

1. article	artical	articale	artacle
2. necesary	necessary	necessery	neccesary
3. acomodate	accomodate	accommodate	acommodate
4. knowlige	knowledge	knowlage	knowlege
5. emphasise	emphasize	emphesize	emphesise
6. injustice	injustise	enjustice	injustece
7. privilage	privelige	privilege	priviledge
8. momentum	mommentum	momuntem	momentim
9. proceedure	proccedure	proceidure	procedure
10. observence	observance	observanse	obsiervance
11. persestint	persistent	pirsistent	persistant
12. realezation	releazation	realization	reliazation
13. violently	vialently	violantly	violentely

Answers:

1. article	6. injustice	11. persistent
2. necessary	7. privilege	12. realization
3. accommodate	8. momentum	13. violently
4. knowledge	9. procedure	
5. emphasize	10. observance	

Figure 3.5 **Math Skills Test**

Time: 15 minutes

Add:

2	¾	3,6078.34	35 + 18 + 54 + 87 =
12	½	8,7089.01	
7	⅜	901.56	43.2 + 76.32 + 2.1 =
14	¼	2,3234.01	

Subtract:

70,695	435.40	12,897.43	665.21
10,243	23.43	6,909.54	458.98

Multiply:

34567	5467.87	3 x 4 x 12 =	¾ x ⅔ =
12	.23	½ x 14 =	

3 cases of bolts @ $2.95 per case =

80 acres of land @ $1,908 per acre =

Divide:

432)8796   6.0)761.54

Percentage:

15 is what percent of 75?

What percent of 200 is 10?

What is 40% of 400?

What is 8% of 8,000?

Answers

Add:

2	¾	3,6078.34	35 + 18 + 54 + 87 = 194
12	½	8,7089.01	
7	⅜	901.56	43.2 + 76.32 + 2.1 = 121.62
14	¼	2,3234.01	
35	1 ⅞	124,068.91	

Subtract:

70,695	435.40	12,897.43	665.21
10,243	23.43	6,909.54	458.98
60,452	19.97	5,987.89	206.23

Multiply:

34,567	5,467.87	3 x 4 x 12 = 144	¾ x ⅔ = ½
12	.23	½ x 14 = 7	
414,804	1,257.6101		

3 cases of bolts @ $2.95 per case = $8.85

80 acres of land @ $1,908 per acre = $152,640

Divide:

          20.361111   126.92333

432)8796   6.0)761.54

Percentage:

15 is what percent of 75?	20%
What percent of 200 is 10?	5%
What is 40% of 400?	160
What is 8% of 8,000?	640

Figure 3.6 **Word-Processing Test**

If you can perform the following functions, you will pass most word-processing tests with flying colors.

1. From the subdirectory prompt, enter the command to load the program.
2. Retrieve a document.
3. Change the left/right and top/bottom margins.
4. Change the line spacing to double space.
5. Center the date.
6. Insert two words in a sentence.
7. Delete four words.
8. Cut and move a paragraph to another location.
9. Copy and place another paragraph in a different location.
10. Save and exit the document without exiting the program.
11. Use the print menu to print two copies.
12. Indent a paragraph.
13. Enter underlined text, underlining as you type.
14. Enter boldfaced text, bolding as you type.
15. Insert a hard page break.
16. Use "GOTO."
17. Use subscript.
18. Call up the "Help" screen.
19. Search and replace a word.
20. Merge two fields.
21. In a 70-column screen, clear all tabs; then establish new left-aligned tabs at 1.5", 3.5", 5.5", and 7.5."
22. Use decimal tabs to line up the following: 123.12
                                                 1234.12
                                                 12345.12
23. Create a new document.
24. Exit word processing without saving document.

Figure 3.7 **Spreadsheet Test**

If you can perform the following functions, you will pass most spreadsheet tests without much trouble.

1. Call up the program.
2. Retrieve and/or create spreadsheet.
3. Label a specific cell location.
4. Place a value in a specific cell location.
5. Center-align the label to a column using a command.
6. Insert a row.
7. Delete a column.
8. Move a range of data to another location.
9. Copy a range of data to another location.
10. Use "GOTO."
11. Using the edit command function, change center-aligned label and data.
12. Name a range.
13. Change the cell width of a column.
14. Format to show commas, but no decimal places.
15. Insert a page break.
16. Call up the "Help" screen for data commands.
17. Using the appropriate function, display the sum of a column in a specific location.
18. Save a file.
19. Print.
20. Create and view a bar chart showing Temporary Sales for the last two years of data. Show years on X-axis.
21. Display average sales for 1994 figures in one column.
22. Sort in ascending order using designated column as primary key.
23. Exit.

Figure 3.8 **Windows Test**

Basic Tasks

1. Start Windows from DOS
2. Maximize Window
3. Resize Window
4. Move Window using scroll bar
5. Open Group Window
6. Start Application
7. Exit Windows
8. Access Help Contents
9. Select Help Topic
10. Access Help Search Feature
11. Use Help Search Feature
12. Display Help Definition
13. Access Help History Feature

Intermediate Tasks

14. Arrange Windows
15. Move Application
16. Switch to Window
17. Start Print Manager
18. Delete Print Job
19. Print Document

20. Start File Manager
21. Create Directory
22. Display Files
23. Copy Files
24. Change Drives
25. Select Files
26. Delete Files

Advanced Tasks

27. Start Control Panel
28. Start Printers Application
29. Install Printer
30. Change Port
31. Set Default Printer
32. Minimize Application
33. GOTO DOS Shell
34. Quit DOS Shell
35. Display Task List
36. Switch to Applications
37. Create Group Window
38. Change Group Properties
39. Install Application

Figure 3.9 **Windows Word-Processing Test**

Basic Tasks
1. Start Program from DOS
2. Open, Print, Save Document
3. Exit Program
4. Display Ruler
5. Reveal Codes
6. Use GOTO
7. Select, Cut, Paste Text
8. Copy Text
9. View Multiple Documents
10. Activate Document Window
11. Maximize Document Window
12. Move Between Documents

Intermediate Tasks
13. List Files
14. Retrieve File
15. Print Page Range
16. Access Help Index
17. Access Context Sensitive Help
18. Access Font Dialog Box
19. Change Font
20. Bold Text
21. Center Text
22. Redline Text

23. Undo Formatting
24. Change Margins
25. Indent Multiple Paragraphs
26. Justify Text
27. Indent Single Paragraph
28. Change Line Spacing
29. Insert Page break
30. Clear All Tabs
31. Set Decimal Tab
32. Move Tab
33. Access Speller
34. Skip Proper Name
35. Replace Misspelled Word
36. Automatic Replace

Advanced Tasks
37. Create Style
38. Apply Style
39. Edit Style
40. Create Table
41. Add Row
42. Change Border
43. Insert Graphic
44. Move Graphic
45. Edit Graphic

4 *Time Is Money*

*T*ime is money, and the number of hours available in a year to earn money is finite. Your time is more precious than money, for you can't "buy" more of it. As a self-employed professional, you sell your knowledge, experience, and talent as a package that produces results for agencies and clients. When you sell results by the hour, the value of your time takes on new meaning.

Five factors directly affect the time you have to produce income as well as the amount of income you receive for your efforts. The first is your management of time. Organize yourself to free up as much time as possible for billable hours and for working on your business. The second is knowing how to compute rates for your services that will engender a profit. A third area is the ability to assess your business services for profitability. While you might enjoy adding a new service to your mix, you must be able to compute its profit potential in advance so that you don't spend a lot of precious time finding out it delivers minuscule money for heroic efforts. The fourth is prudently managing money by minimizing the cost of handling it and maximizing the income it generates while in your possession. The last is collecting your client fees in a timely manner.

Factors Affecting Time and Income

1. Time management
2. Realistic and profitable fee computation
3. Assessment for profit potential
4. Prudent money management
5. Timely fee collection

This is the "formula" chapter. It includes a variety of ways to look at expenses, along with several methods to calculate realistic rates for your services. I have included computations that work for projects, agency assignments, and individual consulting efforts. There are tips to help you get a handle on your fixed expenses. Once you do your homework, you can focus on getting paid what you are worth for what you know.

Time

How many hours can a self-employed person work in a year? How much time can skillful time management shake loose for you to earn money? How many angels can dance on the head of a pin? It depends on your viewpoint.

If you start with 40 hours per week times 52 weeks, you get 2,080 available hours (40 hours × 52 weeks = 2,080). You also get no vacation, no holidays, and no sick time. So, from those 2,080 hours deduct 4 weeks vacation and 3 weeks administrative work (7 weeks, or 280 hours). Now your earning base is 1,800 hours (45 weeks). If you are new to this, drumming up business (outside of agency work) will take at least 35 percent of your time (probably more, but we'll use this number). The earning base of billable hours shrinks to 29.25 weeks, or only 1,170 hours each year. That's how many angels will dance on the head of your particular pin, and the number I will use for the formulas that follow.

Rates

Here is a way to figure out the hourly rate for a particular annual salary. For this exercise I am using $50,000 per year for one person with part-time secretary (1/4 time).

1. 40 hours per week × 52 weeks = 2,080 available hours
   $50K divided by 2,080 hours = $24.03 per hour

2. Deduct from that 4 weeks vacation and 3 weeks administrative work (7 weeks, or 280 hours). Now your earning base is 1,800 hours (45 weeks).
   $50K divided by 1800 hours = $27.78 per hour

3. Drumming up business 35 percent of your time reduces the earning base of billable hours to 29.25 weeks, or 1,170 hours.
   $50K divided by 1,170 hours = $42.74 per hour

4. Benefits (pension, insurance) are about 30 percent of your salary, which means you must now earn $65,000 (30 percent of 50K = $15K. $15K + $50K = $65,000)
$65K divided by 1,170 hours = $55.55 per hour.

5. Office expenses (equipment, supplies, rent—at least $100 monthly, even if you work out of your home, $200 secretarial help) estimated at $400 per month, or $4,800. Add to the $65,000.
$69,800 divided by 1,170 hours = $59.66 per hour

6. Profit: 15 percent before taxes brings total to $74,750 or $63.88 per hour
Round it off to $65.00 per hour.

The last component of the formula above, "profit," brings me to my next point. There is an important element to your rate known as the profit margin. It must be figured into all of your services. Wages and profit are two different critters. You cannot determine a profitable hourly rate solely by including overhead and expenses.

Suppose you were offered $500 to give the keynote address at a business function. Your "wages" are $250 per hour for the two hours of the event. Sounds good, doesn't it? Take a closer look. Let's say the function takes place in another city, and you spend many hours preparing the speech. You must travel to and from the event in addition to the time spent there. When you total up the hours, you find you have easily used four days of billable time. So, instead of $250 per hour, you have been paid roughly $15.50 per hour ($500/4 = $125 per day. $125/8 hours per day = $15.62 per hour), on which you will pay the full 15 percent Social Security tax as well as state and federal taxes. You have earned money, but definitely not made a profit. Unless you figure profit into your pricing, you won't make one.

Profit Margin Formula

Use this formula to add a profit margin to your hourly rate. Let's say your rate is $50 per hour. Consider that your "wholesale" rate. If you want a 10 percent profit on your rate of $50 per hour, multiply the $50 by 10 percent. It equals $5, which you then add to the $50 to make it a $55 "adjusted wholesale" rate per hour. A 20 percent profit would be 20 percent × $50 = $10 + $50 = $60 adjusted wholesale rate.

Suppose you sell 200 hours of consulting. If you adjust for a 10 percent profit, you will bill at $55 per hour, or $5 more than the $50. That $5 multiplied by 200 hours equals a $1,000 profit for yourself. A 20 percent margin is $10 multiplied by the 200 hours, or a $2,000 profit. A difference of $5 won't matter much to a client, but in this instance it doubles your profit.

Here is another way to look at it. If you work on a 10 percent margin, you will have to sell $1,000 worth of consulting to offset a $100 loss. If you work on a 20 percent margin, you need sell only half the amount, just $500.

Try several profit margins on for size.

Temporary Agency Rates

Suppose an agency offers you a two-month project at $25 per hour? How should you look at the rate? Lay it out as a balance sheet with the pluses and minuses. The agency pays 50 percent of the Social Security tax (7.5 percent) and contributes to state unemployment, disability, and workers' compensation funds as dictated by the laws of your state. Will there be any perks on the assignment that will save you time and money, such as free lunches, medical coverage, a convenient location, or a minimal commute? For example, if the commute is one hour each way, automatically you would want to negotiate a higher rate. A two-hour-per-day commute takes ten hours of your time each week, approximately eighty hours in the two-month period. That is a sizeable chunk of time.

Figuring Overtime and Base Rates for Agency Work

If you work over forty hours in one week for the same agency, you are entitled to time and a half. Let's say you worked at several rates of pay over the week. How do you find the base rate to use for the time and a half? You take an average of the rates. For example, suppose you worked a 46-hour week that breaks down as follows:

18 hours at $15 per hour

12 hours at $19 per hour

6 hours at $18 per hour

10 hours at $20 per hour

1. Add the rates. ($15+$19+$18+$20=$72)

2. Divide the sum ($72) by the number of rates (4). ($72/4=$18)

3. $18 is the base rate to be multiplied by 1.5. ($18 \times 1.5 = $27)

4. The six hours of overtime will be paid at $27 per hour.

Determining Overhead or Fixed Costs

Your career business and your related ventures are your "business." Every cost incurred for and in your business must be charged to it. Even if you are a sole proprietor, think of your personal salary as a cost, chargeable to the business, and not part of your profit. You must price your services to show a profit. Anything you supply in kind—home office, car, computer—must be evaluated and prorated, then charged against the business as appropriate. All costs must be recovered by the business.

Your overhead includes all the business operating costs that are not directly related to the production of a specific product or service. Generally, these are the fixed monthly expenses such as rent and utilities. If you have engaged in your own business ventures along with agency assignments for six months or so, begin looking at the costs involved by determining a total hourly expense cost. If you are just starting your business ventures, you will have to estimate your anticipated gross sales. Estimate 8 to 10 percent of that number for your fixed costs.

For the moment, let's project that your overhead will be $5,000 annually or $4.27 per hour ($5,000 divided by 1,170 hours per year equals $4.27). If you are making products, and you can make two of them in one hour, then you would add $2.14 to the price of each one. If you are offering a service or working through agencies, add *at least* $4 to your hourly rate.

Before you can do financial projections and budgets, you will need to track your expenses for a month and do the math to get an hourly rate. Use the business and personal expense charts shown in Figure 4.1 and Figure 4.2 as guides. Add and delete categories to reflect your own situation. Take a stab at estimating to see how close to (or far from) the target you are.

Figure 4.1 Business Expense Checklist

	Estimated	Actual	Yearly
Advertising	_____	_____	_____
Answering service (machine/prorated)	_____	_____	_____
Auto and insurance	_____	_____	_____
Books, reference material	_____	_____	_____
Entertainment, promotion	_____	_____	_____
Equipment payment (or saving for future purchase)	_____	_____	_____
Insurance costs (projected, prorated)	_____	_____	_____
Legal services (projected, prorated)	_____	_____	_____
License renewal	_____	_____	_____
Loan payment	_____	_____	_____

	Estimated	Actual	Yearly
Marketing			
Miscellaneous			
Office (rent or % home)			
Printing, supplies (not paid by clients)			
Professional development			
Retirement contribution			
Salary (must cover personal expenses)			
Savings			
Subscriptions			
Tax return preparation			
Taxes (FICA, pension)			
Telephone			
Travel (local, out of town)			
Typing, secretarial services			
Utilities (% in home)			

Figure 4.2 **Monthly Personal Expense Detail**

	Estimated	Actual	Yearly
Auto and insurance			
Charity, donations			
Chump change			
Clothing			
Dental			
Disability insurance			
Electricity			
Entertainment/cable			
Food			
Haircuts, cleaners			
Investments			
Medical and medication			
Medical insurance			
Newspapers, magazines			
Rent/mortgage			
Rental/homeowner's insurance			
Telephone			

Here is another way to look at overhead rates. A 50 percent overhead rate means that you add 50 cents to every dollar of direct labor to recover your total. If you pay out wages of $40 per hour to yourself or to another subcontractor, you must rate the work as *costing you $60* ($.50 × $40 = $20; $40 + $20 = $60). To that $60, you will figure a profit margin of 15 percent or $9 ($60 × 15 percent = $9). Your billing rate is thus $70 per hour ($60 + $9 = $69).

A different way to get some rough figures on your spending is to track your daily expenses for a week and then project them over a year. Once you get a figure for the year, divide again by the number of working days per year for a daily average. Be sure to include that $1 to $2 a day vending machine "expense" multiplied by 5 days per week ($5.00 to $10.00) times 50 weeks per year (allowing 2 weeks of vacation) adds up to $250 to $500 per year.

Three factors weigh heavily in your successful competition in the marketplace: tightly-controlled business costs; continuous and aggressive marketing, a focus on profit-potential activities that bring in revenue. In my case, I had to stop teaching for many community adult education programs because they cannot pay enough for me to recover my costs, much less make a profit. It takes as much of my time and effort to prepare for and teach a seminar where I don't make money as one from where I do.

Break-Even Point

The break-even point is the point at which your annual income from the sales of your services covers your fixed costs. Anything above that number is profit. If you set up spreadsheets to track income and expenses for each of your ventures and keep them current, you can keep tabs throughout the year on what you can afford and what you cannot. Suppose you have decided to charge $30 per hour for your services. Further suppose your yearly costs are $12,000. That would be $10.25 of every consulting hour going to fixed costs ($12,000 divided by 1,170 hours = $10.25). You must sell 400 hours of your services, a little more than one-third of your available time, just to break even ($30 × 400 hours = $12,000). The most you will clear is $23,000 ($35,100 − 12,000 = $23,100). The $30 rate is too low for this overhead figure.

Pricing Psychology

When times are slow, many people consider reducing the price of their services or taking agency assignments at a lower rate.

Don't fall into that trap. First of all, if you reduce your hourly fee by 15 percent, you will have to increase your sales by 15 percent just to offset your loss. If times are slow, it will not be easy to increase sales.

Consider instead *raising your prices*. Yes, you may lose a few clients, but you will attract a very different clientele at the higher price. You may find out that your services are worth considerably more than you thought. Barbara Brabeck tells a story in *Homemade Money* of how she once doubled her price just to keep from saying no to a client. However, instead of declining as expected, the client agreed to the higher price without blinking an eye. Anytime you don't want a job, you might try that maneuver just to see what happens.

Do the same thing with your agency work. Sign up at one or two new temporary staffing services and give your hourly rate a healthy increase. I learned the hard way that taking lower rates in slow times got me offers of lower rates in better times, and with some agencies, I had to renegotiate rates with each job offer. Which brings me to the next point: your image. Never sell your services for less than they are worth. Pricing your services too low, or reducing them immediately if a client questions your rate, is a sure way to lose respect for your services. If you must take a lower price, negotiate a corresponding reduction in what you guarantee to deliver.

Again, this applies to agency rates as well. Don't accept a low rate for highly skilled work. In one situation where I was offered a lower rate, the client wanted proficiency in three software packages. The agency would not come up on the price. I finally said I would be happy to work in one package only for the offered rate. If that wasn't agreeable, they should please find someone else. I got my rate.

Rate Components

There are several components to pricing your services. The first is cost, or what it actually costs you to provide the service (without profit margin). Four other factors also figure into your fee structure:

1. The general cost of living and economic situation in your area.

2. The kind of fees your technical or professional field commands.

3. Your personal qualifications (degrees, professional achievements, fame).

4. What the competition is charging.

In 1996, the *Wall Street Journal* quoted human resources experts who estimated that it typically costs $50,000 for a company to recruit and train one managerial or technical worker, *before* the new worker does any substantial work. Anytime that same work can be done as an interim project or by a temporary employee, it means a big savings to the company, with no "permanent" employee headaches afterward. Employers save anywhere from 20 to 40 percent in payroll costs and employee benefits by using independent contractors. Your hourly rate should take this into consideration.

Try to find out what your service or a similar service is *worth* to clients. Don't overlook what your clients *expect* to pay.

Why are you *worth* your fee? Think it through, believe it, project your belief in it. You may find it necessary to educate the prospective client or temporary help company about why you are worth the price you quoted, and of course you should be prepared to do so. Your *price* is the cost of your service, but the *value* of it is the *worth*.

Charge by the Day. For some jobs it might make more sense to charge by the day. Perhaps the client prefers a daily rate, so it behooves you to have one. If you quote $500 a day, it works out to $62.50 per hour for an eight-hour day. At this time (1998), $500 per day is considered a *modest* consulting fee. The range is $500 to $750.

Cash Flow Formula. Here is another quick, rough, rule-of-thumb formula. You must have enough cash on hand to "buy" your receivables twice. Estimate your receivables (fees owed to you) and double the figure; then set aside cash equaling that amount. Nothing will put you out of business faster than a negative cash flow.

Rough Hourly Rate Formula. Figure out the hourly rate for a full-time, salaried employee doing the same work you will be doing. Multiply the rate by 1.5 (really low), 2.5, 2.8, or 3 to get your hourly rate as a temporary worker. Remember, temporary workers do not receive the untaxed benefits of permanent employees, such as longevity, accrued vacation, sick time or severance pay. However, use these multipliers as a way to get a quick idea. You can then refine the numbers to suit your needs, taking into consideration such factors as prevailing wages in your area.

Stalling on a Price Quote

Almost all clients want a quote for the entire project. No one with budget responsibility will be crazy enough to let you run the meter and just pay you for whatever hours you rack up on a project. If you cost out the job properly, you will find it easier to explain your pricing in negotiations. Take market research, for instance: Clients must often be told how many telephone calls it takes to produce one complete survey. You must describe how you work in a matter-of-fact manner—what you are up against and what is involved—or the client may think that you are overcharging.

Occasionally, the client will want a rough, ballpark figure before you have had a chance to do your homework. Here are a few sample answers that will help you hem and haw without seeming to.

"It would be unfair to guess at this point. I need to discuss it more with you."

"I can give you a rough estimate, but it will be on the high side. I need to get some more information."

"There are several options possible, and we need to discuss these before I can give you a sensible estimate."

If a client demands your daily rate immediately, before discussing his or her needs or your credentials, you are wasting your time. Such clients are impossible to deal with on a job, and they always want you to reduce your rates to less than break-even.

Estimating Hours for Long-Term Assignments

Long-term assignments normally do not have logical endings. In nearly all cases, these engagements result in substantially more work and in more diversified areas than originally foreseen, making an estimate of hours impractical. As an alternative, consider guaranteeing a fixed number of days per week or month if you are doing this as an independent contractor. Quote a maximum time limit for ending the job, or for renegotiating its scope and price. For instance, you might want to work for the client three days per week for two months. You will need to agree on the number of hours you will be on the premises if you quote a daily rate. Also, set a payment schedule—weekly, or the first and fifteenth of the month, for example. Do not quote a "not to exceed" price or a minimum-maximum dollar amount. The client may want more days, and you could take a substantial loss.

Tips for Managing Flexible Income

As pointed out earlier, with flexible income comes a responsibility to manage it prudently. That includes tracking and soliciting payment for the billable time you sell. Another aspect of it is "aging" your accounts, that is, paying on time but as late as you can, while collecting as promptly as you can from those who owe you money.

Are you minimizing the cost of handling money and maximizing the income it generates while in your possession? To minimize costs, keep tight control over bank fees, interest payments, late charges, and penalties. To maximize income, investigate sweep accounts that move noninterest-bearing deposits into money market accounts that earn income.

Put at least one savings habit on automatic pilot. If you work for agencies, have money deducted from each paycheck for a savings account. Another idea is to open an account at an out-of-town credit union and save a small amount from each paycheck. (Out of sight, out of mind—and you are less likely to withdraw funds frivolously.)

Establish a simple system for keeping informed on the financial status of your business on a regular basis. Daily, you should have at your fingertips the amounts of cash on hand, a bank balance, summary of sales and cash receipts, money paid out by cash or check, and the correction of any errors from previous reports. Weekly, you should be able to review a listing of which accounts need a call because they are overdue, a listing of what you owe to whom, and information on whether there is an early payment discount.

Take a long hard look at your investments. Find out exactly what you are paying in fees and commissions, how your investments are allocated, and what distinguishes one mutual fund in your portfolio from another. If you have two or more that seem to have the same approach, thin them out.

Centralize and automate your bill paying. Consider using software that allows you to write checks and offers financial management options as well. Assign one box for bills and related correspondence. Supply it with envelopes, stamps, address labels, pens, a calculator, a stapler, and paper clips. Whenever you get a bill, dump it in the box. Weekly, or at least twice monthly, pay the bills. That way you will never lose a bill.

Pay off any holiday spending quickly. Transfer all balances to the credit card that has the lowest rate and pay it off in big chunks, that is, if transfer fees (bank fees for transferring funds) are negligible or nonexistent. Check the rates on all of your cards. Renegotiate lower ones where you can.

If you haven't already done so, take the time to figure your net worth (your assets less your liabilities).

Keep your expenses in line. Consider using a higher deductible for automobile or medical insurance policies. Higher deductibles are not always a good deal, so do the math calculations before you decide to make changes. Another area to look into is a lower-cost telephone service. (For further information, check the Appendix A under *Telephones.*)

Learn how to develop and use your net working capital rather than borrow from the bank.

Timely Fee Collection

The agreement between you and a customer does not have to be written in complex legal terms, witnessed, or notarized. An exchange of letters or faxes that include your payment policy, other ground rules, and that confirm the transaction is often all that's needed. A letter agreement is less intimidating than a more formal document, but it is just as valid legally. Do become familiar with this method of doing business. Remember *The Economist*'s prediction, "By the year 2005 fully 90 percent of all jobs in the U.S. will be contractual in nature." That is less than seven years from now.

Credit Policy

One of the biggest problems with small businesses and credit policies is their *lack* of any policy. Too often, in the exhilaration of closing a sale or beginning a project, the amount is agreed upon, but the terms are left hazy. A typical credit policy will cover how much credit you'll extend and under what circumstances. Clients who do not pay you for ninety days are using your money without interest to finance their business or personal projects.

Steps to Take Before Beginning Work for a Client

1. Communicate your credit policy as it pertains to the work you will do for the client.
2. Get one of the following: a signed contract, a letter agreement, an order form, or a purchase order.
3. Get a deposit, if possible.

Design a simple form that states your policy (see Figure 4.3). Get the client's address, telephone number, Social Security number, driver's license number, bank name and branch, and employer's name and address (if applicable). Before doing business with a partnership, collect the same specifics on all partners, since, in most cases, each is fully responsible for the liabilities of the enterprise. Have your form state your payment policy and other ground rules. The front-end work you put into your accounts receivable system is every bit as important as the tail-end (actually collecting the bills), and that means collecting information about each potential client. You can use a duly signed credit application or agreement as proof to banks and suppliers that you have been given permission to do a credit check. Ask for references that would be considered a discretionary expense by some (doctors, department stores), unlike a supplier who could cut off goods necessary to conduct business if not paid on time. In general, customers will always give their best three references. Another example of discretionary expense is a service that would not be terminated immediately, such as a utility. Is the client frequently thirty to sixty days in arrears with the telephone or electric company?

The first time you receive a check from a client, photocopy it for the bank information. Add it to the client's file.

Ask yourself the following questions before you write your policy:

1. Will you require deposits in advance? How much work will you complete before payment must be made? How do you want to be paid? Personal checks? Credit cards?

2. To what extent do you guarantee satisfaction?

3. If the client wishes to terminate the amount of agreed-upon services, how much notice will you require? Will you charge penalties? How much?

4. What are your credit terms, including due dates, early payment discounts, and late-payment penalties? Under what circumstances will you expect advance payment? These terms will be stated clearly on your purchase orders, delivery receipts, invoices, and spelled out in your contracts.

If you give discounts for payment in less than thirty days, you are generously paying your client to take a no-interest loan. On a $100 invoice, a 2 percent discount allows the client to use $98 of your funds, and *you* pay the client a $2 reward for doing so. On the other hand, quick payment helps your cash flow and means less billing paperwork. Which is the greater benefit to you?

Check References

Calling to check references is simple. For bank references, give your name and your company name. Say that you want to check a credit rating on a customer. Ask how long the account has been open, the average balance, and

Figure 4.3 **Sample Credit Application**

Date:_____

Business Information	Business Type
Name:	Proprietorship:
Legal (if different):	Partnership:
Address:	Parent Company:
City: State: Zip:	Corporation:
No. of employees: In business since:	Division:

Company Principals Responsible for Business Transactions

Name	Title	Address

Bank References

Bank:	Contact:
Branch:	Address:
Account #:	Telephone:

Trade References

Company	Contact	Telephone	Account Open Since

Confirmation of Information Accuracy and Release of Authority to Verify

I hereby verify that the above information is correct. The information included in this credit application is for use by YOUR FIRM NAME to determine the amount and conditions of credit to be extended. I understand that YOUR FIRM NAME may also utilize the other sources of credit which it considers necessary in making this determination. Further, I hereby authorize the bank and trade references listed here to release the information necessary to assist YOUR FIRM in establishing a line of credit.

X_____   _____   _____
Signature   Title   Date

Policy Statement: **Initial orders from new accounts will not be processed unless accompanied by the information requested above. Terms are net 30 days from date of invoice unless otherwise stated.**

whether there have been any problems with the account. (The client's signa-ture on the credit application grants permission to release information. You may need to fax a copy to the bank.)

With vendor references, you are basically asking the same questions as you asked the bank. Say you wish to speak to the bookkeeper. Give your name and your company name, and ask to check a credit rating on a customer. Inquire how long the account has been open, the highest amount of credit granted, and how the customer pays (on time? late? very slow?).

Give some thought ahead of time to how you will handle a client who doesn't give complete information, or who has a poor credit history.

Collection Policy

To prevent problems collecting your fees, insist on definitive clauses in your agreements that specify exactly when payment should be made on each invoice. If you don't get advance payments, either weekly or monthly, you will need to conduct a thorough credit search, including bank references. Avoid billing disputes by presenting invoices that itemize all work performed. Try not to finance other companies, not even for thirty days.

In spite of your best efforts, disputes will arise from time to time, or a client will not pay as obligated. Here are three strategies other self-employed profes-sionals have used to collect payment:

1. Present the invoice to the CEO in person. This works best in a small company. In large corporations, present directly to a honcho higher in the food chain than your contact minnow.

2. Insist on payment before continuing work.

3. Hold back important information or implementation steps until the in-voice is paid.

Contract Basics

A contract records the agreement reached. Negotiations should be con-cluded *before* a contract is drawn up and signed, not afterward. The reason for writing the agreement on paper is to guard against the frailties of human memory and to avoid later disputes. Don't think of a contract as a means to win or to protect yourself against a lawsuit. Its main purpose should be *to clarify* the agreement rather than to enforce it. Therefore, it should be understandable. Spell out all the details, and answer all the questions before they are asked.

A contract is not legal unless there is an exchange: something of value (services and/or products) to be given for something of value received (money). In legal terminology this is known as "consideration," and it should be stated clearly in the contract.

Prepare Before Offering a Contract

List everything you want to cover. Look at other contracts. Any library will have ample reference material for you to review. Also, if you look under a specific profession, you can find examples of contracts used in that profession. For instance, accounting contracts will have special clauses that are important to include for accounting but wouldn't be appropriate for writers. Trade organizations also have samples. Herman Holtz's *The Complete Guide to Consulting Contracts: How to Understand, Draft, and Negotiate Contracts That Work* has more than forty model agreements and clauses to customize form contracts. After you draft your contract, take a few days to think it over before you present it.

In addition to the names and signatures of the parties involved, a contract also needs to contain certain other basic components:

1. Dates for signing, beginning work, ending work, and any progress dates.

2. Scope of the services to be rendered.

3. Explanation of payments to be made.

4. Method of cancellation.

5. Method of returning any funds or property exchanged if the contract is terminated.

6. A clause that protects you if the work is stopped in progress through no fault of yours. (Think downsize!)

7. A clause that explains what will happen if work is late.

Always do your homework to gain an understanding of the other party. And when you are negotiating, don't get emotional or take things personally. Think creatively. Be willing to say no. Keep your word.

Receiving a Client's Contract

A client's "standard" agreement will contain clauses that protect the interests of the client. This protection may be inequitable to you. Certain words or phrases, listed below, should signal to you that there is trouble ahead. In some instances, you may want to do some legal research before rewriting the clauses, or you may want to seek legal counsel. In any event, you should try to have the following clauses deleted, or at least rewritten to be less onerous.

Indemnification Clauses that have you indemnifying the client if various problems occur mean you are promising to repay the client for losses or damages. These clauses usually contain the words "indemnify" or "hold harmless" and require you to defend or repay the client for such things as problems with the IRS or other agencies, injuries and damages arising from your services, or intellectual property "infringement." You should always refuse to agree to such clauses, but you should be prepared to offer substitute language for the client to consider. This is what negotiation is all about.

Insurance Requirements It is not unreasonable for a client to expect you to maintain liability coverage. Read carefully to see if a clause requires you to maintain excessive insurance coverage. If you are unable to delete the excessive coverage clause, you might consider requiring substantially more compensation for your work.

Noncompetition Restrictions Beware of businesses that want to restrict you from working for competitors. In essence, that limits your ability to earn a living. The Nolo *Independent Contractor's Legal Guide* suggests that in those instances where you can't get the clause deleted, you might consider not performing the same services for competitors named in the contract. (An example would be, "For the duration of this contract, Contractor agrees to perform no services for XYZ Company.")

Confidentiality Provisions Be sure that any confidentiality provision is not worded so broadly as to make it impossible to work for anyone else. For example, "Consultant agrees not to use or disclose Client's proprietary or confidential information except as directed by Client." The provision neglects to define what information *is* confidential and what information *is not,* and it could be interpreted so broadly as to encompass *all* information.

Termination at Will Some clients add clauses that allow them to terminate the agreement for no reason (as opposed to a breach of contract provision) with ten days' notice. If the client insists on such a provision, you should have the same termination rights as the client.

Time Is of the Essence "Time is of the essence" clauses sometimes appear in the portions dealing with project deadlines. If the contract contains this clause, clients can sue you for damages as well as terminate the contract for even a slight delay in performance. In these instances, it also means the client is not held to contractual obligations and need not pay you.

Beware of any contract where a client says, "Don't worry about that paragraph" or, "We never enforce that clause." In fact, beware of that particular client, too.

Letter Agreements

A letter agreement is shorter and less formal than a contract, although it serves the same purpose (see Figures 4.4 and 4.5). At the very least, it must include a description of the services to be performed, the fees charged, the deadlines and schedule of payment, and reimbursement of materials and expenses. Other optional provisions might include limiting your liability if something goes wrong, ownership of intellectual property (written article or other work), requiring the client to pay late fees for late payments, and provisions covering mediation or attorney fees in case of disputes. Letter agreements work well for brief projects or where relatively little money is involved. If your project is a complex one and involves substantial money, or if the client is troublesome and you are concerned about disputes, you are better off with a contract.

Figure 4.4 **Sample Letter Agreement**

Temp Strategically! Seminar

Mr. John J. Bigelow
Barnard College
116th Street and Broadway
New York, NY 10032

Dear Mr. Bigelow:

This is to confirm our appointment at 10:00 A.M. on Thursday, July 16, 1998, at which time we will discuss the specifics of my tailoring a *Temp Strategically!* seminar for your Career Services fall programs. I will begin the project following this meeting. I expect the total time for completion (including the custom handout materials) to be approximately eight (8) hours. This is in addition to the four (4) hours for the actual presentation of the seminar scheduled for October 12, 1998. As we discussed, "tailoring" and "presentation" are billed at different rates. The presentation contract is attached for your review and signature.

As we discussed, at this stage of the project my hourly fee will be $75, plus any expenses incurred on your behalf.

The payment may be handled in one of two ways:

1. You may deposit an advance retainer with me, and I will invoice against the retainer.

2. I will present you with an invoice for the total amount due at our pre-seminar meeting on January 15, payment in full being due within ten (10) days.

If the terms of this letter and the attached contract meet with your understanding and agreement, I would appreciate your signing both copies of each and returning one copy of each to me in the envelope provided.

I look forward to working with you on this project.

Sincerely,

Diane L. Thrailkill

enc.

P. O. Box 8335, Chelsea Station, New York, NY 10016 (212) 989-4534

Figure 4.5 **Form Agreement**

Client: _____

Address: _____

_____

Contact: _____

Services to be provided: _____

Reports/presentations: _____

On client's premises: _____   On consultant's premises: _____

Other or special arrangements: _____

Start date: _____   Target completion date: _____

Fees: $_____   per _____   Est. hours: _____   Est. fee/cost: _____

Other costs: _____   for_____

Advance retainer: _____   Terms for balance: _____

Notes, special provisions: _____

_____

_____

Joanne J. Doe, Consultant   Client Big Bucks

By: _____   By: _____

Date: _____   Date: _____

Invoicing Clients

Your invoice should contain your company name, address, and telephone; the client's name; an invoice number; the date; the client's purchase order or contract number (if any); the terms of payment; the time period covered by the invoice; a brief description of the services you performed; and details of your billing method (by the hour, by the day, etc.). If you're billing separately for expenses or materials, add the amounts of these items. Then calculate the total amount due and add your signature. Make it easy for them to pay you by including a self-addressed return envelope. Make two copies of the invoice. Send the original to the client, one copy goes to your file and use the extra one as a tracking copy in a follow-up file (see Figure 4.6).

Figure 4.6 **Sample Invoice**

Jasper Smythe
1024 Marigold Drive
Seattle, Washington 98101
(603) 675-2365

Date: 9/30/98
Invoice #:   604-98
Your Order #: B-7865
Terms: Net 30
Time period: 9/1/98–9/30/98

To: Andrea Entero
                   Accounting Department
                   Everything's Rosy Florists
                   65 Washington Drive
                   Seattle, Washington 98111

Services: Consulting services of Jasper Smythe for advertising campaign,
                   64 hours @ $75 per hour.
Expenses: None
Materials: None
Total Due: $4,800

Signed: _____
                              Jasper Smythe

Purchase Orders

Purchase orders are documents used by a company to authorize payment for your services. Find out if the client requires a purchase order for payment. Some companies are so rigid about it that you will not be paid without one, even if you have a signed contract. If your client uses purchase orders, make sure you have one before beginning any work (see Figure 4.7).

Figure 4.7 **Sample Purchase Order**

Purchase Order: #10599A

Kramer Business Products
200 West Houston St.
New York, NY 10003
(212) 889-7634

Vendor: Al-Wes Electric Services
38 West Eighth Street
New York, NY 10014
212-564-9889

Date: July 8, 1998

Delivery Date: July 18, 1998

Terms: $75 per hour labor, plus parts. Total labor price not to exceed $600.

**Description of
Services:**   Contractor will rewire electrical switch box connecting the three offices and replace
parts at cost plus 10 percent.

Authorized by: _____
Martin Quonones, Office Manager

Late Payments and Bounced Checks

When should the first call be made to a delinquent account? As soon as the account becomes late. In the present economic climate, a business could close its doors in sixty to ninety days. Your call lets the client know you pay close attention to business. If it takes 120 days to collect on your accounts receivable, and you are paying your own bills within thirty days, what do you think happens to your cash flow?

A check that is returned for insufficient funds can only be redeposited once. For a fee, you can ask your bank to collect it for you. Your bank will send the check to the originating bank with instructions to deposit it the minute there are enough funds to cover the amount. The originating bank will then hold it for thirty days.

Another approach you might consider, depending on your relationship with the client, is to call the client before redepositing to see if there are sufficient funds.

If the check bounces again, some people advise sending a certified letter to notify the client that you intend to turn the matter over to an attorney. Personally, I think that's a waste of time. The kind of person who deliberately passes bad checks won't be scared by a threatening letter. Consider, instead, taking action in small claims court. If you feel there was a deliberate attempt to defraud, send copies of the check and a letter of explanation to your local district attorney. While law enforcement personnel can't collect the money for you, their inquiries or intervention might make the client reconsider his/her action.

Small Claims Court

Small claims court is an informal court for monetary claims in small amounts with limits that range from $1,500 (Alabama, Kentucky) to $10,000 (some jurisdictions in Virginia). Each state sets its own monetary limit, and in each it is relatively uncomplicated to file and present a claim.

Two important questions must be answered before filing a suit: (1) Do you have a case? There is a big difference between having something bad happen to you and actually having grounds for a lawsuit. (2) If you win, can you collect? Don't bother suing a broke deadbeat.

Any number of books and articles will take you through the process. One of the best books I have read on the subject is Nolo's *Everybody's Guide to Small Claims Court* by attorney Ralph Warner, one of the founders of the self-help law movement. This easy-to-read, jargon-free book takes you through the steps to prepare a case, present it, and then collect a judgment.

What Price Innovation? Quantify Everything!

It's easier to increase profits by decreasing costs than it is to increase sales. This is because of the high cost of marketing and landing a new customer. Get in the habit of figuring unit prices for your supplies and services. You can use the concept to cull your less profitable endeavors and/or decide whether to raise your prices.

Is a Service Worth Doing?

Begin to analyze your portfolio of skills by taking a look at the work you have done for the past six months. Which of your activities produced the bulk of total income for the period? Which produced the smallest portion? Which had the greatest expense connected to it? Is your price structure realistic? Do you charge enough for what you do?

When you discover a service that is not profitable, consider how you might turn it around. Can you raise the price without losing clients? Can you reduce the costs of providing it? Can you perform it more efficiently? Should you continue it as is, combine it with another service, or discontinue it altogether?

Either teach yourself how to set up your books (or your software) to deliver the information that follows, or consult with a professional to do it for you.

Overhead Costs. How much they are, and whether they are constant or fluctuating.

Sales Figures. Dollar figures, frequency of sales, types of sales/clients, trends up or down, if any.

Cost of Sales. Total cost of landing and completing every project or assignment.

Markup. How much you are adding to your total estimated cost of each project so that you can meet all expenses and realize a profit.

Profit. Surplus overall costs for each job, in total, and as an average.

What About New Services in the Portfolio?

Before getting too involved in the development and marketing of a new service, ask yourself the following questions.

1. If the new service were fully implemented, what would be the ultimate contribution to my performance?

2. Does it have application to any other area of my business?

3. Does it conflict with any aspect of my business enterprises?

4. Will the new service help me reach my overall objectives?

5. Is anything standing in the way of my implementing it? Is any aspect of it proprietary and subject to trademark protection? (If you have an approach that is uniquely yours, it is considered proprietary, and you have the exclusive right to market and sell it. You will want to take steps to protect it by registering it as a trademark or service mark.)

6. Do I have the resources to implement it without impairing any of my other objectives? Can it be sold through my established channels? Is it convertible to other media and applicable across other markets?

7. Where will I get additional resources if I need them?

8. Is it tangible and packageable? Can I express it as a book, manual, newsletter, seminar, audiotape, videotape, or software?

Subcontracting

From time to time you may need to subcontract other professionals to work with you on larger projects. If you use subcontractors, always mark up their rates either implicitly in your overall quote or explicitly as a handling charge. Thus, $250 becomes $300 per day. Compensate yourself for bringing in, overseeing, and managing the subcontractors. Always quote "fee plus expenses." The biggest hazard of subcontracting is hiring semi-competence. If you are not directly familiar with the person's work, you can take several steps to avoid problems:

1. Require references, and check them thoroughly.

2. Whether you hire by the hour or by the day, structure the work so that you are not paying for unproductive time.

3. Reach agreement on what is to be done, when it is due, and the quality or standard expected by you. Your letter agreement should both explain the standard and state the agreed-upon price of services.

4. Make it clear that payment will be made only when you accept the work as meeting the standard.

Wisdom from Mark Twain

Always do right. This will gratify some people and astonish the rest.

Don't part with your illusions. When they are gone, you may still exist, but you have ceased to live.

It is better to keep your mouth shut and appear stupid than to open it and remove all doubt. (Remember this one if you haven't done your homework.)

Read on to learn how to make the best use of your time on an assignment.

FURTHER READING

The Complete Guide to Consulting Contracts: How to Understand, Draft, and Negotiate Contracts that Work, Herman Holtz, Upstart Publishing Company 2nd edition, 1995.

The Contract and Fee-getting Guide for Consultants and Professionals, Howard Shenson, John Wiley & Sons, 1990.

Freelancing Made Simple, Larry E. Hand, Doubleday, 1995.

The Frugal Entrepreneur, Terri Lonier, Portico Press, 1996. Creative ways to save time, energy and money in your business.

Homemade Money, Barbara Brabec, Betterway Books, 5th edition, 1994. Comprehensive guide to anything and everything connected to home-based businesses. An excellent reference for anyone who is self-employed.

How to Become a Successful Consultant in Your Own Field, Hubert Bermont, Prima Publishing, 1994

How to Succeed as an Independent Consultant, Herman Holtz, John Wiley & Sons, 1993.

If Time is Money, No Wonder I'm Not Rich, Mary L. Sprouse, Simon & Schuster, 1993.

The Independent Consultant's Q&A Book, Lawrence W. Tuller, Bob Adams, Inc., 1993.

Money Smart Secrets for the Self-Employed, Linda Stern, Random House, 1997. A practical guide full of great tips to maximize your income while minimizing taxes.

National Writer's Union Guide to Freelance Rates and Standard Practice, National Writers Union, Betterway Books, 1995.

Priced to Sell, Herman Holtz, Upstart Publishing Company, 1996.

Selling Your Services, Robert Bly, Henry Holt, 1992.

5 *Managing the Assignment: The* Carpe Diem *Temporary*

*T*he helpful tips presented in this chapter are applicable to a wide range of assignments. They are designed to help you get the information you need to do the job, to find your way around a new office quickly, and to organize the work in ways that will free up blocks of time that can be used for your own pursuits.

There is a commonality of function among the same job titles regardless of where the work is performed. A sales manager for IBM will execute some of the same functions as a sales manager for Procter & Gamble, although the specifics of their jobs may be different. The same holds true for temporary work. Certain aspects of all temporary assignments will be the same, whatever form the work takes. An obvious example is that a temporary worker, at whatever level or position, will be unfamiliar with other employees, the physical plant, and the corporate culture of a new assignment. And not knowing these things will make an impact on how work is accomplished on the job.

Image

Most of us have spent the bulk of our careers in places where power was defined by position and title. People who have never worked as a temporary before are concerned about their image, and rightly so. When the evolution of this "new order" is complete, it is said that power will be defined by the skills we bring to the marketplace. But we are not there yet, and as intergalactic travelers among strange, new corporate worlds, we are concerned about image.

How will you be perceived as a temporary? Employees at some sites may regard you as less than an equal, or not regard you at all, thereby rendering you invisible. There will be clients who treat you as an employee who is there to do their bidding (however ill-advised their bidding may be), rather than as an independent entrepreneur selling a valuable service and entitled to function as a business colleague. Whether you are there as an agency temporary or as a consultant, you must think of yourself as an independent contractor and assess yourself and your services appropriately. You are delivering a valuable service to your agency and to the client. You are trading your knowledge and special abilities for money.

Unless you firmly believe in your ability and competence to do everything the job requires, it is unlikely you will project an image that will make anyone else believe it either. Your true value to the client and agency, what you are being paid for, is *results,* not your time. Time is only the measure by which you calculate your charges; it is not the commodity you sell. You sell results. If you believe it, so will others.

First Impressions

Keep professional demeanor uppermost in your mind at all times. Remember, your "throwaway job" (if that is how you are looking at temporary work) is someone else's career, and it is taking place on the premises of your agency's client.

I recommend arriving fifteen minutes early on the first day. There will always be people who are leery of temporary employees, who are afraid "the temp won't show," and your early arrival allays that fear. You are paid for the time. Be sure to include it on your time sheet.

Shortly after you arrive at the assignment, call the agency to give your telephone number and extension. As a matter of courtesy, tell your "supervisor" that you must make the call, so it won't be perceived that you walked in and immediately began using the telephone for business or personal calls. Make a note of the time you arrived and the telephone number of the work station on your portable organizer. During the day, record the length of your lunch break and the time you leave. This same information is recorded on the timesheet. Keeping a duplicate of the information gives you a convenient record of the work and the rate if there is any discrepancy on a later paycheck. Also, having your own records means that if you leave any personal belongings behind, you can retrieve them without involving the agency.

It is not unusual to be left waiting anywhere from fifteen minutes to half an hour in the reception area for a human resources person to take you to your work station. This is especially true at large companies. Ask to use a courtesy telephone to notify the agency of your arrival. (I have never been refused. When there isn't a courtesy telephone, the receptionist has called for me.) You can call again later with your telephone number. You are paid for the waiting time.

If you do not carry a cellular telephone, call home to check your messages hourly. Give your name, location, and extension to the client's receptionist also. This ensures your receiving telephone calls or having messages taken if you are away from your desk.

Relay the work station number to your other agencies. When you expect to work longer than one day, you can call agencies over the course of the assignment. If the assignment is for only one day and you must find work for the remainder of the week, make sure you talk to all of your counselors. It is acceptable to call agencies from the job; it is, after all, your livelihood. Sometimes you may be without a convenient telephone. Don't be shy about asking for the use of a telephone during a lunch break to make your agency calls. Rarely have I had to do this, but no one has ever refused my request. (Agencies will relay messages to you through the client's Human Resources Department if you don't have a direct line.)

Even when everyone has your work number, continue to check your voice mail or answering machine messages. Agency counselors can, and often do, misplace scraps of paper with telephone numbers scribbled on them.

At the end of the shift, say goodbye to people and thank them for their help, or for the courtesies extended to you. If you have found them obnoxious, perhaps you can manage a "good luck with your project." They are your agency's clients, and another temporary may have a different experience there.

The Work Environment

Ideally, someone in the department will be assigned to show you around and introduce you to coworkers, your work station will have the supplies you need to do the work, the telephone list/book will be handy, and there will be someone to give you directions about what is expected. If you are really lucky, there will be a one-page instruction sheet about the office routine.

That's the ideal situation.

Almost without exception you will work in clean, safe, and comfortable surroundings. But there are the occasional exceptions. In a "special project" spot at a famous cosmetics company, I was expected to sit on a canvas deck chair and use a computer that had been turned to one side on the vice president's desk while she carried on as usual with meetings and telephone calls. I said no and, oddly enough, another work space was found for me to use.

Don't ever hesitate to ask for, or insist on, whatever you need to make your work space habitable—including a move to a different location. In addition, you need a safe place to store your purse if you carry one. A graciously firm attitude usually does the trick.

Temporaries who rely on public transportation and are requested to work late (past 8:00 P.M.) are usually sent home by taxi. The manager provides a signed voucher for the company's car service. Inquire what the company policy is before agreeing to stay late. That includes asking about transportation and/or escort to a deserted parking area. Don't be foolishly macho about this. Muggers are equal opportunity predators.

On occasion you will have to share work space or equipment. Most of the time people are considerate and this turns out okay. Occasionally they are not so okay. If the environment is intolerable and you are unable to rectify the situation tactfully, tell the agency. Perhaps a counselor can come up with a solution or have you moved to a different location. If not, tough out the day. Ask for a replacement. Don't return to the company.

Sometimes you are taken to your work station by someone from Human Resources who doesn't know much about the job. Or your guide may be harried because the regular person is out, or extra help is needed. Even when people are knowledgeable, you won't always be given the information you need to do a good job. You have to know what questions to ask. Regular employees often assume that you know their company procedures. (I have never understood how they think we get the knowledge. Clairvoyance? Osmosis?)

Ask three important questions:

Whom do I work for? Get names, locations, and telephone numbers. A preoccupied employee can drop you off at a vacant desk, mutter a few vague instructions amid non sequiturs, and then rush off leaving you unsure of your supervisor's identity.

Who will answer my questions? Don't assume that other department members either have the information you need or want to be bothered. Request a specific person to answer your questions.

Which telephone number is mine, and how does the system work? Don't assume your telephone number is the prefix of the company's general number added to the four numbers on your telephone. Direct lines can be, and often are, a different prefix.

The Three Most Important Questions

1. Whom do I work for?
2. Who will answer my questions?
3. Which telephone number is mine, and how does the system work?

Find out the location of the following:

copy machine

mail room

water fountains

coffee

cafeteria

fax machine

bathrooms

refrigerator (to store lunch)

vending machines

paper and other necessary supplies

At some point during the day, you may also want to ask any or all of the questions that follow.

Are you expected to answer any telephone lines, and if so, what should you say? (Accounting? Icon Software?)

Who are the other members of your work group? Get a departmental list as well as an internal telephone directory.

Do you need access codes (such as client/matter numbers) or cards to work equipment or doors? For instance, accountants and attorneys use client numbers, matter numbers and attorney/accountant numbers as part of their record keeping for billable hours. These numbers are keyed in (to bill the client) in order to work the copy machine, facsimile, or telephone. These numbers are also needed to complete forms to request a messenger or to send mail. Get a backup administrative code to use if a number is inoperable. Sometimes the system won't be up-to-date, and the client number won't work.

What is the name of the messenger service? It is seldom listed on the Rolodex under "M" for messenger. Will forms or account numbers be needed?

What is the number for technical support (or the LAN administrator if you are using a computer on a local area network)?

In busy areas everyone pitches in, managers and VPs included, to cover the telephones. Are you expected to cover telephones for anyone during lunch?

Mail? Will you be expected to pick it up from the mail room? Is there mail coming to your position that you should open or handle in some way? When is the last pickup of the day?

Which courier service do they use? Where are the forms and envelopes kept? When is the last pickup of the day?

Ask who signs the time sheet at the end of the day. Some companies have temps report back to Human Resources. People leave early on Fridays, and you might need an alternate.

I have designed the Temp Template® (Figure 5.1) as a quick reference. It has all the right questions to ask to get the information you need to succeed. Get answers to these questions and you can't fail.

Job Upgrade, Rate Upgrade

By the time a work order was placed with the agency and you appeared on the scene, a company's needs may have changed. The agency selected you because of your skill with computers and your knowledge of five software packages. You arrive to find out your first task is to photocopy a technical manual. The "downgrade" doesn't warrant a change in rate; you are paid at the same professional rate you agreed to accept.

A rate change *should* take place, however, if the job is upgraded materially. For instance, if you were sent to do general mail room work at a general mail room rate and the job turns into "mail room supervisor" because of your competence and initiative, you are entitled to a higher rate of pay. Tell the agency if your job changes drastically, and let the agency handle rate negotiations with their client. Never allow companies to exploit your knowledge and talent for less than an equitable dollar amount.

Earlier in the chapter I described the ideal situation, where the temporary assignment was well planned. A more common scenario is as follows. You are

Figure 5.1 **The Temp Template**®

Everything You Need to Know to Survive the First Assignment . . . and Thereafter

Whom Do I:

... work for?

Get names, telephone numbers, and locations for these people. (You'd be surprised how many times you aren't told.)

... go to with my questions?

Get name, location, and telephone number.

... answer telephones for?

How does the telephone system work? Is there an intercom? How does it work? What do you want me to say when I answer?

... cover for at lunch?

Who covers for me? Are lunch times "assigned"?

... receive mail for?

Do I distribute it? open it? date-stamp it? Where is the date stamp? Where is the mail room? Is mail delivered, or do I pick it up?

Who/What:

... signs my time sheet?

Manager? Personnel person? Alternate signer?

... messenger service do you use?

Get telephone and account numbers, and special forms if used.

... car service do you use?

Get telephone and account numbers, and special forms if used.

... courier service do you use?

Where are the forms/envelopes kept? Does the service pick up automatically, or do you call?

Where Is/Are the:

... women's/men's room? Do I need a key? . . . a code?
... Xerox machine? Are codes or access cards used?
... fax machine? Handy list of fax numbers? . . . forms or top sheets for the fax?

... paper and other supplies?
... water fountain, coffee? Is the coffee free?
... vending machines, cafeteria? Is the food worth eating? Is it cheap?

1. Ask for a telephone list for people in the department and an internal telephone book.
2. For law or accounting firms, get the attorney (or accountant), client, and matter numbers.
3. Ask for the number to the firm's technical support or LAN administrator.
4. Find out their document/file-naming protocol and the directory/subdirectory paths for retrieval.
5. Find out when the last mail pickup is.

taken to the work station to find that the VP who is in charge of the project and scheduled to brief you is in a lengthy meeting until lunchtime. You are left alone in an unfamiliar cubicle with a locked desk, no instructions, and no one who knows the password for the computer. This is why you should always carry personal work—material to read, letters to write, etc.

When I first began doing temporary work and ended up with nothing to do, I would go from person to person asking if I could assist with any work. I wanted overtime money, and I felt compelled to earn it. I got a lot of startled looks. People are territorial about their work, and "helping" is not necessarily acceptable behavior in some offices. In some places it is a "group secret" how little work there is, so I was upsetting the status quo by speeding up the assembly line.

Work doesn't always happen in a steady flow, especially when you drop in from outer space and have no other projects in progress. There are peaks and valleys; nothing for an hour or two, then you may be buried for the next six. Just understand that this happens, and come prepared to look industrious with your own projects if necessary.

As a matter of course, always carry an envelope with time sheets from each of your agencies. If, however, you find yourself without the right time sheet on a job, you can use company letterhead to write a memo containing the necessary information and signatures in lieu of a time sheet (see Figure 5.2).

As I mentioned earlier, I find it helpful to keep track of all the places I work in my portable organizer. I record the information from my assignment form, adding to it the work station telephone number and the person I actually reported to. I use this as a permanent record for income tax purposes.

On-the-Job General Tips

Your on-the-job mind-set is a commitment to the substance of the work itself, how it showcases your talent as a "quick study," and what you will learn from it. Entrepreneurial temporaries focus on the project, assimilate the knowledge, complete the assignment, and move on. I don't mean to be tiresome about this, but remember to assess each project or assignment for its potential to: (1) expand your present skills or experience, (2) develop new skills, and (3) increase your ability to acquire another project. Entrepreneurial temporaries develop a talent for recognizing opportunity and creating their own jobs.

Use discretion in making telephone calls. On a new assignment I limit my short telephone calls to agencies. Depending on the company and general climate, I may or may not make other calls.

Figure 5.2 **Sample Time Sheet Substitute**

HERETIC MEDIA COMPANY
3124 Iconoclast Lane
Noncommittal, ND 50609

June 29, 1998

Oscar Herman
Abracadabra Temps
4 Union Square
Noncommittal, ND 50609

Dear Mr. Herman:

This is to confirm that David Gervais worked for us on June 27, 1998, from 9:00 A.M. to 5:00 P.M., less one hour for lunch, for a total of 7 hours. His Social Security number is 565-51-5503.

Yours very truly,

Susan Weinstein   (Your Supervisor)
Manager   (Her Title)

The letter doesn't have to be a writing masterpiece. Just be sure to write it on company letterhead and include

1. *Your name*

2. *The dates worked*

3. *The hours worked, less breaks*

4. *Your Social Security number*

5. *Name and title of your supervisor*

6. *The supervisor's signature*

All pros leave behind a brief written report about the work they completed on an assignment. Some write personal notes; others leave a list or fill out a form they have designed and photocopied.

Label a manila folder "completed work." (You can attach a Post-it or a sheet of paper to the folder instead of a label.) Place copies of completed work inside the folder. Attach a note explaining what you did, where you put things, how you have named documents, and any other pertinent information that would be helpful.

If you don't like to write notes, design a form specific to the type of work you do that can be completed and left behind to simplify the process of relaying information. Figure 5.3 is for a secretary, and may give you some ideas.

Quickly Find Your Way Around an Unfamiliar Department

Make a seating chart of the cubicles and offices around you. List name, title, extension, and any other information that will be useful to you.

Figure 5.3 Sample Temporary Assignment Record

Work Completed

DOCUMENTS

For	Document Name/Location	Description
1. Sam Yee	c:\wpwin\docs\1998rate.xyz	Rate comparison spread
2.		
3.		

TRAVEL ARRANGEMENTS

For	Date of Trip	Arrangement
1. Jerry Jackson	11/2–4/97	AA #605 to Knoxville, AA#506 return
2.		
3.		

MEETINGS SCHEDULED

For	Date	Meet Who	Where
1.			
2.			

TELEPHONE MESSAGES

For	Caller	Date/Time	Telephone Number
1.			
2.			

Name: _____   Agency: _____

Date: _____

Simplify the departmental telephone list. Make a photocopy of it (where feasible, not when it is a book). Highlight the frequently called names. If no list exists, and the department is a manageable size, compile one.

Compose a quick-reference internal distribution list that includes mail drops and telephone numbers (handwritten is fine; it's a tool, not a contest entry). Every time you send material to another department, add the information to your list.

On longer assignments, if you find yourself distributing material to the same bunch of people, make up a pile of buck slips with mail drops.

Whenever possible, replace plain telephone message pads with ones that make carbonless copies. This gives you an archive of messages and telephone numbers taken during your tenure and a reference tool to find people quickly.

Work stations with voice mail: Change the greeting to reflect your presence if you will be there for more than a day or two.

"Tom Dorato's line, this is Jason Carter. Tom is out of the office through Wednesday this week and I'm filling in. Please leave a message." Change back to the standard greeting at the end of the assignment.

Planning Ahead

Prepare a file for each of the companies you work at. Take a sample piece of letterhead, a copy of the telephone sheet, instructions for transferring calls and retrieving voice mail, the seating chart you made, computer notes, and record your rates. Make a list of helpful/hateful people, the kind of work you did, and your notes on the day-to-day routine (use the Temp Template for ideas). You will be well prepared on your next assignment there.

On-the-Job Problems

Here are situations that crop up from time to time, along with short-term solutions.

Everyone Tries to Give You Work. Ask your supervisor to act as a clearinghouse. Have people deliver any work to the supervisor for prioritizing. This works every time.

Smoker in Area. Ask to sit someplace else, ask for an electric fan, ask someone in the Human Resources Department for a fan.

Questions About Your Hourly Rate. If other temporaries inquire about my rate, I will give the range that should be paid for the work I am performing. (I run into too many temporaries who are being exploited and I feel an obligation to educate them.) When permanent employees ask, I tell them to check with the Human Resources Department.

Curious Employees. Employees sometimes let their curiosity override good manners and ask rude, personal questions. My personal favorite is the vice president who asked me in all sincerity, "What do you *really* do? You seem so normal." You don't owe anyone the story of your life or the circumstances that led you to become a consultant, an independent contractor, or a temporary.

Personality Conflict. Every now and then you may run into a situation where, even though you are performing your assignment well, the people you are working for don't like you—and you know it. Maybe it's because you are self-confident and do the work quickly. Maybe it's because you aren't deferential enough to please their sense of self-importance. Whatever the reason, they will probably terminate the assignment by the end of the day. Agency and temp professionals are aware of this phenomenon and do not take it to heart. This is not to imply that it is not unpleasant when it happens, but it's not the end of the world either. Sometimes it works the other way: The client loves you and always requests you, but you would rather panhandle on a street corner than ever work there again. I don't think it is particularly wise to share these unflattering perceptions of the client with the agency. Instead, through one ruse or another, make yourself unavailable for work whenever requested by that client.

Socializing. In friendly companies, coworkers will make an effort to include temporaries in their conversations, office parties, and lunch plans. Usually I thank the inviter profusely but regretfully decline, for if I'm not doing their work, I have my own. Temporaries with different agendas, such as seeking employment within the company, will handle it differently.

Long-Term Assignments

In order to earn overtime dollars, you must put in your forty-plus weekly hours at one agency. If you bounce around on one- and two-day assignments for several agencies, you can easily put in over forty hours, but you won't be paid time and a half. Companies looking for a long-term person may offer you the job. Companies not looking for a long-term person may offer you the job. It still amazes me how often this happens.

An assignment is referred to as "long term" if it is longer than one or two weeks. Reality is often something entirely different. A long-term assignment can mean anywhere from one day to infinity, especially if it is an "indef" as they say in the trade. This term is usually given to assignments for which a permanent person is being sought. Occasionally it is bestowed upon jobs that no one wants for very long. Companies will employ a series of interim workers for these mind-numbing monstrosities, replacing the burned-out temps with fresh ones as needed.

If you take a long-term slot, check with your supervisor at least once a week that the job is continuing. This can be done casually. A division head may come in one morning and issue an edict, "No more temps." Human Resources may announce that the position has been filled internally and that the new person is reporting tomorrow. Either edict can be communicated to you, the "disposable" temp, at 5:00 P.M., effectively fouling up your schedule for the rest of the week.

When I accept a long-term assignment, the only thing I tell my other agencies is that my assignment is for a week. First of all, I may not want to stay for two months. If the job works out and I want to do it, I say I've been asked to stay on for another week or two. I take it one week at a time. At any given moment, I maintain relationships with six to eight agencies. When I take a long-term assignment, I call my counselors every few weeks to touch base, let them know I'm extending for another few weeks, and make sure they have my telephone number. I call between 10:00 A.M. and 3:00 P.M. when they aren't as busy.

Staying in touch pays off. If you need work in a hurry because something happens to your assignment, it's nice to have counselors remember who you are.

Long-Term Tip

Try to work with the person you are replacing for at least one day prior to her/his leave. It makes for a more orderly transition. This is especially helpful when you are filling in during a maternity leave, or while the company interviews for a permanent replacement. However, if you are taking over an administrative assistant or secretarial position, avoid working with the employee for more than one day. These jobs are not that complicated and rarely have enough work to keep two people busy. The person leaving is often awkward at training a replacement, and the two of you end up tripping over each other in a confined space.

Organize Assignments to Secure Maximum Personal Time

Without exception, the client's work is completed first, getting it out of the way. This keeps the client happy and allows temporaries to follow their own pursuits with a clear conscience. The key is organization.

Daily. Begin each day with a plan for what you want to accomplish and a to-do list. Schedule personal errands before and after work rather than during a lunch break.

Try to finish one task before beginning another. Group tasks for maximum efficiency. For instance, do a block of telephone calls, compose several short letters.

If you spend a sizable portion of time looking for things, you need to organize yourself better.

Before I leave the assignment for the day, I make a list of materials I need for the next day: correspondence I must refer to, telephone numbers, reference material. Use expandable, letter-sized plastic file envelopes to transport personal work back and forth from job to home. They come in several colors, are lightweight, and won't get dogeared. Use a colored "completed" folder inside the file envelope to carry home completed work. It saves time packing, unpacking, and looking through folders.

After I arrive home, I unpack for the day before I relax. Using my list prepared on the job, I repack for the next day. That way I don't have to think in the morning.

It pays to take the time to organize a work station if you will be there for a few days. You have the advantage of coming into a position with an open mind and a fresh pair of eyes. Look at the job as a consultant; make it better for yourself. Being able to find unfamiliar work easily and dispatch it quickly gives you more free time.

The "Traveling" Temporary

Bear in mind that you will be traveling between companies and your home office. Here are suggestions that others have found helpful.

1. Develop a system for yourself that keeps your personal work organized and easily carried from one assignment to another.

2. Devise a method to transport and easily set up personal files at a temporary desk. Use colored hanging files and folders for quick identifi-

cation. Keep backup material for telephone calls in a red folder, data entry material in a green one, and so forth.

3. Keep your computer work in a personal subdirectory on the job as well as on diskette (your backup).

4. Devise a system to prevent accidental deletion or overwriting of data that you transport between work and home. Not all software lists the time of update, and in a hurry you can forget and overwrite the wrong file. The simple method I came up with uses a date and designated location as part of the file name. It tells me at a glance when and where the file was updated. For instance, a file called "IBM-agr8.16c" was edited last on August 16 and saved on the hard disk at the job.

   A: = 3 1/2″ floppies (The file name will use A.)

   C: = assignment hard disk (Work saved on client's computer will use C.)

   D: = home hard disk (Work saved on home hard disk will use D.)

5. Use your planner/organizer to record telephone messages, expenses, and mileage (if applicable) as well as appointments.

6. Keep all receipts together in one place, such as a designated pocket in your briefcase or an envelope insert in your portable organizer.

7. Project information stays together and travels well in three-ring notebooks.

8. Create "action" and "reference" pockets in your portable system. Perhaps two colors of folders. Enclose a copy of your home file index for reference. Chapter 8 has tips on how to create one easily.

9. Anytime you receive someone's business card, make a note on the card of the date, the event and place, and any pertinent information you need to follow up on.

10. Carry blank diskettes with you daily. When you need one, you usually need it NOW (your printer stops working, someone else must use your computer for a while). Diskettes can be hard to come by in some places. Rather than spend an hour trying to get one, I carry my own— formatted and brightly colored for easy identification.

11. Not all companies have the latest version of software, and utility programs help you easily find and manage unfamiliar files. Consider taking an uncomplicated utility program with you daily. Office personnel

can be vague about the location of their document files, and very few have a naming protocol, much less one that makes sense.

12. These useful items pack easily and don't take up much space: stationery, envelopes, postage stamps, cleaner packets for screens and keyboards, alcohol wipes for telephones (often you are filling in for sick people), subway and bus maps, tokens for public transportation. Band-Aids for paper cuts, bank deposit slips, tissue packets, straws for sodas (I hate drinking out of cans). Sometimes I carry a paperback dictionary and thesaurus. I am still amazed at the number of offices that have neither.

13. During the last half hour of the day, plan what you must take home and what you must bring in the next morning.

14. It is important to organize for a weekly agenda as well as a daily one, and to devise a follow-up system that works for you. I hope the following description of how I do it gives you some ideas.

Late Sunday afternoon I plan and organize work for the week. This takes anywhere from thirty minutes to one hour. I make a three-column to-do list of everything I want to accomplish (readable, but believe me, no work of art). The columns are entitled Must Do, Should Do, Can Do. Then I pull out files, letters, research material, telephone numbers, whatever I may need for the entire week. I separate it into categories and place in the appropriate colored, labeled folders. I select several items to take with me. I also pack my lunch. The less thinking I have to do on a Monday morning, the better. Each morning I select a few more items to complete on the job.

Seasonal Considerations. Temporary work has seasonal ups and downs. Business slows down in weeks with holidays, people leave early, work dwindles. Many companies are reluctant to hire temporaries because of this. Temps working day to day will pick up only two or three days for the week. Try to land a week-long assignment in these weeks: Presidents' Day, Memorial Day, Good Friday/Easter, Passover, Fourth of July, Labor Day, Rosh Hashanah, Yom Kippur, Christmas, New Year's Eve/Day. That way you are protected. You won't be paid for the holidays, but you are assured work on the days preceding and following them.

Try to land a month-long spot in June, which is traditionally a sluggish month for professional temps. I have a theory why this is so. School lets out, and all of the eager college students who work for peanuts-an-hour rates hit the agencies. By July, however, the students want to put in some beach or pool time, and the agencies suddenly remember their more seasoned temps. I don't know if this is what really happens, but June *is* a slow month.

Check Cashing. If an agency doesn't have a free check-cashing arrangement, take your paycheck to the branch bank it is drawn on (usually convenient to the agency). In most instances, they will cash it for you without question with proper identification. If the teller gives you a hard time, speak to the branch manager.

Increase Your Paycheck Painlessly. Hourly pay is calculated in quarter-hour increments. Bring a lunch whenever possible and you won't waste time looking for a reasonable place to eat. Eat at your desk while you work, and get paid for lunch. Or take a fifteen-minute lunch if you want. You are there to earn money and accomplish your agenda, not necessarily to enjoy a leisurely lunch.

When there is ample work and the office is open early, each morning arrive fifteen to thirty minutes early and get right to work. You will be surprised how quickly the extra time adds up to a fatter paycheck. Most of the time your supervisor will be pleased at your initiative and eagerness to work. Use common sense here. Do this only if there is enough work to warrant it. Managers who do not want you to put in extra hours will make it a point to tell you. I leave my time sheet on the desk so that the manager can look it over at any time.

Become computer literate, no matter what your specialty is. Apprentice yourself to someone by offering to do mundane tasks for a little instruction. Use free time to learn more.

Take every opportunity to learn another software package on the job—and be paid for learning. Volunteer.

Suppose someone asks if you know Excel. You can answer that you have "played around" with it a little, or you can immediately find out if a complicated procedure is wanted. Most of the time you will be asked to do glorified data entry, but it gets you started on a new package and with someone training you. Ask for a copy of the manual to teach yourself more functions. More skills equal more money. After you have worked with the new software, let your agencies know about it—but don't inflate your proficiency.

Whenever work stations have software manuals, use them to teach yourself another function or two, or some shortcuts. Teach yourself how to use unfamiliar software packages during free time. Get paid to go to school.

On my first temporary assignment, I was a secretarial ornament whose sole function was to sit at a desk and answer the occasional telephone call. To pass the time I took the software manual and literally went from "A" to "Z" teaching myself unfamiliar functions. Then I compiled a shortcut sheet that I shared with other temporaries.

Obtaining or Upgrading Computer Skills

Learning how to use the computer takes a commitment of time and energy that is more akin to learning a musical instrument than learning how to program your VCR.

Look into the local adult and continuing education programs for nearby school districts, colleges, and YWCA/YMCAs for inexpensive classes. All it takes is a telephone call to request a catalogue of classes.

Consider calling the instructors to ask about private sessions. Two or so hours of concentrated instruction will rarely cost more than a class and is often a better use of your time.

1. Take the time to learn one software program really well. After that, the world is yours. Each software package in a genre (word processing, spreadsheet, database) will use the same logic and similar, if not identical, functions. The difference will be the keystrokes used for the execution. But you need to be familiar with the full range of functions.

2. Don't sign up for instruction until you know you will have the opportunity to use the program afterward. The old adage, "Use it or lose it" applies to computers too.

3. Don't try to learn two programs simultaneously; you will confuse them. I meet far too many job seekers who have signed up for word processing and spreadsheet classes. I try to talk them into dropping one program until they are more comfortable with the computer in general and have learned, and are *using,* one program proficiently.

Computer Viruses

Companies are frequent targets of computer viruses deposited by disgruntled employees "getting even" for real or imagined wrongs. By using a number of different systems, you risk contaminating your diskettes and hard drive unless you have good virus software that you keep updated. Check Appendix A, *Computer Virus Software* for suggestions.

The Internet can be a source not only of viruses but also of virus hoaxes. Here is one way to tell a hoax. If the "warning" indicates that it is by the Federal Communications Commission (FCC), be advised that the FCC has not and never will disseminate warnings on viruses. It is not part of their job.

Regarding e-mail as a virus source: Reading a mail message does not actually execute the mail message; you are reading it from the Internet. Trojans and viruses have been found as executable attachments to mail messages, but they must be extracted and executed to do any harm.

For detailed information on viruses and virus hoaxes, check out the information provided by the U.S. Department of Energy Computer Incident Advisory Capability (CIAC) or the National Computer Security Association (see Appendix A for contact information).

Show Off

In addition to leaving completed work in a folder with a note attached, consider leaving behind a nonthreatening improvement to make the work site a better place. Here are three suggestions to get you started.

1. Something as simple as printing out directories for diskettes is helpful. Attach the printout to the diskette with tape. I always hope to educate those who scribble hieroglyphics on the label that there just might be a better way to do it.

2. "Computerize" a form the employees use a typewriter to complete. On medical and dental forms, certain information—name, address, date of birth, Social Security number—must be completed with every claim. Once the form is on a computer, that information never has to be filled in again.

3. Make up a one-page instruction sheet explaining the position to a "temporary employee." I do this when I'm in the spot for longer than a week. Think how much more a company would get for its "temp dollar" with something like Figure 5.4.

Troubleshooting on the Job

Somehow You Lost the Menu and Can't Find It Again

One way that always works is to return to the DOS prompt and the root directory to execute the autoexec.bat command. To return to root directory:

At the DOS prompt type C: (press ENTER)

then type CD\ (press ENTER)

at C: \ type AUTOEXEC.BAT (press ENTER).

In addition, many menu systems will return if you type MENU (press ENTER).

Figure 5.4 **Sample Instructions for the Temporary Secretary**

General:	The "Daily Appointment Forms" are in the red folder on desk. Ron must fill one out and give to Reggie (mail person) by 10:00 A.M.
	Make two copies of all memos and letters. Please leave these in blue folder marked "File."
Messengers:	Notify Frances in Reception (0) and she will call the messenger. Prepare the package or envelope and take to her for pickup.
Supplies:	Stationery is in the first drawer under the PC. Envelopes and junk paper are under the printer. The hall supply closet has other office supplies.
Telephones:	Your extension is 229, Ron Smith is 231, Sarah Allen is 241. Please answer phone with the greeting, "Communications." Both Ron and Sarah will pick up calls if they are in the office. Please answer for them on the third ring.
	Press 9 for an outside line. For area codes outside 212, press 81, wait for a tone, then press area code and number. Reception can be reached by pressing 0. A list of telephone numbers for other staff members is taped to the top pullout section on right-hand side of desk.
PC:	When you turn on the PC, you will be asked for your password. Ron has a sheet with that information and directions to the work directories.
Printer:	You share a printer with Mike at the adjacent work station.

How to Get Help When No One Knows How to Do It

Call equipment and software help lines. To get information from the technical support staff, you must have available to give them (1) the serial number of the equipment or software and (2) the company name and department.

The help telephone numbers are often posted on the equipment. Software help numbers can be found in the software manual.

Errant fax Machine

Every now and then someone sending a fax will key in the wrong number—the number of your work station. Technology is grand until it goes awry. The fax keeps trying to get a signal and automatically calls you every few minutes, driving you crazy. Find out the number of the company's fax and transfer the call. When the document prints out, call the sender to transmit it again, this time to the correct number.

Precautions for Everyone

Be careful and tactful when presenting suggestions for improvement. People are often defensive about their way of doing things. If you meet with resistance, don't get into an argument over it.

Be cautious about displaying extensive knowledge of computers. Technically illiterate employees get nervous that you might be (1) spreading computer viruses, (2) stealing their company's secrets, (3) hacking into whatever, or (4) all of the above.

Be sure that any books or diskettes, or other materials that you bring into the company are clearly marked with your name. This is one of the reasons I use brightly colored diskettes; they are less likely to be confused with the company's.

Use common sense doing your personal work. I have gone on assignments to companies where reading at a desk—even business magazines, technical manuals, and newspapers—is forbidden. (Obviously, I never returned.) On the other hand, I've had a manager ask me if I had a book to read because there wouldn't be much work for about an hour or so.

Company policies vary. If you're not sure something is okay, ask.

Special Tips for Administrative/Support Staff/Word Processing

Here are a variety of time-saving ideas to help you quickly organize the assignment, produce the work, and still have free time to follow your own pursuits.

Organizing

1. Create a new subdirectory called "current." Use it for work that you do during the assignment. This will go a long way toward speeding up searches for files. People use hard disks as vast storage bins, naming each and every fragment of data. This results in temps searching for files in a morass of unfamiliar names. At the end of the assignment you can:

   a. Copy the "current" documents (the ones that you worked on) back into the general directory and delete the "current" subdirectory.

  b. Copy the "current" directory onto a diskette and delete it from the hard disk.

  c. Leave instructions telling the permanent employee how to get into the subdirectory, letting her/him decide what to do with the directory. Assume a lack of knowledge on the part of the employee and write explicit directions. For any documents you create, institute a naming protocol to convey as much information about the document or file as possible.

2. Place footers on all your work that list the file name and path. Some temps use the automatic date code in footers to accurately track updates.

3. Print out the directories for the diskettes you are to use. It takes the guesswork out of what files are on them.

4. Set up templates for faxes, memos, and courier forms. Keep these together on a separate diskette. It gives you the ability to grind out work immediately.

5. Automate routine functions using macros. Macros are a set of instructions that are executed by one or two keystrokes. An example of a repetitive short phrase is the closing for a letter:

Yours very truly,
Roberta R. Roberts
Vice President, Financial Planning

Instead of typing this closing for endless letters, your own correspondence included, you would press one or two keys to activate the macro; the phrase types itself.

Teach yourself how to do macros if you don't already know. As you did with templates, save the macros on diskettes and edit them as needed on the job. Don't reinvent the wheel for each assignment.

6. Use the "copy" function to build a correspondence name and address list. This enables you to quickly find and print out unfamiliar addresses on envelopes or labels. Here is a simple way to do it:

  a. Save the file after typing the letter; open another window; name it "corr.lst."

  b. Highlight and copy the name and address to "corr.lst"; save.
     Each time you type a letter, add the name and address alphabetically

to "corr.lst." Print out the list and you have a quick reference tool as well.

7. Use mail merges to quickly dispatch multiple letters. Teach yourself how to do it if you don't already know.

8. Prevent the mixups that often occur with documents undergoing multiple revisions by using a different colored paper for each draft.

9. Unless specifically told to do otherwise, I do all word-processing correspondence on separate pages of one document. This keeps the client's work organized and in one place for easy access. I make the first page a log where I record who wrote the letter or memo, who received it, the date, and the subject. The second page is the most current document. The last page of the file is the chronological first document of the week (or month). I print out the log (see Figure 5.5) and leave it for the regular secretary. The log has the file name as a footer.

   On longer assignments, you can set up monthly correspondence files for documents. Thus, SEPT–98.COR, OCT–98.COR hold correspondence for the months of September and October 1998.

10. Save documents frequently, especially if you are part of a LAN. Having several hours of work wiped out because of electrical fluctuations or network failures is more than depressing.

Figure 5.5 **Sample Log**
Document Log for Week of 12/10/98 (*The log itself is page 1*)

12/14	(Page 2)	MJB letter to Harold Smith re resignation
12/13	(Page 3)	ARB memo to Drafting Department re specs
12/12	(Page 4)	ARB letter to Human Resources re vacation
12/10	(Page 5)	ARB letter to Martha Covey re fees

Document name and path appear as a footer:
c:\ mm\ docs\ wk12-10.cor (correspondence for the week of December 10)

Dixie Darr's Portfolio of Skills

As a free agent working out of a home office, Dixie Darr is a master of what can be done with a portfolio of skills. She balances work on short- and long-term projects with part-time assignments. She is a business writer, the editor/publisher of *Accidental Entrepreneur,* and an adult learning consultant. She gives corporate seminars on returning to college as an adult and develops training materials for corporate clients. She presents her own seminars on self-employment and writes on numerous business topics as well as public relations. Her multiple and varied sources of income give her great freedom and a resilient safety net.

She highly recommends becoming a good networker. All of her projects come about through fairly casual, long-term networking. She publishes a one-page monthly marketing newsletter—full of news, resources, and "fun stuff." It lets people know what she is doing and keeps her name in front of them on a regular basis.

Dixie's advice to other entrepreneurial temporaries?

"Expect the unexpected. Opportunities arise at the oddest times and under the strangest circumstances. Say 'Yes!' whenever possible. One thing leads to another. Be useful to other people, hang out with other entrepreneurs. Pay attention to your intuition. Be willing to do whatever it takes to stay self-employed."

6 *Marketing and Selling Your Services*

*T*here are literally hundreds, if not thousands, of books, videos, Web sites, and audiotapes on the topic of marketing and selling services or products. It would be impossible to condense even the highlights of what is available, much less all of that information, into this chapter.

What I do hope to accomplish here, however, is to pass along some basic concepts and tips, to impress upon you the need to develop some degree of expertise, to remind you that a small business is not a *little* big business, and to help you avoid drowning in a sea of information by pointing you in the direction of helpful *expert* resources. My own personal favorite marketing guru is Jay Levinson. He is the author of the "Guerrilla" marketing books and audiotapes, all of which are full of useful information and creative marketing ideas that don't cost a fortune to implement.

Every self-employed person is in the marketing business; it is not optional. Expect to be a salesperson for your venture. Think of these efforts as business development; there is nothing difficult about it. You will use your natural enthusiasm for what you do to promote your business, and you will learn how to solicit new business in a manner that suits your style. The secret of success is the systematic pursuit of leads and the avoidance of "analysis paralysis." If you engage in endless analysis, you can successfully avoid marketing and selling by having no time for it. *Selling* is the act of asking for and getting the order. *Marketing* is the process of deciding what order to ask for and how to go about getting it. *Success* comes from planning and preparation. Plan and prepare.

When she speaks before organizations and groups on the topic of finding work, Renee Cohen, a freelance medical writer and editor, encourages her audience to act like detectives on the trail of new clients and opportunities.

Take the reading of newspapers, for instance. Renee says,

> *I study the local paper and the* New York Times *various* JOB *classified sections—all of the section. For the Sunday Times, that means the backs of the Week in Review and Money & Business sections. Biotech companies, medical foundations, and research organizations need "other" personnel, controllers, administrative assistants, database experts. In their ads for the "other" personnel, these organizations often identify themselves as being in the health care/medical field or they say that knowledge of medical terminology or medical trends is required. And then I contact these people and identify myself and my skills.*

Use Renee's technique with your own area of expertise.

What? Another Plan?

Yes, another plan, albeit a brief one.

However, your first task is to come up with a short description of what it is that you do, one that adapts to any conversation. Write it down, commit it to memory, and practice reading it and saying it until the words are second nature to you. When people ask what it is that you do, this is what you tell them. It must express the essence and benefits of your business, not its features. It is your primary selling tool.

Now your mission is to come up with a marketing scheme expressed in a maximum of seven sentences. Brevity makes the scheme easier to use, and avoids your becoming overwhelmed by yet another plan. It is important to have a planned approach to your marketing and to commit to it. (This includes marketing your services to agencies for interim work.) Not only does it strengthen your identity, but the planned approach is essential to your business survival and growth. Even when you have developed relationships and a customer base, your marketing continues. The market is constantly changing, and people have short memories (especially true at temporary help companies). If your competitors aren't marketing, it will give you an edge. If they are, it enables you to hold on to your old customers. Now that you have them, you have to keep them and keep yourself in their minds for future projects. Always follow up with both agencies and clients. Clients may have friends, family, or colleagues who can use your services. Agencies may have similar projects in the works. As Jay Levinson says, "familiarity breeds sales."

Most formal marketing plans contain all of the same elements as the one below, perhaps in a somewhat different order. Use one (and only one) sentence for each topic.

1. State the benefit to consumers. Find that which is interesting or unique about what you do and translate it into a meaningful benefit. People buy benefits, not features. Remember that features are the characteristics of a product or service. The benefits are how they help the user.

2. What business are you in? Include your positioning in the marketplace.
   Deluxe Gift Baskets at Budget Prices!

3. What is your target market?
   Downsized corporations, small businesses.

4. Advertising strategy? Concentrate on what you are equipped to do, not what you would like to do. Your emphasis is not on how many strategies you can come up with, but on how *well* you implement the few.

5. Position or niche?
   Champagne looks for beer-budget costs.

6. Tools and techniques?
   Targeted direct mail, radio advertising.

7. Budget and timetable? Be realistic about what you *can* do as one person or with hired help.

Commit to your plan and implement it for at least three months. Then set aside time to look at which strategies were the most effective and which were the least. If the results are less than stellar, consider meeting with a small business marketing consultant for a fresh approach.

The First Client and/or the First Temporary Help Agency

Working with your first client helps you to develop a methodology—the tools, processes, and techniques you will use to deliver results. This also applies to the first time you work for a temporary help company. The concept of your own business or practice becomes a reality. This reality will be reflected when you sell your services or register with another agency, making your questioning more insightful and your presentation more convincing. The trick is getting over the hurdle of the first one. For new clients, especially, it helps to have references from other work you have done. If you are just starting out, you might consider asking an associate or boss at your former firm where you performed the same function to give you a reference. Another idea—to be used only with extreme caution—is to offer to work for a portion, maybe even one-half, of your fee in exchange for favorable future references. Choose the candidate carefully; don't get exploited for your efforts.

Do a little homework before you approach any potential client or agency. Be ready to speak about your past achievements as well as answer questions about what it is you do. Write out some of the achievements, along with the traits and skills it took to accomplish them. Be prepared to answer personal questions and to balance *listening* with telling your story. If you can, gather and analyze information about potential clients' achievements and/or competitors. Your focus will be on what you can do for them, relating your past projects to their needs.

Twelve Tips to Get You Started

1. A past employer might consider you for a specific project, since your expertise and knowledge of the company make you especially qualified. Consider targeting the firm you just left, particularly if you know of projects that need doing. Think about potential assignments and write a proposal.

2. Consider working as second banana to another consultant who has more work than he or she can handle.

3. If you have a specialty, work for specialty temporary help agencies for a while to get a feel for the type of projects contingent workers are used for. This will help you to develop a pitch for your services.

4. Look through the employment classified ads. Call companies to offer your services as a consultant while they search for the right person for the job. Use Renee Cohen's approach and answer the ad "even if you don't have all of the skills they want (desktop publishing, Internet research, spreadsheet, database, two foreign languages, and playing the clarinet)." Renee maintains that those who advertise for a full-time person won't be able to find quite that person. Your answer should make it clear that you are ready to work right now. Skip the ads where you are asked to send a letter to Human Resources, unless the match is nearly perfect, or unless the organization is so small that HR might mean the office manager or the managing editor. Even if the organi-

zation finds the right full-time person, Renee says "that individual will have so many meetings to attend, so many presentations and telephone calls, that he or she will still need a freelance to meet deadlines and busy periods."

5. Nonprofit organizations need additional people during their fund drives. Find out what the drives are, when they are held, and who is in charge of staffing them; then offer your services.

6. Consider running a Situation Wanted advertisement describing your services in one of the trade papers. Before parting with any money for this approach, read current ads and call a few of the people who advertised. Ask what kind of response they had to their ad. Look in the library at various papers if you don't know where to advertise.

7. If you want to work as a freelance office temporary, have the ad appear in Thursday's paper whenever possible. Office managers begin thinking about staffing for the next week at this point. Your ad should mention being paid on a per diem basis. You want to be paid at the end of the day on a short assignment, not sixty days later.

8. Research the seasonal needs or likely special projects of industries or individual companies. Make direct contact with those in charge if you can, rather than through human resources departments. Local papers often furnish leads in their announcements of who is heading up which fund-raiser or charity event of the month.

9. Numerous large companies maintain their own temporary work force. Query human resources departments directly. You will receive a higher hourly rate than agencies pay, but less than freelancing.

10. Freelance office temporaries often adopt the prospecting technique that agency sales reps use: making cold calls to all of the offices in a building. Chat with the receptionist to get the name of the correct person to contact. Sometimes it is possible to talk briefly with him or her. You can always leave your business card with the receptionist.

11. Your business network is another good source for leads.

12. Attorneys frequently use a variety of freelance services.

New Client Research: Plan and Prepare

Pursue new clients aggressively and continually; nothing ever stays the same. Your contacts will leave for other opportunities, companies merge, go out of business, reorganize, and change emphasis. Every new addition to your clientele helps you to grow, diversify, and—more important—be less dependent on the clients you have.

As you prepare to approach potential clients or to make a presentation, here is the type of information worth having on the tip of your tongue or at your fingertips. The suggestions below are to give you ideas. Not all of your calls will require information this complete.

You should know the company locations and the name of the founder, president, and other operating officers. Know the type of service and/or products it produces and the number of employees. Find out the gross and net sales for the past three years, who their competition is, and how well the company is doing by comparison. Learn what you can about the business strategy, corporate culture, and/or national or local economic events affecting the company. Read any recent articles about them. Of course you will have researched the name and title of the best person to contact. However, try to find out other information about this person—length of time with the company, positions held, accomplishments, and where previously employed.

New Client Research

1. Company locations
2. Founder, president, other operating officers
3. Service and products
4. Number of employees
5. Gross and net sales for past three years
6. Competition
7. Business strategy, corporate culture
8. Recent articles about company
9. Name, title, information about best person to pitch

Marketing Letter

If you intend to make your initial contact by letter, you are more likely to get the letter read as well as generate interest if you include the following elements.

1. State something you know about the organization. *I am impressed with your quality control record over the past twenty years and the less than 4 percent "need for repair within five years" rate for your products.*

2. Give information about yourself, including specific accomplishments. *I have over fifteen years of experience in the field and have published two books on the subject.*

3. Make a proposal that could boost their productivity. *Using my patented technique, I can help you shave another 1 or 2 percent from your rate.*

4. Take the initiative. *I will call you in ten days.*

Seek feedback on any marketing effort and cut your losses early. You can waste months chasing a bad idea or trying to sell to someone who, for whatever reason, likes to jerk people around.

Telephoning Potential and Established Clients

More plan and prepare. Doing a little homework makes telephoning clients easier and gives better odds for a successful call, whatever your agenda. Before you pick up the telephone, have it very clear in your mind why you are making the call. Know what information you hope to get, as well as what information you wish to convey. How much of the client's time will you need? What is your plan if you reach the secretary, assistant, receptionist, or end up in voice mail?

List the items that you want to discuss. Put the most important ones first. Have backup papers handy, along with any files you may wish to refer to. Write out a script and practice it; don't read it to the client, though. Some people find putting a mirror by the telephone and watching themselves talk helps them to relax and chat more comfortably.

Bypassing Voice Mail

Just as a matter of course, always ask for a private extension number to eliminate going through the fresh hell of a punch menu. If you get the fax number, you can fax ahead to set up a time for the call. Call it a telephone appointment, and leave a choice of two times when you are available to take the return call. If you don't get a return call, see if their operator will assist you with another number to call, or if the client can be paged. Persist, leaving a different message each time.

When you run into someone who is always unreachable, work with the secretary to find out the best time to call. Ask the secretary if the person comes in early. With the direct line you can call early in the morning, between 7:30 and 8:30. Try calling after work at 5:30 or 6:00, or call during lunch, between 12:15 and 12:45.

Word-of-Mouth Advertising

Initiate word-of-mouth advertising by starting a referral program. Give brochures to new clients, ask for recommendations, give discounts for referrals. Don't leave the referrals to chance. Ask colleagues and clients for the names of others to contact. Ask for permission to use the referrer's name.

Educate existing clients about your referral program. Ask for testimonial letters, positive comments you can quote. Doing this strengthens clients' commitment to you. They understand you are in the market for more clients, and the letters give you a selling tool to present to new accounts. A "no" from one of them can flag a problem that needs fixing, and that is a good thing.

Remind clients periodically that you want their business, perhaps sending them a flyer offering "$100 discount on your next invoice when you refer someone to us."

The Secret of Successful Word-of-Mouth Advertising

- Initiate a referral program.
- Educate existing clients about referral program.
- Remind them periodically.

Ten Tips for Frugal Marketing

1. Treat the business cards of your contacts with respect. Ask for an extra one to pass along to someone else, then do it.

2. Develop a short survey on a business trend, problem, or national issue; no more than five or so questions. Call one hundred successful businesses you think will have the answers. It sets you up as an expert to be quoted, and you can use the survey results in promotional and press materials.

3. Find ways to congratulate people.

4. Ask the referrals for referrals.

5. Believe the 80/20 rule: You get 80 percent of your business from 20 percent of your clients. Learn to refer problem clients to your competitors.

6. Any time you have mail going out to clients, make the most of your postage:

- Do you have an attractive order form to enclose that lists all of your services?

- Does your letterhead state your one-sentence positioning statement? *The best customer service on the East Coast!*

- Did you include a brochure, a business card, a discount coupon, or a notice about your referral program?

7. Make the most of your business cards; they can serve as unique and informative brochures. Investigate the Adnet infocards to see if this concept would be appropriate for your services. (Check Appendix A under *Business Card Brochures*).

8. Use postcards to acknowledge orders, or as thank-yous. They require less postage than letters, and a handwritten message will invariably be read.

9. Read your junk mail. (I know, I know. This tip may not appeal to everyone.) Ask yourself if you can help this business, team up on advertising or promotion, refer clients and receive referrals. Look at the layout; maybe saving it for ideas (in a specific file, not as clutter). Can either you or your clients use it?

10. Offer your service or product as a prize for a community fund-raiser and receive the kind of publicity and goodwill that can't be bought at any price.

World-class speaker Dottie Walters counsels her audience, "If you can conceive it and believe it, you can achieve it. Ignore those with no vision." She illustrates her point with the following excerpt from history.

Orville and Wilbur Wright invited the whole town to watch their plane fly at Kitty Hawk. Although much of the town already thought the two men were crazy, and a number of the townspeople had actually signed a petition to have them incarcerated in an insane asylum. Only five people came to watch the flight. And then it flew.

"Ignore those with no vision."

The Networking Connection

Networking is the process of building links to other people who can extend your reach, strengthen your knowledge, use your services, or help you reach those who can. Staying in touch with former colleagues, clients, information providers, or literally anyone who touches your business life constitutes worthwhile networking. Technology strengthens your ability to network effectively. Telephone communication is routine, online communication is rapidly becoming so.

Look into networking groups, local alumni chapters, professional associations. There are referral or "tip" clubs that hold weekly meetings for members to exchange business cards and information about their businesses to pass along to friends and acquaintances looking for expertise. If you are thinking of joining such a group, visit several meetings before doing so (most allow this). Be sure you like the members of the group—you will be spending a lot of time with them. Several are listed in Appendix A under *Networking: Business Tip Groups*.

Conferences, seminars, trade shows, and workshops offer opportunities to network with peers, customers, and clients. Their names are added to lists and programs, helping you identify potential business associates. Giving a presentation at these functions nets you free advertising in their publications (newsletters, journals, magazines). Use the gatherings as a hunting ground for future business and a listening post for what is of interest to your clients. Cherry-pick, though, and don't waste time with irrelevant sessions and people. Always ask yourself, does this function serve your clients? Does it make your business prosper? There is no requirement to stay in boring meetings and useless sessions.

Your suppliers, too, become a part of your business network. Consider swapping talent or services with a computer consultant (to keep you updated on hardware and software), a telephone consultant, a proofreader, a freelance writer, a marketing consultant, or a bookkeeper.

The six networking tips below are from Pam Murray, a popular keynote speaker, trainer, and consultant who helps businesses and individuals with the "people" side of success. Among her publications is *127 Ways to Build a Powerful Network,* a booklet guide to solving some of the most common people-connection problems.

1. Establish a critical core of five to eight people who are vital to your success in different ways, such as a mentor, a super lead generator, a commiserator/encourager, an idea genius, and a truth-teller.

2. Establish stables—groups of people in compatible industries you can call on or refer others to.

3. Make sure you are in other people's groups. Let them know you would love their referrals.

4. Think of people in your stables as your partners.

5. Re-evaluate your network at least twice per year. As you change, so will your network. Let go of those who are simply not interested in recip-rocal activities or to whom you do not feel confident about giving leads.

6. Spend 80 percent of your networking time with the 20 percent in your network who will bring you the most reciprocal results.

Networking Guidelines

1. Schedule time for networking.
2. Set goals.
3. Each day call at least one person you've talked to in the past. (One call a day is *not* a big deal.)
4. Use a script if it makes you more comfortable initially. "My reason for call-ing you is . . ." "I would like to know (or discuss or pick your brain). . . ."

Business Cards

Another networking expert you should know about is Susan RoAne, an author and keynote speaker based in the San Francisco Bay Area. Most of the tips in this section on business cards come from her funny and informative book, *How to Work a Room* and are quoted by permission.

Most of us take business cards for granted. We grab a fistful before leaving the office. We give some out if asked for one. We collect other people's cards, fail to note any information about them, and some time later (a week or three years), these potentially valuable resources surface—dog-eared—and we no longer have a clue why we have the card and who the contact is.

This is not the purpose of your business cards. Their purpose is to give peo-ple a tangible, physical way to remember you and something they can slip di-rectly into a Rolodex or a card file. This is also how you should use other people's cards.

1. Make sure that your name, your company name, and your telephone number are readable. Select a typeface that is big enough and clear enough so that even Baby Boomers who are now in their forties and fifties don't need a magnifying glass or four-foot arms to read the card.

2. Devise a system for carrying your own cards and for collecting cards from others. RoAne uses a large cigarette case, with a baseball card to divide her cards from those she has collected. Filing a card is helpful only if you can retrieve it by remembering the person's name and why you wanted to contact that particular person. Tip #3 will help you remember.

3. Make a few notes on the card—as soon as possible—to jog your memory about the person (jazz lover, marathon runner, and so forth).

4. Bring enough cards. No one wants to take home a scrap of paper that you grabbed in a hurry to write your name and number on. The excuse, "I just gave out my last card" is questionable and smacks of poor planning.

5. Never leave home without them! You never know who you will run into. The ever-dedicated RoAne keeps cards in the pocket of her running suit.

6. Do NOT pass out brochures. Brochures are expensive. They are meant for people who are genuinely interested in doing business with you. They are also bulky. People at a reception have no place to put them. Brochures are also a great way to follow up, so don't waste that opportunity by giving them away at the first meeting.

7. If you want to give your card to someone but they have not asked for it, ask for theirs first. Most people will respond in kind, especially if you hold your own card conspicuously, as if you are ready to trade.

8. Avoid "sticky" situations. Don't reach for the buffet with one hand and your card with another.

9. Pass out your cards discriminately. Not everyone should have your business card. Keep your own safety and sanity in mind. *The exchange of cards should follow a conversation in which rapport has been established.* Ask yourself if you actually want this person to call you.

Susan RoAne: Open Minds Lead to Open Roads

In 1982, there was a massive layoff of teachers in the San Francisco Bay Area. Susan was one of the teachers who lost a job and as a result found herself informally counseling her colleagues on career alternatives for teachers. The counseling led to presenting a series of workshops on the same subject. When the series quickly sold out and accumulated a waiting list of one hundred, it dawned on her that she had a business. The rest, as they say, is history.

Her favorite temp story is that of her late friend, Chuck Montgomery. Chuck, an accomplished pianist, also had a master's degree in English from Ole Miss. In an effort to have a less pressured job and life, he left teaching and began temping. His keyboard skills as a musician served him well when he took a temporary assignment as a typist at Bank of America. The people who gave him typing to do began noticing that their correspondence and reports always read better after Chuck worked on them. When they finally asked him about this, he owned up to his advanced degree. One thing led to another, and they hired him full-time. He eventually became a vice president and continued working for the bank until his untimely death in 1992.

Keep an open mind. You never know where it might lead you.

FURTHER READING

Any marketing books by Jay Conrad Levinson and/or Dr. Jeffrey Lant.

Getting Publicity, Tana Fletcher and Julia Rockler, Self-Counsel Press, 1995.

Marketing Without Advertising, Michael Phillips and Salli Raspberry, Nolo Press, 2nd edition.

The New Publicity Kit, Jeanette Smith, John Wiley & Sons, 1995.

Uncommon Marketing Techniques, Jeffrey Dobkin, Danielle Adams Publishing Company, 1997.

Which Ad Pulled Best? Philip Burton and Scott Purvis, NTC Business Books, 8th edition, 1996.

See also the following topics in Appendix A:

Brochures and Mailing Pieces

Business Card Brochures

Business Cards, Letterhead, Forms

Networking

7 *Credit, Taxes, and Professional Advisers*

*T*he variable income your business ventures generate changes the business deductions for your taxes. It also changes how the IRS views you in terms of audit potential and how credit card companies and financial institutions evaluate you as a credit risk.

The IRS View: IRS auditors salivate over taxpayers who are entrepreneurs, consultants, freelancers, have home offices, and/or variable income.

The Credit Industry View: You *are* your business. Forget about drawing lines between business and personal obligations, whether by incorporation or by other means. Lenders do not set themselves up to watch business loans go bad while the business owner's personal assets remain untouched. Everything will be neatly tied together before the first dollar is lent.

This chapter is about credit, the inevitability of taxes, avoiding death by audit, and choosing professional advisers wisely.

Personal Credit and Credit Cards

Until 1996, states could limit the fees charged by any card sold to its citizens. A U.S. Supreme Court decision changed that. It ruled that credit card fees are "interest" and therefore subject to state regulations. Those rules are set by a bank's home state, not the cardholder's state. So many banks have put their credit card operations in states such as Delaware and South Dakota, where the sky's the limit on interest and fees.

Fees and Interest

As we discussed in Chapter 4, prudent money management requires minimizing the cost of handling it, and that includes keeping credit costs in check. In order to do so, you have to know what incurs the charges. The credit card annual fees and introductory interest rates generally stay low because consumers keep an eye on them. What cards lose on the front end, however, they more than make up for with a diversified array of fees and interest computations. Here's how they do it.

- **Late fees:** Traditionally, you had thirty days to pay. Today, the average is eighteen days. If you don't pay on time, late fees run anywhere from $15 to $25. In 1996 the average penalty was $13. By 1998 the average had jumped to $20.

- **Billing method:** Most cards use your average daily balance for calculating interest charges. The growing trend is toward **two-cycle billing.** Two-cycle billing doesn't affect you if you always pay in full or always carry a balance. **It penalizes the people who pay in full for a while, then carry a balance.** *It charges you an extra month's interest every time that happens.*

- **Penalty interest rates:** If you pay late, exceed your credit limit, or have a deteriorating credit report, credit card companies raise your interest rate by anywhere from 3 to 10 percent for a year or more.

- **Compounding rates:** Most cards compound your loan interest monthly, but a few are switching to daily compounding, which costs you more. The giveaway phrase is "daily periodic rate."

- **Cash advance fees:** Most cards charge interest immediately, with no thirty-day grace period for payment. In addition, they charge an interest rate 2 to 6 percent higher than they do on other unpaid balances *in addition to* a cash advance fee of 2 to 5 percent.

- **Balance transfers:** These transfers can be treated as purchases, but some cards treat them as costly cash advances. Be sure to check out how a company classifies this transaction before signing up for a new card with a low introductory rate and making a transfer with attached costs that more than offset the savings in interest rate.

- **Slamming:** Slamming is when you're charged for extra services that you didn't order. Watch for extras on your account statement such as a shopping service or credit, life, disability, or unemployment insurance.

Three Strategies to Offset Credit Costs

Negotiate a Better Rate. Call the customer service lines of your present cards and ask them to match the competitive rates of other card offers in order to keep you as a customer. They may not match the other rate exactly, but chances are that you will still get a lower one. *You won't unless you ask!*

Find the Right Card. There is no one-size-fits-all, generic credit card. Depending on your financial habits, you will find that some cards suit you better than others.

- *If you pay off your balance in full each month,* look for a card with no annual fee and no late fee.
  USAA Federal Savings Bank 800-922-9092
  United National Bank 800-242-7600
  Broadway National Bank (available in Texas only) 800-531-7650

- *If you occasionally carry a balance to finance a large purchase,* use a card that offers a generous grace period for new purchases. This will give you at least one month free of interest.
  American Express/Centurion Bank Optima (True Grace) 800-467-8462
  Citizens Bank 800-438-9222

- *If you carry balances on several cards,* choose the card with a low introductory rate followed by the lowest rate you can get when the introductory period ends. Consolidate your credit card balances on the low-rate card and pay off as much as you can as soon as you can.
  First USA Bank, 6.9 percent for six months, then 13.9 percent fixed rate 800-347-7887
  Bank of Boston, 6.4 percent for six months, then 12 percent variable rate 800-252-2273
  The KeySmart Card (800-539-2969) rewards users who pay off more of their balance. Clear 5 percent or more of the amount owed and KeyBank calculates the next month's interest at its lowest rate (range 8.9 percent to 11.9 percent).

- *Must you sometimes take cash advances?* Few credit cards offer grace periods on cash advances, so you should try to avoid taking them. Two banks offer a twenty-five day grace period:
  Arkansas Federal Credit Card Services 800-477-3348
  Fidelity National Bank 800-753-2900

Find a Low-Rate and/or No-Fee Card. Here are places to look for credit cards with low annual rates and no annual fees.

- Check your local area first. Local banks and credit unions often have the lowest-priced cards. Some credit unions have open membership. For example, I opened a savings account with Self-Help Credit Union, located in North Carolina, because they are committed to grass-roots economic development and make loans to first-time home buyers, worker cooperatives, worker-owned businesses, and businesses owned by minorities and women. Call them at 800-747-3205. For more information on finding other open-membership credit unions, contact the Credit Union National Association for a list of those in your areas.

- Both *Money* magazine and *Barron's,* a weekly financial paper, list credit cards with the current lowest annual percentage rates in each issue.

- CardTrak provides a list of low-rate and low-fee cards from bigger banks.

- Bankcard Holders of America, a nonprofit organization funded solely by membership dues ($18 per year), has lists for cards that are secured, have no annual fee, and have low interest rates. Call them at 540-389-5445.

Credit Card Safety

Take a few minutes to make a record of your credit cards and membership cards. Spread the cards on a copier, and make several copies. Put a copy in your home file and another in your safety deposit box if you have one.

Destroy all old ATM and credit card receipts and any promotional mailings from credit card companies with your account number on them. Professional criminals specialize in "dumpster diving" and use the stolen numbers to pay for mail-order merchandise and to make long-distance calls from public telephones. Recently, our local police precinct issued a warning in a community newspaper. A group was operating in our neighborhood the evening before each trash pickup. We made it so easy for them with our paper refuse neatly bundled for recycling. Members of the group methodically collected information from selected addresses over a period of weeks until they had enough to start ordering merchandise. These criminals are thorough, persistent, and professional. The same professionals work the public telephone areas in airports to pick up credit card numbers from travelers placing calls. Sometimes they secure the number by observation, at other times by pressing the "last number dialed" button on the telephone. I found this hard to believe—until it happened to me. A month after I returned home from California, the credit card I carried on the trip started showing charges for calls all over the U.S. The only time I had used it was to call my daughter from the San Diego airport.

Credit Bureaus

More than ever before, you need to check for errors in your consumer credit report. The bureaus are reducing our credit histories to a single-number "score." That score distills everything that credit bureaus know about our debts, such as how many years we've had credit cards, how much credit we use, and how many times we've paid bills late. Naturally, we don't have access to our scores; they are released only to people who inquire about us. The most commonly used system was created by Fair, Isaac & Co. in San Rafael, California. It puts our score anywhere from 800 (borrow money from us, please!) to 300 (surely, you jest). Scores change as new information comes in. We may have different scores from different bureaus because of errors in our file.

At the end of 1997, a new set of amendments to the Fair Credit Reporting Act (FCRA) took effect. They expand consumer rights and make it easier to enforce the rules. The new law says that disputed data removed from your file cannot be reinserted unless the creditor certifies that it is accurate, in which case the credit bureaus must notify you. *For the first time, creditors in all states will be held liable for their errors in an individual's report,* as a violation of the FCRA. While creditors cannot be sued for making mistakes, lawsuits will generally be possible if they don't correct a mistake once it has been pointed out, or if they reinsert erroneous data in a file. Creditors will have to tell credit bureaus if an account is in dispute and reveal whether an individual closed an account voluntarily. (Accounts closed by creditors work against the consumer.) Another amendment stipulates that national credit bureaus must supply a toll-free number answered by people, not a recorded message.

Under the new changes, if a consumer challenges a report and its accuracy cannot be verified within seventy-five days, the negative items must then be stricken by reason of default. Under the FCRA, individuals also have the right to insert a one hundred-word consumer statement into the credit report telling their side of the story. Lenders say these statements weigh heavily in credit decisions, but most consumers simply don't know that they have the right to add to their own files. Free reports are required for victims of credit fraud, people on welfare, and unemployed people intending to look for work within the next two months. At present, the only credit bureau offering a free annual report is Experian (formerly TRW). Their telephone number is 800–682–7654.

Laws for Consumer Protection

According to a Federal Trade Commission regulation, if you receive a solicitation saying that you have "preapproved" credit, and you accept, the bank must grant you the credit. Banks and credit card companies may not use that phrase as an enticement; if they use it, they must grant it. [Regulation 16 C.F., section 604 (3) (A) (6)].

Every printed credit card offer is required by law to display a "Schumer box" (Figure 7.1). It is so named for Congressman Charles Schumer, who sponsored an amendment to the 1988 law that created it. The box details the interest rate, interest computation method, grace period, and other fees as a neat little synopsis of the offer. Be wary of any offer that doesn't display the box.

Figure 7.1 **Schumer Box**

ANNUAL PERCENTAGE RATE	5.9% fixed through the first five billing cycles, thereafter a fixed rate of 15.95%.
Grace Period for Repayment of the Balance for Purchases	Not less than 25 days from the date of the periodic statement (provided you paid your previous balance in full by the due date).
Annual Membership Fee	None
MINIMUM PERIODIC FINANCE CHARGE	$0.50
Transaction Fee for Purchases of Wire Transfers, Money Orders, and Gaming Chips	None
Method of Computing the Balance for Purchases	Average daily balance (including new transactions).

The Federal Fair Credit Billing Act lays out the following ground rules for disputing charges with a credit card company.

1. You must notify the creditor in writing. Your letter must include your name, address, account number, and a copy of the disputed bill (and any receipts or canceled checks that support your claim). I suggest that you close with, "I expect to hear from you about this matter within the thirty days allowed by law."

2. Your letter must be acknowledged within thirty days.

3. The matter must be resolved within two billing periods or ninety days, whichever is sooner. If the credit company fails to meet its obligations

under the time limit, it may not be able to collect the full amount owed, even if you are the one in error.

4. If you continue to disagree and refuse to pay, the credit company can report you delinquent to the credit bureau, restrict your credit, and institute collection proceedings. However, it must inform the credit bureau that the amount is under dispute. It must also report to you the name and address of any credit bureau or reporting agency that it contacts.

If a bank refuses to reverse an unjust charge for a consumer purchase, you are protected by law if your item cost more than $50 and was bought in your home state or within one hundred miles of your address. You may also be protected if you used a credit card to buy by telephone, mail, or the Internet from a company that advertises in your state or sent you material such as a catalogue. The level of protection varies from state to state, but generally you are covered. You have to make a good-faith effort to resolve your problem with the merchant. Report the problem immediately in writing and ask for a refund or other fix. Keep copies of your correspondence, as well as written notes of your telephone conversations. The law helps you only if you haven't paid for the item in full. The card issuer can erase an outstanding amount but won't recover money you've already paid. The card issuer must investigate. (During that time it cannot close your account or report you as delinquent but can report that a payment is in dispute.) In turn, you are able to withhold payment only on that one transaction. There is no time limit on asking for a charge back. The card issuer can charge the disputed payment back to the merchant's bank. If you are found to owe the money and refuse to pay, the card issuer can report you as delinquent and blacken your credit standing. You can add your side of the story to your credit report.

Please note: The dispute must be over a consumer purchase. The law doesn't cover items used in business, including home businesses.

Debt Danger Ratio

Experts use a *debt danger ratio* to assess your financial health. The ratio is a percentage of the amount of debt you carry to your annual income (debt ÷ annual income = debt danger ratio). If your ratio is more than 25 percent, and well on the way to 33.3 percent, you're headed for trouble. If the amount of your debt is more than 36 percent of your income, most banks will immediately deny a mortgage loan.

Here are tips from professional financial planners on how to reduce debt.

1. List each of your loans, how much you owe (too many people have only a hazy idea), the minimum monthly payment, and the interest rate. Total it.

2. Restructure your debt to reduce the cost of interest. You can transfer credit card balances to lower-rate cards, or consolidate consumer loans on a credit union loan or home equity line of credit. Don't use either to run up more debt.

3. Increase your monthly debt reduction budget, even if only by a small amount. For example, if you were paying off a balance of $5,000 at 18 percent with payments of $100 per month, it would take thirty-nine years and four months to retire the balance. Increasing the monthly amount to $125 saves you five years and three months in time, and reaps a saving of $10,666 in interest.

4. Make one-shot reductions in your loan balances. Have a garage sale and use all the proceeds to pay off debt.

5. Consider using your savings to reduce balances, especially if you pay 18 percent interest and the money in the savings account earns 5 percent.

6. Pay the minimum amount on lower-rate loans. Funnel the extra money toward the loan with the highest rate.

7. Keep on paying the same amount each month, or more when you can, even though your loan balance goes down. Once you've erased the highest rate, go to the next highest, still paying at least the fixed amount.

8. Work your way down the list, debt by debt.

Business Credit

Until you've developed a good track record in business, many commercial banks and other traditional lenders will be reluctant to extend credit to you. If you are in the early stages of your business, either as a start-up or with a business plan, product samples, and no revenue, your best bet is to approach more nontraditional lending sources.

However, you will still need a good business plan as an extension of your personal assets. Be prepared to demonstrate convincingly what the money will be used for and how you will be able to repay it under different contingencies, such as a recession or becoming seriously ill or disabled.

Nontraditional Lending Sources

Friends, relatives, partners
Local development corporations
State and local governments offering low-interest micro loans
Private foundations offering program-related investments
Credit unions featuring small business lending
Universities with targeted research and development funds

Traditional Lending

You can approach a commercial bank if you have full business and pilot programs in place, or if you have been in operation for some time and have documented revenues and expenses. Your best bet is to submit an application to a bank where you have an established relationship. If you do not have one, lenders recommend that you ask an experienced accountant or lawyer to contact a bank and present your proposal. You must have chosen a legal designation, such as sole proprietorship or corporation, and have executed the necessary documentation for your small business before approaching a bank or other lender.

The process by which traditional lenders judge a business creditworthy is called credit analysis. There are five components to it, the "five C's" of credit analysis: Capacity, Capital, Collateral, Conditions, and Character.

Capacity to repay is the most critical of the five factors. In order to know exactly how you intend to repay the loan, the prospective lender will want to look at the cash flow from the business, the timing of the repayment, your contingency plan, and the probability of successful repayment. Your payment history on existing credit relationships—personal or commercial—will be considered an indicator of future payment performance.

Capital, the money you have personally invested in the business, is an indication of how much you have at risk should the business fail.

Collateral, or guarantees, are additional forms of security you can provide the lender. Giving a lender collateral means that you pledge an asset you own, such as your home.

Conditions focus on the intended purpose of the loan. Will the money be used for working capital, additional equipment, or inventory? The lender will also consider the local economic climate and conditions both within your industry and in other industries that could affect your business.

Character is the general impression you make on the potential lender or investor. The lender will form a subjective opinion about whether you are sufficiently trustworthy to repay the loan or generate a return on funds invested in your company. Your educational background and experience in business and in your industry will be reviewed. The quality of your references and the background and experience levels of your employees will also be taken into consideration.

Internal Revenue Service

Avoiding Audit

As self-employed professionals who engage in several forms of employment (including consulting), work from a home office, and have flexible and varied incomes, we are ripe melons waiting to be cracked open by the IRS auditors.

Once upon a time, the IRS plucked the wrong melon for a two-year audit, Amir D. Aczel, Ph.D. Dr. Aczel is associate professor of statistics at Bentley College in Waltham, Massachusetts, and an expert in the field. Dr. Aczel fielded his audit in such a way that the IRS ended up refunding money to him. But the experience was so execrable that Dr. Aczel spent the next three years conducting an analysis of the factors that trigger audits and then wrote a book about it, *How to Beat the IRS at Its Own Game: Strategies to Avoid and Fight an Audit* (terrific book—read it!). The detailed ratios and strategies Dr. Aczel writes about give us melons a fighting chance. (*Attack of the Killer Melons*, a new cult classic!) Here are a few of Dr. Aczel's audit-avoiding tips:

1. Avoid nice round numbers, such as $10,000 instead of $9899.91.

2. Avoid inconsistencies across years. If your daughter changes her name, let the IRS know, so that they won't think you are claiming a bogus dependent.

3. Check to see that your IRS information agrees with the information on your state return.

4. Don't leave large shifts of income and/or expenses from year to year unexplained.

5. Explain everything. Use convincing, valid, written (typed) explanations for everything you claim. The computer will DIF-tag you for the audit (explained in the next paragraph), but a human IRS employee will then look at the selected returns.

Each year the IRS selects a random number of tax returns for a thorough scrutiny under the Taxpayer Compliance Measurement program that analyzes all items on tax returns. Most audits result from a screening of tax returns by the "discriminant function system" (DIF) computer program that assigns scores according to a secret mathematical formula. Tax experts generally agree on several items that trigger audits:

failure to list all sources of income

use of a high-percentage formula to compute deductions for rental property or a home business

high deductions relative to income

Here are more of Dr. Aczel's findings, following extensive statistical analysis of 1,289 returns:

1. Taxpayers whose expenses on Schedule A itemized deductions are 44 percent or more of their earnings have a high risk of audit.

2. Those whose expenses on Schedule C (profit/loss) are greater than 63 percent of earnings face a high probability of audit.

3. Written explanations of unusual items go a long way to reducing your chances of being selected for an audit. Explain everything.

4. If you fit into any of the following profiles, you are a likely candidate for an audit: small business owner, entrepreneur, consultant, freelancer, farmer, waiter, caterer, physician.

5. Returns that have deductions for bad debts or casualty losses face a higher probability of audit.

6. Excessive charitable giving, high medical expenses, and use of a home office deduction result in a higher probability of audit.

In addition, meticulous documentation should be kept if you have deductions in the following areas:

barter

home office

business travel

business entertainment

Organizing Business Expense Categories

Your tax reporting will be facilitated if you categorize and separate your expense receipts. At the end of the year, it will take less time to total each category and prepare summary expense sheets for the tax preparer.

I use a numerical accordion file that has thirty-one compartments to categorize the expenses. I print out my expense categories in alphabetical order on labels and place them over the numbered partitions. At the end of the year I total the receipts in each category and give the summary sheets to my tax preparer. She takes the appropriate percentages for deductions and depreciation and completes the myriad forms for all of it.

Possible Self-Employed Deductions

accounting/bookkeeping services	legal services
advertising, public relations	membersip dues
answering service machine	moving expenses (>35 miles)
bad debts (costs incurred to collect)	newspapers, periodicals, books
bank account/checks/fees	office equipment
business cards	office supplies
business travel/transportation	postage
cleaning services/supplies	printing/copying services
education	repair services
entertainment	safety deposit box rental
equipment/furniture rental	stationary
financial planning services	subcontracting fees
gifts and holiday cards	telephone answering machine/ service
interest paid on business loans	
insurance/special riders	tools, supplies
IRA/Keogh contributions	uniforms
late tax payments	voice mail

Qualifying the Home Office as a Tax Deduction

The IRS qualifies a home office as space that is used ". . . exclusively and regularly for activities to a trade or business, and is either (1) the principal place of business or (2) a place to meet and deal with patients, clients, or customers or (3) located in a separate, free-standing structure." The business must show a net profit, no matter how small. It cannot be a hobby or a passive activity such as managing investments.

If the taxpayer works as someone else's employee and *is not* self-employed, the home office must be (1) a condition of employment and (2) for the employer's convenience, not the employee's.

Indirect expenses such as utilities, real estate taxes, and depreciation are permitted on a percentage basis. To determine what percent to use in your calculations, first figure out what percent the net square footage your home office is in relation to the total square footage of your home. This is the percentage that you deduct.

Indirect Expenses A percentage deduction may be used for the following items:

child care/invalid care (so you can work)

depreciation of home

insurance premiums

mortgage interest

rent

repairs (furnace, roof)

services (trash/snow removal, yard maintenance)

utilities

Direct expenses

decorating/remodeling costs (not capital improvements)

inexpensive furnishings (large purchases are depreciated)

repairs such as rewiring, flooring

Remember, everyone is different. Run the deductions by a tax person for a careful check, or consult with the IRS.

Qualifying the Business as a Tax Deduction

Unless the business shows a profit in three out of five years, it may be considered a hobby. The IRS decides if a business is legitimate on the basis of nine criteria. While you don't have to meet all nine points, the number you do meet gives a general idea of the seriousness of your intent. Therefore, keep records of your expenses and of your failures (rejection letters, fruitless sales calls, etc.). Here are the IRS's nine criteria:

1. The activity is carried on in a business-like manner.

2. The amount of time and effort spent on it indicates you intend to make it profitable.

3. You are dependent on the income from the activity for your livelihood.

4. The business losses are due to circumstances beyond your control, or they are normal in the start-up phase of your type of business.

5. You change your methods of operation in an attempt to improve the profitability of the activity.

6. The activity makes a profit in some years, and the amount of the profit.

7. You and your advisers have the knowledge needed to carry on the activity as a successful business.

8. In the past you were successful in making a profit in similar activities.

9. You can expect to make a future profit from the appreciation of the assets used in the activity.

Taxes for the Self-Employed

The "self-employment" tax is the money you pay for Social Security and Medicare. As a W-2 employee, 6.2 percent of your salary up to $65,400 goes to Social Security and another 1.45 percent goes to Medicare; your employer pays the other half. As a 1099 worker, you pay the entire amount, 15.3 percent of your income.

Keep in mind that expense deductions against the business will save in taxes. According to Linda Stern, author of *Money Smart Secrets for the Self-Employed*, if you are in the 28 percent federal tax bracket, your state/local income tax is around 6 percent, and your self-employment tax is roughly 12 percent, the marginal tax rate on business income is 46 percent. In other words, a $200 software program costs you $108 after taxes. Her book is full of other tax-saving and money management tips. I highly recommend it.

Business Records: How Long Do You Keep Them?

For tax documents, the general rule is that receipts may be discarded three years from the date the tax return is filed or two years after the tax is paid, whichever is later. For example, your 1998 taxes will be due on April 15, 1999. The records should be kept until April 15, 2001. For taxpayers with self-employment income, complicated investments, or significant capital gains, six years is a better number. That is because the IRS has six years to audit if it thinks income has been underreported by more than 25 percent. If you file a fraudulent return, or don't file one at all, there is no time limit in prosecuting you.

Some personal records must be kept forever (or **until you sell the item**):

expensive insured items such as jewelry, furs, art, etc.

investments

property records

home improvement

escrow or settlement statements

refinancing

Self-Employed Business Records

Six years

accounts payable/accounts receivable ledgers

expired contracts

employee time reports

disability and sick benefit records

former employee records

W-4 forms (withholding statements)

freight bills

Eight years

payroll records, including canceled payroll checks, time reports, and
   earning records

Indefinitely

tax returns (Form 4506 is the "Request for Copy of Tax Form," should
   you wish to get a copy of a missing return)

depreciable assets (for three years after you sell) computer, office equipment

IRA records (for three years after funds are withdrawn)

Safety Deposit Boxes

The annual rental of these boxes is tax deductible. What do you keep in them?

legal documents; stock certificates; property deeds; marriage, and birth certificates

insurance policies; photographs of valuables in case of fire or theft

an equipment and furniture inventory of your home and office

a copy of your will if the original is stored elsewhere

Taxpayers' Fifteen Most Common Mistakes

Just as failed small businesses repeat identical mistakes, so do the intrepid taxpayers. From our friends at the IRS comes this list of common mistakes:

1. Failure to include receipts from charitable organizations for gifts of $250 or more. Without receipts the deduction could be disallowed.

2. Failure to deduct state and local taxes that were paid in the current year for a liability from a previous year. If additional 1998 taxes were paid in 1999, those taxes are deductible on the 1999 return.

3. Failure to report a state and local tax refund on the federal return. This results in an underpayment of taxes. Not all state and local refunds are taxable. Taxpayers who did not itemize in the year in which those taxes were paid but just took the standard deduction, then do not have to include the tax refund in their income.

4. Failure to consider the consequences of the alternative minimum tax, resulting in a large debt to the IRS.

5. Failure to file a Schedule C for net profit and loss from business, and most likely nonpayment of self-employment tax or Social Security tax. Taxpayers who make this mistake often put income that should be on Schedule C on line 21 of Form 1040.

6. Failure to claim the earned income tax credit, a special break for low-income workers, which can be worth as much as $3,110. To claim it, you must complete the IRS earned income credit worksheet and enter the credit on line 57 of Form 1040 or line 29c of Form 1040A.

7. Failure to include a Social Security number for any child listed as a dependent results in a delay in processing the return.

8. Understatement of the cost basis of mutual fund shares by failing to include dividends reinvested in fund produces an overstatement of the capital gain and results in a higher tax.

9. Overpayment of the Social Security tax. Big earners who change jobs during the year may have paid taxes on more income than the $65,400 Social Security base. Fix it by taking a credit for excess on line 59 of Form 1040.

10. Failure to deduct points paid in a mortgage refinancing. This deduction should be taken over the life of the mortgage and not all in the same year of refinancing.

11. Failure to deduct the appropriate share of taxes paid at closing on the purchase of a home. If the former owner prepaid taxes, the new owner repays a pro rata share of those taxes. Many taxpayers forget because they never get a receipt from the tax authorities.

12. Failure to deduct the cost of self-employed health insurance. The percentage allowed keeps changing. Those who err on this one can file an amended return.

13. Failure to claim all the dependents to which they are entitled, such as elderly parents who do not live with them; or failure to claim for a full year for a dependent who dies during the year. (There are five tests to determine the qualification for dependents.)

14. Failure to use the most advantageous tax status. Single parents with children should list themselves as the head of household. Couples should be sure that filing separate returns is not cheaper than filing a joint return.

15. Failure to calculate the underpayment penalty on Form 2210. Those who did not pay enough taxes during the year could come up with a lower penalty than the IRS.

Independent Contractor

In recent articles about the perils of temporary employment, one of the facts cited is that workers are paid as independent contractors. Employers have a number of obligations to regular employees that they do not have to independent contractors (freelancers, consultants). For permanent employees, they pay into those funds that provide workers' compensation, unemployment insurance, and state disability benefits; and they withhold employment taxes from paychecks. On the other hand, independent contractors are paid on a 1099 form, and no deductions are taken out.

The IRS considers as independent contractors those who operate under written or oral agreements that define work to be performed by a given date for an hourly or fixed amount from which no taxes are deducted. Independent contractors pay quarterly taxes. The IRS has twenty "qualifying rules" to distinguish independent businesspeople who offer services to multiple clients from employees who work for one employer. Questionable cases are decided on an individual basis. Appendix B lists the IRS's twenty qualifying rules for independent contractors.

A great resource and reference book on this topic is Nolo Press's *Wage Slave No More: The Independent Contractor's Legal Guide.* Along with outlining "everything an independent contractor should know," it comes with a disk with form contracts, business correspondence, and business/legal forms.

That contract workers are widely used is well known. What is just coming to light is that as many as 20 percent of them are people who have returned to their old companies, many after having been pushed off payrolls or lured off with lucrative buyouts. New surveys are beginning to document this growing trend in which companies and employees feel less obligated to each other.

Not only do we have the IRS and its twenty qualifiers, but the Supreme Court has issued six criteria to determine whether a person is an employee or independent contractor. The Court's guidelines are:

1. The extent to which the services in question are an integral part of the employer's business (the more integral, the more it shows employee-employer relationship).

2. The permanency of the relationship (the more permanent, the more it shows employee-employer relationship).

3. The amount of the contractor's investment in facilities and equipment (the more substantial, the more evidence of the contractor's independence).

4. The nature and degree of control by the principal (the more control, the more evidence of an employer-employee relationship).

5. The extent of the contractor's opportunities for profit and loss (the more opportunity, the more evidence of the contractor's independence).

6. The amount of initiative, judgment, or foresight in open-market competition with others required for success (the more of these, the more evidence of the contractor's independence).

Agency Wages

Agencies withhold taxes and FICA according to the number of exemptions listed on the temporary's Form W-2. A sizable number of them do not withhold taxes if the temp works for only one day. Some will pay temps as independent contractors, withholding no taxes or FICA, and filing a 1099 at the end of the year if wages exceed $600.

Finding Professional Advisers

Business Advisers or Do-It-Yourself?

Many small businesses have never used a lawyer and will never have to—that is, unless they enter into long-term agreements (such as partnerships, cooperatives, distributor/exclusive dealer agreements, licensing/franchising arrangements, or royalty contracts) or buy property or a business. While certain transactions are easy enough to do on your own, the question becomes one of the best use of your time. Take incorporation, for instance. There are many books in the library that can help you, but there will be *time* involved in researching and understanding the pros and cons as they apply to you. By the time you figure out what to do, you could have paid an attorney for a consultation and still saved money. On the other hand, something as quick and simple as a copyright application involves only filling out a form and mailing a check with it. You do not need to hire an attorney to do it for you. Selectively get the help you need.

Questions to Ask Potential Advisers Before Hiring Them

Before you talk with any professional, have some idea of your plans and objectives. Make a list of questions. Compile information about the business or personal financial decisions under consideration so that you can ask specific questions. Some general questions apply to all professional advisers offering their services.

1. Make sure the person is licensed to practice in your state.

2. Talk frankly about fees. They will depend on the type of services you require, the prevailing costs in the community, and the complexity of your work.

3. Talk to the professional personally before committing yourself. If he or she will not talk on the telephone other than in vague generalities, call someone else. If you do have a conversation, does the person make sense, or does he/she speak in technical jargon?

4. Ask what percentage of his/her income comes from fees paid by clients versus commissions from the products he/she sells. Anything less than 100 percent means that you are speaking to a salesperson with a vested interest in recommending certain strategies and product purchases.

5. Does the expert perform professional services in more than one area of specialization? Be wary of someone who claims expertise in more than one area.

6. Ask if liability insurance is carried.

7. Inquire if the fee includes a written report of strategies and product recommendations that you can implement on your own. Avoid advisers who charge an hourly rate to make you feel you are not working with a salesperson, but give generic advice and recommend only commission-based products.

Guidelines for Choosing a Professional Adviser

1. Proper licensing.
2. Fees in line with prevailing rates.
3. Does not speak in jargon and vague generalities.
4. Derives income from client fees, not product commissions.
5. Expertise confined to one area.
6. Carries liability insurance.
7. Provides a written report of strategies and product recommendations.

Investment Advisers/Financial Planners

A good planner has the expertise to analyze insurance policies, identify the hidden risks of investment products, and understand your tax and estate-planning issues. You don't need a paid adviser to tell you that it makes sense to participate in a tax-deferred retirement savings plan or to have a disability insurance policy. You want someone who will work with you to clarify and prioritize your major goals, establish the cost and timetable for fulfilling them, and give you practical advice that is simple to implement.

Financial advisers use numerous certifications as evidence of their professional competency. A "Certified Financial Planner" (CFP) is an individual who has passed courses in such areas as investments and estate planning as well as a comprehensive examination on these topics. CFPs are required to have three years of work experience and to participate in continuing education courses. A "Chartered Financial Consultant" (ChFC) has passed a financial services curriculum with an emphasis on life insurance. In addition, ChFCs must have three years of work experience and participate in continuing education courses. "Personal Financial Specialist" (PFS) is the designation given to accountants who have passed a test covering retirement planning and related topics, whose annual practice has included 750 hours of financial planning over three years, and who participate in continuing education courses. A "master of financial planning" (MFP) is a graduate of a university granting this advanced degree in a financial services curriculum.

On the other hand, "investment advisers" are merely individuals who are paid to offer financial advice. However, investment advisers must register with the Securities and Exchange Commission (SEC). They must file a Form ADV, a lengthy document that asks for very specific information, such as a breakdown of their sources of income and the details of their relationships and affiliations with other companies. You can ask prospective advisers to send you a copy of their ADV for review, or you can get it from the SEC by calling 800-732-0330.

Investment Adviser Referrals. As always, ask friends and business colleagues for recommendations. Failing that, there are professional groups that will refer you to financial planners in your community as well.

Referral Groups

American Institute of Certified Public Accountants (AICPA)
    888-999-9256   http://www.aicpa.org
American Society of CLU and ChFC
    888-243-2258
Institute of Certified Financial Planners (ICFP)
    800-282-7526   http://www.icfp.org
International Association for Financial Planning
    800-945-4237   http://www.iafp.org
National Association of Personal Financial Advisers (NAPFA)
    888-333-6659   http://www.napfa.org

Background Checks and Complaint Registration. For a fee of $39, the Mortgage Asset Research Institute will run a comprehensive background check on a planner, investment adviser, or broker. It will cover any disciplinary actions from self-regulatory groups and legal judgments levied against them. Call the Institute at 800-822-0416. The CFP Board of Standards (888-237-6275) keeps disciplinary records of planners holding its credential. For securities dealers, call the National Association of Securities Dealers Regulation (800-289-9999). For referrals to state securities commissioners, call the North American Securities Administrators Association (888-846-2722) or the SEC.

Insurance Advisers

Speak with people in your field who are engaged in similar activities. Ask for referrals from other small business owners, the Chamber of Commerce, or small business council in your community. Professional associations are good sources for liability checklists to assist the assessment of your needs and for group insurance that targets your specialty.

Another avenue for referrals and information is the Internet. Check Appendix A under *Insurance (Business)* and *Insurance Quotes* for a variety of sources to contact, both online and by telephone.

The following helpful tips on buying insurance wisely come from Terri Lonier, author of *Working Solo* and *The Frugal Entrepreneur.*

1. Know your needs; be prepared to answer questions about your business, both current and planned.

2. Consider higher deductibles. (Caution: Do the math involved to see if you are really saving any money.)

3. Another way to save is to "piggyback" on other plans. Centralizing all of your insurance with one company can bring significant discounts.

4. Comparison shop among several companies.

5. Don't buy on cost alone. Good service goes a long way. So does a reputation for prompt settlement of claims.

6. Keep complete and accurate records.

7. Keep your agent up-to-date on changes in your business.

Business Pursuits Endorsement. Regular homeowners' or renters' policies will *not* cover business equipment, supplies or inventory, or losses due to fires that may be caused by such things. A business pursuits endorsement (BPE) is a good answer, since it offers some liability coverage for people in your home for business purposes as well as for materials and products you are storing. If you are storing over $3,000 of inventory, you should probably get a separate fire, vandalism, and theft policy. Business riders on your home insurance carry no personal liability coverage for your business.

Replacement Value Insurance. For about 15 percent more yearly, you can obtain replacement value insurance on personal possessions. It pays whatever the cost is to replace any item that has been damaged or destroyed, regardless of its age at the time of loss, up to the limits of your policy. A loss of business furnishing and equipment is figured on a depreciable basis and is limited to the amounts shown on your special business rider.

Tax Advisers

Which professional do you need, a tax expert or an accountant? That depends on the complexity of your business activities. You will probably want to find a good accountant if your business endeavors require putting together financial statements, if your financial statements require an audit or a review, or if you need help preparing business loan applications or special reports to government agencies.

In any event, stay away from storefront operations that spring up every tax season. Most of the people who work for these chains are relatively inexperienced, minimally trained, and usually familiar only with uncomplicated tax problems. In looking for an adviser, take the same approach as you did to finding an insurance person. Ask for referrals from colleagues in your field, from associates in professional organizations, and so forth. Check Appendix A under *Tax Advice.*

Legal Advisers

Nolo Press is the largest publisher of self-help law books and a name synonymous with high quality and user-friendly books and software. It was started by two Legal Aid lawyers who were fed up with the fact that the average person couldn't find affordable legal information and advice. Twenty-five years ago, they began writing law books in plain English for nonlawyers. Today Nolo Press publishes more than one hundred titles and has five million copies of its books in print. Check Appendix A under *Lawyers* for further information.

Nolo furnishes legal information online twenty-four hours a day, access to helpful articles on a wide variety of topics, selected chapters from Nolo books, downloadable demos of their software, and online seminars with lawyer authors and other experts.

Keep a dual vision. Think back to what it was like when you first learned to drive a car. You focused on the six feet in front of you. That's the same way it is when you start your business. You're thinking about only what's going to happen in the next few weeks. As you get to be a better driver—or as your business matures—you learn to have a dual focus. You can attend to what's right in front of you, but you also cast your eyes farther down the road, so you can be better prepared for what's coming. As you become more comfortable driving your business, you also become more aware of what/who else is on the road, and you pay attention to other elements that will impact your ability to navigate the road well.

—Terri Lonier

FURTHER READING

Credit

Credit Repair, attorney Robin Leonard, Nolo Press, 1996. Includes worksheets and
    sample letters.
The Guerrilla Guide to Credit Repair, Todd Bierman and Nathaniel Wice, St. Martin's
    Press, 1994. Step-by-step guide with sample letters.
Money Troubles: Legal Strategies to Cope with Your Debts, attorney Robin Leonard,
    Nolo Press, 1997. Includes worksheets and sample letters.

Taxes

Being Self-Employed, Holmes F. Crouch, Allyear Tax Guides, 1994.
Dealing with the IRS, Scott Miller and Thomas Guy, Creek Bend Publishing Com-
    pany, 1992.
Disagreeing with the IRS, Holmes F. Crouch, Allyear Tax Guides, 1993.
The Ernst & Young Income Tax Guide, Ernst and Young, John Wiley & Sons, yearly.
H&R Block Income Tax Guide, H&R Block, Fireside, yearly.
How to Beat the IRS at Its Own Game: Strategies to Avoid and Fight an Audit, Amir
    D. Aczel, Ph.D, Four Walls Eight Windows, 1995.
How to Pay Zero Taxes, Jeff Schnepper, ed., McGraw-Hill, 1998.
J. K. Lasser's Your Income Tax, J. K. Lasser Institute, Macmillan General Reference,
    1998.
101 Tax Loopholes for the Middle Class, Sean Smith, Bantam Doubleday Dell, 1998.

Stand Up to the IRS, Frederick Daily, Nolo Press, 1994.

Tax Planning for the One-Person Business, James Bucheister, Rayve Productions, Inc., 1994.

What the IRS Doesn't Want You to Know, Martin Kaplan and Naomi Weiss, Random House, 3rd edition, 1997.

Your Tax Questions Answered, Ed Slott, Plymouth Press, 1998.

8 *The Office at Home: Time Management and Problem Solving*

*A*lthough the statistics may vary a bit depending on the source, it is estimated that around thirty-nine million people are working from home either full- or part-time. Telecommuting accounts for over eight million of those workers, while an additional six million are wage-earning and salaried employees who work at home after business hours. Home-based businesses number about twenty-five million.

As anyone who has ever done it will tell you, working at home involves both practical and psychological adjustments. Under the practical heading are the issues of appropriate space, lack of privacy from family members, interruptions by well-meaning neighbors and friends who think it is okay to call or drop by anytime. The distractions of operating a home and being part of a family provide endless ways to collide with business work, and a disciplined detachment from household routines must be a priority if you want to be successful. Under the heading of psychological adjustment, we deal with workaholism, loneliness, self-motivation, discipline, and productivity.

Loneliness is relative, and people who choose to work at home usually value their privacy. But everyone requires a certain amount of social interaction to remain alert to the realities of running a business. Most books on home offices or self-employment mention the psychological factors to varying degrees. Working for yourself is very different from working for someone else. Your private and professional lives overlap. There is no longer the separation by physical distance of going to work or the psychological distance of allegiance, or lack thereof, to a corporation. This lack of distance is a mixed blessing; my own adjustment was rocky at best.

As a new consultant I felt isolated, lonely, constantly worried about money. I had joined a business group, but the meetings were monthly. The other members had been in business for a while and seemed secure in their professional dealings; I wasn't. Working at home also brought me face to face with personality traits I hadn't noticed in myself before.

For most of my life, I had fancied myself as somewhat of a loner. I went to work, to work. While I might exchange pleasantries with coworkers, I didn't necessarily socialize all that much. It shocked me to find out how much I needed to be around people, whether I socialized with them or not.

Furthermore, in the past I had taken pride in being a bit of a workaholic. This tendency to push myself until I literally dropped grew and flourished as I worked at home. My loneliness and worry supplied the fuel for working even harder. There truly is work to do twenty-four hours a day for the energetic and enterprising person. After I caught myself enough times still in my nightgown at eight o'clock in the evening and realized I hadn't even bothered to dress that day, much less comb my hair, I decided that my new lifestyle was at best unhealthy, and that it certainly wasn't making me happy. To alleviate some of the stress, I decided to take an undemanding job (to have a steady income and be around people) while I built my practice slowly as a part-time computer consultant.

Knowing what I do now, at that point I should have signed up at temp agencies. But I had to learn that lesson the hard way. Instead, I swallowed my pride, rewrote my resume to reflect new, downscaled aspirations, and went looking for a permanent job.

Undemanding Job #1

Within three weeks I accepted a position as executive assistant to the president of a small investment firm of dubious integrity and reputation. My first week on the job, I found they expected me to work a fifty-hour week with neither a lunch nor any other kind of break.

"That's why we pay for your lunch," they said.

And no overtime pay.

"Executive assistants don't get overtime," they said.

In addition, I was expected to serve lunch to the male staff members, hotshot vice presidents all. Since I couldn't afford to walk out, I came in defiantly not one minute before 9:00 A.M. and left promptly at 5:00 P.M. I "served" lunch by placing unpacked bags of food orders on the conference room table and calling out, "Lunch is here."

It took an endless ninety days to find another "undemanding" job, it being hard to schedule interviews without a lunch break. I said nothing until I had received and cashed the paycheck that compensated me through my last day there. At 10:00 A.M., cash safely tucked away in purse, I entered my boss's office, handed him my building pass and key, resigned, and walked out.

Undemanding Job #2

The second job was with the private company of a semiretired broadcast mogul. In addition to the staff of people he normally maintained to administer his personal life, Mr. Mogul had hired a talented and charming man to analyze potentially lucrative venture capital investments for his consideration. My job was to assist him. To give you some idea of the office atmosphere, all staff members (save one) spoke Mr. Mogul's name thusly: "Mr.," pause, assume revential tone, "Mogul." The job itself consisted of researching and reading all sorts of interesting publications, analyzing business plans, and making up stories to cover a certain Boss Charming's long absences from the office.

I began working there in April; my promised raise (a pittance, but money nonetheless) was scheduled for October. October came, but Boss Charming was so caught up in his personal affairs that he kept neglecting to implement the raise despite my weekly reminders. Instead, one morning he surprised me with the announcement that he had tendered his resignation.

To cap it all, Mr. Mogul decided to come out of retirement, consequently lost interest in venture capital investing, and closed out the business. Thus endeth Job #2.

Before he left, though, Boss Charming put aside personal problems long enough to make one telephone call on my behalf to a principal of the newly formed Loathsome & Schlock, as I later called them, to pitch my skills, my plight, and my low salary. As you know from the *Preface*, my employment with them lasted ninety days. When they ended their partnership, I became a temp.

How much better off I would have been registering with a few agencies in the beginning. Indeed, if time is money, think how much of it I wasted in job search activities and interviewing alone. I put in a good amount of unpaid overtime too, in hopes of salary increases that never materialized.

And none of this takes into consideration the aggravation or the stress.

Do as I Say, Not as I Did: Tips to Counter Isolation

Connecting is a good way to learn how others like yourself have solved similar business problems, as well as to discover new projects that you might work on jointly with another colleague.

1. Join several professional/business associations, networking groups, and/or personal-interest organizations and attend their meetings and functions. Monitor their publications for annual meetings and special events that interest you. Business magazines advertise specialized meetings that cross individual professional lines. Request information, and talk with others who have attended. Ask for a calendar of upcoming events at conference centers, Chambers of Commerce, economic development councils, adult and continuing education programs at universities and colleges. A useful resource to guide you along these lines is *127 Ways to Build a Powerful Network* by Pam Murray.

2. Become a savvy networker to get the most out of your membership participation. If you are shy about meeting and socializing with new people, do some reading on the topic. Susan RoAne has books, audiotapes, and a Web site (http://www.susanroane.com) to help you: *How to Work a Room: The Secrets of Savvy Networking;* and, most recently, *What Do I Say Next?* She even furnishes a script of what to say to break the ice. See Chapter 6 for more networking information and tips.

3. Schedule at least one social activity each week, with old friends or new ones.

Telecommuting

There may be periods when you choose to be one of the 8.1 million telecommuters. Telecommuting offers more flexible hours and working conditions. It also eliminates the time and expense of daily commuting and the diverse work-related expenses of lunches, wardrobe, and child care. To some extent it avoids having to attend useless meetings and being embroiled in office politics. In addition, its flexibility enables people with disabilities and those caring for young children or the infirm to continue working. The same qualities that spell success in a career business are among those that best describe a successful telecommuter: self-starter, self-disciplined, flexible and goal-oriented, good planner and time manager, one who enjoys working independently.

On the negative side, telecommuting brings isolation. Depending on the company, some workers may lose certain employee benefits or find it harder to advance their careers. Many of the adjustment problems are similar to those of the self-employed working in a home office.

In the last few years, some companies have established a number of electronic neighborhood centers as an alternative to work stations in the home. They contain various types of computers and other office equipment not practical to have in one's home. Employees commute a short distance instead of to a central office location. At the moment, the centers are concentrated mostly in Los Angeles. If they are successful, no doubt the concept will spread to other cities.

Telecommuters Stay in Touch

A little initiative can keep you in the professional mainstream during those periods you may telecommute.

1. Keep your home days to a minimum, and never use them during "crunch" time.

2. Cultivate coworkers who will keep you posted on current rumors and gossip.

3. Ask a coworker or secretary to check your inbox on the days you are home.

4. Offer your home as a meeting place.

5. Use your e-mail to remember birthdays and anniversaries, or to send congratulations for promotions.

6. Use a combination of telephone, fax, and computer to stay connected to office events.

Set Up the Home Office to Avoid "Common Mistakes"

The "those ignorant of history are doomed to repeat it syndrome" applies to setting up a home office. Experts on the topic of home offices have their own list of the most common mistakes people make: wrong location, a lack of dedicated space, inappropriate furniture and equipment, the lack of filing space coupled with an unworkable filing system, a shortage of book and storage space, and an excess of clutter. Although the kitchen or dining room table may work in a pinch, for the long haul it will not be in your or your business' best interests to continue using it as an office. Dedicated space, even if only the corner of a quiet room arranged with a creative use of ready-to-assemble furniture, will at least put you in a business setting.

Sometimes you don't need more storage space, you just need to store things differently. Get some graph paper and try sketching different layouts. Look through catalogues for furniture, shelving, and space savers. Consult a professional organizer (they come in all price ranges) for assistance. Consider your expenses in this endeavor as an investment in the future. You will recover your costs in time saved and aggravation avoided.

Pay attention to ergonomics and comfort when you purchase a chair and desk. Most communities have ample places to buy used office furniture, and used items of good quality are a much better choice than cheap new stuff. (I bought a cheap file cabinet once, and I still have nightmares about it.) Don't overlook the ready-to-assemble furniture that is reasonably priced and often designed to fit in unusual spaces.

Again, with comfort in mind, purchase a few of the little things that make life easier: a cordless telephone, or a telephone headset if you are on the telephone constantly. Get a decent copy holder if you spend a lot of time at the computer. A digital postage scale saves time, effort, money, and the annoyance of trips to the post office. A paper shredder will make sure that your business and personal papers that must be bundled for recycling are useless to professional "dumpster divers."

Competing with the Big Guys

You need to look into business support and backup services that make you more responsive to your clients. Although your value may be that you deliver a unique, one-on-one service and your competitive edge may come from your knowledge and skill, your large corporate customers cannot hit zero or the pound key on their telephone to transfer to your receptionist. Consider a live answering service, a pager, or a "follow me" telephone service. With this service, an electronic voice answers and asks for the caller's name. It offers the choice of leaving a message or holding while the system tries to track you down from the three locations you previously programmed into the system. Vendors offering this service are listed in the Appendix A under Telephone *Follow Me Service.*

Something as simple as spending time at the library to check the Yellow Pages of other cities for the ads of services and/or products similar to yours will give you a good idea of how you measure up.

You want to be yourself, of course, but don't hesitate to seek professional help in those areas where you might need assistance. If you are not artistic, find a professional to design your business cards, stationery, and brochures. Consider using a professional to record your answering machine or voice-mail message if that is best for your business. If your writing ability leaves a lot to be desired, or you want a "second opinion" to polish your copy, find a freelance writer and/or editor to assist you. Are you insecure about your presentation or speech-making skills? Get videotaped and coached.

Before hiring any professional to assist you, it pays to interview him or her in person. Ask for estimates from several in the field. Look at and compare their portfolios. Don't forget to ask for—then check—their references.

Productivity

Time is money; if you waste time, you are wasting money. Your productivity is therefore tied to how well you are organized. You can only "save" time by wasting less of it. If you earn $50,000 a year and waste thirty minutes each day due to disorganization (lost telephone numbers, misplaced files), you are costing yourself approximately $3,074 a year. Save thirty seconds every five minutes, and by the end of the day you have saved one hour.

Ordinarily, when we think of working productively, we think about getting lots of things done and getting them done quickly. However, the way to be truly productive is to get the *right* things done. The key is to spend your time on the activity that is going to bring in the money. When you work for someone else, you develop sloppy habits in this regard (as well as a related profligate attitude towards office supplies). Start asking yourself: What is the best use of my time now? Am I wasting my time? What should I do? Why and When? Is there a way to simplify this task?

Become aware of how long tasks take; it helps you to plan more effectively. Divide the time allowed by the work you want to accomplish. If you have two hours set aside to make telephone calls and have eight calls to make, each call is allotted approximately fifteen minutes. Does that seem right to you? Do you need more time? Less time? By calculating ahead, you will plan more realistically.

Fourteen Productivity Tips

1. In the beginning, keep to a schedule that is similar to your regular office routine until you are used to managing your time in the new setting. Set business hours and work during that time. Try to do the bulk of your work at the time of day when your energy and concentration levels are highest.

2. Have your telephone answering machine or voice mail screen calls until you have educated friends not to call you during business hours. When I am writing, I turn the telephone ringer off and retrieve my messages at the end of the day. That way, I'm not even tempted to pick up the telephone.

3. Keep a dated master to-do list to keep track of your current business tasks, as well as to remind you what you have to do in the future. Always note any unfinished business, work, or future projects. Never put a piece of paper representing unfinished work into a folder unless you have recorded it. Cross off tasks you have completed. Save your old lists in a folder in date order. (Don't use the same to-do list for both personal and business items: Keep "pick up dry cleaning" separate from "work on monthly sales report.")

4. Get in the habit of doing the administrative things immediately. If you don't create a pile, it doesn't have to be filed. If your credit policy is to expect payment upon the delivery of your services, you don't have to mail an invoice. If you handle a complaint now, you won't have to call back later. When interviewing a supplier, if you inquire about the firm's policy for making good on errors, you won't have any surprises later.

5. Set up routines to take care of details automatically, such as filing receipts, making follow-up marketing calls, sending thank-you notes, ordering supplies, etc.

6. Make a "to-call" list and an "awaiting callback" list. Attach related paperwork to the list, and make a notation on your calendar as a reminder. Call people as soon as possible. Don't waste energy thinking, "I've got to call this guy." By procrastinating, you risk finding the "guy" has a full schedule or is absent on an out-of-town trip.

7. Set aside a specific time each morning or afternoon to deal with incoming paperwork. If an item concerns you, write it on your master list. If it concerns someone else, pass it along. If it is not important, get rid of it.

8. Evaluate all of the magazines and periodicals that you receive in terms of their importance to you and schedule a time to read them. There is no such thing as free time. It doesn't drop out of the sky unattached or labeled "free." Schedule an appointment with yourself, and mark it on your calendar. If you don't want to read the material, cancel the subscription.

9. Whenever you purchase new software, register your purchase and record the customer support number and software registration number in an easily accessible place. Put all of the diskettes or CD's in one place. Remove outdated and unused software programs from your hard drive and discard the old manuals.

10. Use the same technique you do on a temporary assignment and bundle tasks. Do a bunch of the same type at once: ordering or buying supplies, going to the copy shop, paying bills, data entry, and so forth.

11. Add fudge factors and buffer time to any schedule you devise. Anticipate and allow for delays, late deliveries, broken commitments, and out-of-town trips.

12. Piggyback your activities to accomplish more than just one thing. Suppose you are asked to speak before a group. Ask yourself how many uses you can make out of it. It is an opportunity to pass out business material, get press coverage, send invitations to key people, and no doubt something else as well.

13. Use daily rituals to gear up for and wind down from work each day.

14. Don't forget to schedule activities with friends as well as attending a networking event *every week*. Lonely workaholics don't have much fun.

Clutter

Ahhh . . . the eternal question is not, "To be or not to be?" but "Do I keep it or throw it away?" Clutter is a reminder of something that needs to be handled. Clutter is a postponement of the decision about what to do with it. You have not established a place for "the things."

Here's how to get rid of clutter. Ask yourself, do I really need or want this? If it requires any action by you, it goes on your calendar, on your to-do list, or into your action files. If it requires no action and you want to keep it, make a notation of where to file it and date your notation. If you want to pass it along to a colleague, put it in an envelope and address it. Everything else, toss.

Organizing and File Systems

There is no right or wrong way to organize; there's only the way that works for you, and whether or not you like it. If, however, what you are organizing will affect other people, it needs to work for them as well. And as with organizing, there is no "right" way to do a filing system; the logic of how you will remember filed items is much too personal. If you expect others (an assistant, perhaps) to use the system, then the logic must make sense to them as well. Keep it simple. File an item for how you will use it (or remember it), rather than where you got it. If you think cross-referencing is necessary, write "see also . . ." on the folder.

Many time-management experts suggest saving time by handwriting the labels on file folders rather than typing them. I disagree. I think handwritten labels are hard to read and look sloppy and unprofessional. But I don't think they should be typed on a typewriter either. Instead, I suggest putting the filing system on your computer. The benefits gained far outweigh the initial investment of time. Here's how to do it.

1. Start with what you have. Make a list of all of your files. Put the list on the computer and sort it alphabetically. Plan on keeping all future labels in this document. The immediate benefit is that you also know exactly what files you have and if there are any duplicates.

2. It is easier to reorganize and add to your present system if a printout of existing files is available.

3. The next time you add a label, add it alphabetically. The font I use is an easy-to-read Universal Condensed Bold, 16 point. I insert a date code at the beginning of the file list. (The first label is the current date.) You will always have an updated list of your files for reference. I like to keep a copy of the list at my desk.

4. I keep my folders in hanging files, even though they take up more room. I guess it is a matter of preference. I print out the labels twice to cover the hanging files.

5. Expandable file pockets hold file folders and use less space in a file drawer. I like to use expandable file pockets to hold frequently used folders that are not in the same category. I also use them for transporting files to and from assignments.

6. Establish an annual File Clean-Out Day. Religiously celebrate it.

Problem Solving

All problems, business and personal, have solutions. They may not be easy or pleasant ones, or the ones we would hope for, but solutions exist in some form or another. The trick is to find the best one for your needs. Sometimes just going through the process of defining what happened leads to the answer. If you take an unconventional look at the situation, you may discover a creative or unusual resolution to your dilemma. Here are some suggestions on how to do this.

Define the Problem. What exactly happened? What started the problem? Did something occur that wasn't supposed to? Did something break that was supposed to operate? Were there unexpected results?

Determine Its Nature or Type. Is this a human, equipment, situational, or operational problem? Is it transitory or recurring?

Find a Creative Solution or Spin-off.

1. Are there other ways to use it as it exists? What if it is modified?

2. Is there a way to *adapt* it? What else is it like? What other ideas come to mind?

3. Is it possible to *alter* its slant? Change the meaning, shape, color, use, etc.?

4. Can I *expand* it? Add more time or greater frequency? Stronger, higher, longer, thicker? Extra value? Duplicate? Multiply?

5. What about *reducing?* Condensing? Lowering? Shortening? What can I subtract or leave out? Streamline? Split up?

6. Will anything work as a *substitute?* What or who else? Other ingredients, materials, processes, places?

7. What about *rearranging?* Interchanging parts? Adding another pattern, layout, sequence? Changing the pace or schedule?

8. Can it be *reversed?* Turned backward, upside down?

9. Is there some way to *combine* it with another? Blend, alloy, assortment? Combine units, purposes, appeals, ideas?

Wisdom means keeping a sense of the fallibility of all our views and opinions, and of the uncertainty and instability of the things we most count on.

Gerald Brenan, *Thoughts in a Dry Season*

Future shock is the disorientation that affects an individual, a corporation or a country when (s)he or it is overwhelmed by change and the prospect of change. It is the consequence of having to make too many decisions about too many new and unfamiliar problems in too short a time. Future shock is more than a metaphor. It is a form of personal and social breakdown. We are in collision with tomorrow. Future shock has arrived.

Alvin Toffler, *The Observer,* 1972

FURTHER READING

The Home Office and Small Business Answer Book, Janet Attard, Henry Holt & Company, 1993.

If You Haven't Got the Time to Do It Right, When Will You Find the Time to Do It Over?, Jeffrey J. Mayer, Simon & Schuster, 1990.

Organized to Be the Best, Susan Silver, Adams-Hall Publishing, 3rd Edition, 1995.

Organizing Your Home Office for Success, Lisa Kanarek, Penguin Books, 1993.

Paper Clips to Printers, Dean and Jessica King, Penguin Books, 1996. This is a terrific reference source, full of information on how to manage your home office efficiently and economically.

Taming the Paper Tiger, Barbara Hemphill, Kiplinger's Book and Tapes, 1990.

Time Management for Dummies, Jeffrey J. Mayer, IDG Books, 1995.

Winning the Fight Between You and Your Desk, Jeffrey J. Mayer, HarperBusiness, 1993.

The Work-at-Home Sourcebook, Lynie Arden, Live Oak Publications, 6th edition, 1996.

9 *Medical and Disability Insurance*

*I*f you were a large company, your Human Resources Department would handle personnel issues, from state and federal regulation conformance to workers' compensation, OSHA, and unemployment and disability insurance compliance. All this is in addition to the usual hiring/firing process, employee benefits, and pensions. When you serve as your own human resources director you need, at the very least, a nodding acquaintance with certain laws as they pertain to your business pursuits. You need not be expert in these areas, but you should be aware that specific information exists and should know where to find it. You should also recognize at what point to seek professional help.

Health and pension benefits have been an entitlement of "permanent" work for so long in the United States that many Americans are at a loss when their employment ends and COBRA benefits run out. Ask anyone what is the biggest drawback to temporary employment, and I am willing to bet the answer will be the "lack of benefits"—meaning, of course, the lack of low-cost (or no-cost) medical, dental, and disability insurance, and other perquisites of a conventional full-time job. Deteriorating working conditions have been an unfortunate side effect of the drastic changes in the employment climate. Many have found, to their dismay, that a job as the sole source of a benefit package can have serious drawbacks. It holds them in bondage, immobilizing their careers in dead-end or sweat-shop jobs for fear of losing medical coverage. In essence, they have become indentured servants. Doesn't it make more sense to acquire medical and pension benefits independently? Once you have your benefits package in place—that is, those perks necessary and important to you—you will never be trapped in work you loathe simply to keep medical insurance for yourself and your family. *That* is freedom.

Are there any affordable options when COBRA runs out? Let's start with some general guidelines that apply to all insurance policies before tackling the hard one: finding adequate and affordable medical coverage.

All Insurance Policies

Insurance policies are legal contracts. Compare several plans, and read each one carefully. Be sure that you understand all of the provisions. Then compare the plans' respective benefits before you make a buying decision. Marketing or sales literature is no substitute for the actual policy. Request a summary of each policy's benefits. The summaries will give you an outline of coverage for comparison, but read the policy itself before you buy.

Ask for the company's ratings. The A. M. Best Company, Standard & Poor's Corporation, and Moody's all rate insurance companies after analyzing their financial records.

Don't be afraid to ask your insurance agent to explain anything that is unclear. If you are not satisfied with an agent's answers, ask to contact someone in the company directly. Good agents and good companies want you to know what you are buying.

If you find after purchasing a policy that it doesn't meet your needs, you generally have ten to thirty days (it varies by company and state) to return the policy and get your money back.

Choosing Insurance Policies

1. Read each plan carefully, then compare.
2. Ask for the company ratings from A. M. Best, Standard & Poor's, or Moody's
3. Request each policy's benefit summary, then compare.
4. Ask your insurance agent to explain anything that is unclear.
5. If you are dissatisfied after the purchase, you may return the policy for refund within ten to thirty days.

Medical Insurance

As a self-employed professional, you do not have the clout of a large corporation. If you express dissatisfaction with the administration of your health plan, you can't threaten to find another plan and switch several thousand subscribers right along with you. That fact alone underscores why it is essential to understand how the insurance system works and how to manipulate it to get the coverage and care you need. Just as you manage temporary employment agencies, so must you manage the insurance company or the managed care bureaucracy to get the most for your dollar.

What Are the Options?

Until such time there is some form of universal health coverage, available medical insurance comes in three flavors: (1) temporary or short-term plans to tide you over while you explore your options; (2) plans with access to coverage, tied to membership in organizations, unions, and associations that offer access to some form of coverage; or (3) individual coverage through an HMO or private carrier. There may be a fourth option on the horizon, a network of health care providers offering services at discounted prices. The National Association of Part-Time and Temporary Employees (NAPTE) offers its members access to such a service.

Temporary Health Insurance

Temporary insurance is sometimes an appropriate fill-in if you are in between policies, if you are waiting for new plan coverage to begin, or while you are investigating and comparing several plans. These plans generally offer restrictive coverage for thirty-day periods, up to six months. Their definitions of "preexisting conditions" limit the coverage considerably. *Depending on the maximum allowed by state law, it can be any illness or condition for which you have received treatment in the last five years.* Don't just read the plan, *scrutinize* it before parting with money.

Membership Organizations

Sometimes a modest membership fee makes it worthwhile to join an association to gain access to group medical benefits. The problem is, the same few companies insure most of the organizations, and the bulk of them "cherry-pick" the people they insure and the states they insure them in. If your place of residence, your age, and/or your ability to pass a physical examination meet their specifications, the insurance is yours. If not, you keep looking.

Twelve organizations providing access to a wide variety of medical coverage are listed in the Resources section at the end of this chapter. They all have modest membership requirements and fees.

Managed Care

As of February 1997, more than fifty million Americans were enrolled in HMOs. Nearly 75 percent of those who receive health insurance through their employers are covered by some type of managed care plan, up from 51 percent just two years ago. A consumer advocate organization recently compared the massive changes and exponential growth of managed care to the fall of the Soviet Union—no one could have predicted it, and we are not really sure how to respond to the new world order. Insiders say this is where the insurance industry is headed. In ten years, managed care will be the *only* choice available. If this turns out to be true, *now* is the time to learn how to make managed care serve your needs.

Know the Enemy

In 1997 alone, managed care inspired the introduction of approximately one thousand bills in forty-nine state legislatures, often with bipartisan support. All were designed to curb excessive abuse or medical decisions based on financial gain of the company rather than medical need of patients, and to assure that consumers would receive decent care. By the end of 1997, forty-one state legislatures had passed almost two hundred new laws to regulate aspects of managed care plans in response to widespread consumer complaints that cost cutting had lowered the quality of medical care in such plans. Consumer advocates generally consider that Connecticut, New Jersey, New York, and Texas have the strongest laws.

There are five main types of managed care:

1. **Individual Practice Association (IPA).** Physicians are prepaid a monthly rate for service to members (called capitation).

2. **Group Model HMO.** The HMO contracts with a group of physicians to provide health care services. Physicians continue to practice in their own offices but pool and distribute income based on an agreed-upon plan.

3. **Network Model HMO.** An HMO contracts with several physician groups and doctors, who may share in savings but may also provide care to other, non-HMO patients.

4. In the **Staff Model,** the doctors are employees of the HMO.

5. In the **Preferred Provider Organization (PPO),** the HMO contracts with a selected group of doctors who agree to reduced reimbursement and payment.

The HMO's main attraction is that it provides members with affordable health care. The premiums are generally lower, and there is no deductible un-

less the member goes outside the network (most allow outside treatment because the marketplace has forced them to). The copayments are minimal, usually $5 to $15 for an office visit and $2 to $10 for prescriptions. Many HMO
contracts cover preventive health care as well.

HMOs are accredited by the National Center for Quality Assurance
(NCQA), an independent, nonprofit organization originally formed by the insurance industry to head off government regulation. The NCQA has come up
with fifty "standards and measurements" for HMO quality. If a plan doesn't
comply with a sufficient number of these "standards" or has even one defi-
ciency that poses a risk to their definition of "quality of care," the NCQA denies
accreditation. The guidelines are voluntary, and the NCQA has no enforcement powers. A plan denied accreditation may reapply to go through the
process again, or it may sue. As of late March 1997, studies showed no correlation between a plan's level of accreditation and its profitability or membership
growth. Nearly 50 percent of all HMOs have not bothered to apply for NCQA
accreditation.

There are two additional contenders in the budding health care quality
movement that show, in my opinion, less self-serving obeisance to HMOs than
the NCQA. The Medical Outcomes Survey evaluates people's general health,
and at some time in the future it should show which plans do the best for their
members. It was designed by a senior scientist at Boston's New England Medical Center. The new Foundation for Accountability (FACCT) is developing
standards for judging how well HMOs manage specific illnesses. HMOs are
more apt to have data on how well their stock is doing than on how well they
are handling illness.

Beginning in 1997, the Health Care Financing Administration (HCFA),
which administers Medicare, required NCQA-type performance data from all
HMOs that take Medicare patients. It is predicted that sometime in 1998 they
will require FACCT-type data as well.

How the Gatekeeper System Works

Primary Care Physician (PCP). Subscribers must choose a "gatekeeper" primary
care physician from a list of member doctors. Generally, those joining an HMO
must change family doctors, something that people do not like to do. All treatment, decisions, and referrals are funneled through the PCP, who may have in-
frequent and inconvenient office hours. (When I called to find one for myself,
there were several on the list who had office hours only one day per week, and
one who had hours from 10:00–noon on Tuesdays. No, I am not making this up.)

Formulary. The formulary is the gatekeeper for prescriptions. There are two types. "Open" formulary has a comprehensive selection of drugs and ostensibly allows physicians to choose any one of them. "Closed" or, in HMO jargon, "preferred" refers to a highly limited number of choices in select therapeutic categories. The HMO will pay only for the drugs on that list except in special circumstances. Their selection is financially rather than medically determined. New, expensive drugs may not be on the list.

What most people don't understand is that all drug formulations are unique; that is the basis of their patents. If a generic drug is "bioequivalent," it enters the bloodstream at the same rate and to the same extent as the brand name. It contains the same amount of active ingredients, is provided in the same dosage form, and will be labeled in the same manner. That still leaves plenty of room for the variables of inactive ingredients and individual response that cause troublesome side effects or allergic reactions to the formula. Generic drugs *are not exactly the same as the brand name and should not be substituted indiscriminately.*

Evaluating the HMO Plan

As all medical care moves closer to the HMO structure, newspapers are printing more and more horror stories about HMOs. The complaints against HMOs usually center on the required use of HMO physicians and their formulary and "approved" practices based on financial rather than medical criteria. To that end, there are two financial criteria with the potential for adverse consequences that you should know about: capitation and withhold funds.

Capitation. This is the fixed amount a plan plays to a doctor whether or not care was provided to a patient. It creates an incentive for the doctor to limit the number of referrals to specialists, office visits, and diagnostic tests and to deny hospital admissions whenever possible.

Withhold Funds. This is sometimes called a specialist or referral fund. The plan withholds a portion of the doctor's fee until the end of the year. At year-end, the withholds of all doctors are totaled and used to pay for specialist referrals. Whatever is left is distributed to all doctors in the plan. The fund's annual surplus (think of it as a bonus fund) is directly related to low specialist referrals.

Although you may have limited options or few actual choices in selecting a plan, you can still ask questions about it and secure its plan satisfaction rankings from state reports. The *state insurance commissioner's office* (located in your state capital) should have consumer information available, such as a list of HMOs in nearby locations, insurer *complaint ratios* (the ratio of unhappy plan members to the total plan membership) and the *rate of payout* (Does the HMO pay its claims?). A payout rate should be in the 60 to 75 percent range. If it is less, then the plan is either severely limiting coverage or it is hassling the doctors/practitioners.

In New York, for instance, available reports include the State Insurance Department's yearly report on the complaint rankings and a consumer guide to evaluating HMOs. In addition, the City of New York Public Advocate's Office publishes a report that gives comprehensive and detailed information, both negative and positive, about the HMOs in the area, along with advice on how to get good service from them. Check with your local or state officials to see if similar reports are available in your area.

A list of contact telephone numbers for each state's insurance commissioner appears at the end of this chapter. In California HMOs are regulated under the Department of Corporations.

Here are suggestions to help you determine if a plan is for you. I have included evaluation guidelines for conventional indemnity plans at the end of the chapter. You might want to take a look at those guidelines as well.

The first thing you must do is to request, *then read,* the member handbook and enrollee agreement. Next, begin requesting further information and asking specific questions.

1. Ask the plan to provide you with a list of its network providers—including doctors, hospitals, home health care agencies, and skilled nursing facilities. How do they make sure that the doctors are competent and all of their credentials are valid?

2. How many primary care physicians are in their network? How many are board certified? Does the plan track the number of PCPs who are taking new patients? If yes, what percentage are accepting new patients?

3. Does the plan track the average wait for an appointment with the PCP and the average wait to see a specialist? If so, what is it? (one to three months is the average).

4. How does the plan handle chronic conditions? Can a specialist be your PCP? What special services does the plan offer to people with complex medical needs?

5. Find out under what circumstances the HMO will allow you to see a practitioner outside the plan without incurring extra costs.

6. What services must be authorized in advance?

7. What is their definition of an emergency? Is it the "prudent layperson" standard? To prevent the HMO from making a patient pay for emergency room charges when the "heart attack" turns out to be the aftermath of a bean burrito, a number of states have passed legislation to require the following definition:

"Emergency Condition" means the sudden onset of a medical or behavioral condition, manifested by symptoms of sufficient severity, including severe pain, that a prudent layperson, possessing an average knowledge of medicine and health, could reasonably expect that, without immediate medical attention, would result in (a) placing the health of the Member in serious jeopardy, or in the case of a behavioral condition, placing the health of the Member or others in serious jeopardy; (b) serious impairment of the Member's bodily functions; (c) serious dysfunction of any body organ or part of the Member; or (d) serious disfigurement of the Member.

8. Will the plan pay for a second opinion outside the network?

9. Are you covered when traveling?

10. Are college-age dependents who are covered under the plan required to return home to receive medical care? This can be a real headache for out-of-state students and bears checking into. Some plans have begun allowing students to designate the college or university health service as their primary care provider to circumvent this obstacle.

11. Can you get a copy of their formulary to see what is included and excluded?

12. Does the plan cover preventive care—flu shots, Pap smears, mammograms, prostate screening—and/or pay a portion of your health club membership?

13. Does the plan prohibit its physicians from discussing treatments with patients other than treatment authorized by the plan ("gag clause")? Who decides what is "medically necessary"?

14. How are the doctors paid—in salary or per patient? How are the doctors rewarded for cost containment?

15. How many doctors left the plan last year (average is 4 percent). How many members left? How many reenrolled in fee-for-service plans? High numbers in these categories indicate a severely restrictive HMO.

16. Remember, "point of service" means the plan will pay 60 or 70 percent of what constitutes a fair fee in *their* judgment. They pay wholesale, you pay retail. Ask for details.

17. Ask if the plan has a "report card" and if the report card has been audited by the NCQA or another outside organization. Ask to receive a copy.

18. Ask what percentage of revenues goes toward treating patients. What percentage goes toward marketing the plan?

19. How can you appeal a decision? How long will it take to complete the process?

20. *Ask about the recent premium history.* HMOs have been busily raising their rates after several years of offering low rates to increase membership bases.

21. Before signing on, check their standings in your state.

Now, how were you treated when you asked for this information? Were representatives knowledgeable and helpful about getting answers for you? This is the courtship phase. If you ran into ignorance, stonewalling, and/or hostility, it won't get better when you are wedded to the plan.

How *You* Can Work the System

First things first, though: Read your member materials. Some plans have "PCP report cards" that help you choose the right doctor for your needs. Some plans have member information lines to search for a doctor on the basis of a convenient location, extended weekday or weekend office hours, board certification—search criteria determined by *your* needs. This saves calling numerous offices to get the information for yourself, as I had to do. My HMO now has a member information line.

If possible, get the name and direct number for a competent service representative from whoever sold you the plan. It is usually the service rep your insurance person deals with. Don't be shy about letting the HMO service rep know who referred you.

Whenever my friend Susana speaks with her service representatives, she records the conversations on her telephone answering machine. She tells the representative that the call is being recorded "to ensure accuracy." Since she started doing this, she finds the service reps much more responsive, helpful, and cooperative than they had been in the past. It's worth a try.

Call the HMO customer service and request a directory of participating specialists if you didn't receive that as a part of your enrollment package.

Determine how the affiliated practitioners—such as physical therapists, podiatrists, and labs—are chosen. It is better to know ahead of time what to expect than to be surprised when you are in need of a service.

Submitting Claims for Out-of-Network Treatment or Consultation

Learn the billing codes for any treatment you receive. Numerous problems can arise from simple miscoding. Of course, keep records and dated correspondence as well.

Know what is on your medical chart. I can't stress the importance of this enough. If you are seeing any specialists at the time you change plans, obtain your own copies of their treatment records. Request a copy of the treatment record for specialists within the plan in order to monitor your treatment. If you are receiving injections from an allergist, this is especially important. My allergies had been stable and under control for two and a half years prior to my changing plans (and, consequently, doctors). The new HMO allergist saved money by giving me just a fraction of the dosage I should have received: 10cc instead of 2,500cc. There were adverse medical consequences because it took a while for me to find out why my allergies were getting worse instead of better. If I had been knowledgeable about my chart, I could have prevented this.

Make up labels that include your name, address, Social Security number, and member number. Whenever you submit a claim, slap a label on every piece of paper you send in. You can add the date of the claim by hand. The claims department will have a hard time losing or misplacing receipts so marked. (Not that material can't still be lost; it is just harder this way.)

What to Do When a Claim Is Denied

Suppose a claim has been denied. First, call the customer service number and find out why. This would certainly be an instance where recording a call would be helpful. Don't take no for an answer; studies show that up to 50 percent of the claims initially rejected are paid upon review. In a May 1998 interview, Christopher Reeve told *USA Today,* "It's in the interest of insurance companies to deny [claims], because only 30 percent of people who are denied fight back. Fight the denial. Always."

Request to handle the matter by telephone conference call. (The participants would be the claims and customer service reps, the doctor and you.) If, perchance, the representative professes to not have conferencing capability, tell him or her you will set up the call. (You will have done your homework and have the conferencing access number handy for AT&T or another carrier.) Say you will call back in five minutes and to please have the participants' telephone numbers ready. Record the session to ensure accuracy.

Do not accept as true any efforts to convince you that the company is devoid of fax machines or direct telephone numbers for its personnel.

Study the explanation of benefits. Return the claim with photocopies of pertinent paragraphs from the benefits contract, along with a note asking for more reimbursement, or requesting peer review, if that is appropriate. Peer review is an evaluation of the total health care provided by medical staff with equivalent training.

Managing Your PCP

While you are not looking for an adversarial relationship here, you must be aware that there may be times when the first PCP you select doesn't work out. In addition, doctors who refer too many patients to specialists or write too many prescriptions outside the formulary are soon dropped by the HMO. While most doctors will put their patients first, we are talking about HMO restrictions that affect their ability to earn a living. If you find your PCP discourages your treatment preferences, it doesn't necessarily mean that you have to take it as a flat denial. Try some of these tactics:

1. Tell the doctor, "I am making a formal request. Are you really denying me this?"

2. Ask if the denial is medically or financially based.

3. Ask if the plan rewards doctors for limiting care. If the medical care offered is not in the best interests of the patient, the PCP is legally liable.

Formulary Questions

Suppose you have been getting along just fine with the PCP but find he/she wants to change your medications. Or, whenever you ask about a new drug, you are discouraged from using it. Try these tactics, and ask these questions:

1. Is there any reason for switching a medication besides prescribing the best drug available for the diagnosed medical condition?

2. Is this substituted drug a cheaper one than the drug I have been receiving? Who recommended the change and why? Does the HMO favor this substitution?

3. How much is the copayment? Is it higher for the nonpreferred drugs?

4. Is the HMO serviced by a pharmaceutical benefit manager that has a contractual arrangement with the manufacturer of the preferred drug?

The City of New York Public Advocate's Office found in its six-month investigation that physicians and pharmacists were being systematically pressured to rewrite or switch prescriptions to cheaper medications favored by drug marketing middlemen retained by the health insurance plans. For a copy of this informative and comprehensive report, *Compromising Your Drug of Choice*, write the Public Advocate's Office, City of New York, 1 Centre Street, 15th floor, New York, NY 10007, or call 212-669-7200.

Filing a Formal Complaint

During my own fight with an HMO to obtain *competent routine care*, I learned the value of knowing whom to call and where to write. Understand that no one is going to take up the fight for you, but it always helps to have a number of resources whom you can notify of your problem. During this time I found the Center for Patient Advocacy (800-846-7444) and am including their tips, along with others of my own.

- First and foremost, always keep accurate records: dates, times, names (first and last) of people you talk to; and copies of all correspondence. You will need to find out who handles the grievance process: the HMO or the medical group under contract. Most HMOs offer their members a toll-free customer service number that uses some form of tracking to record all calls. When you have a complaint and call one of these numbers, you begin a traceable record of concerns, complaints, and grievances.

- If the representative is unable to solve your problem immediately, ask what response time you should expect in this situation. It should not be more than thirty-one days.

- Following your conversation, send a written letter stating your complaint again. Be sure the problem is stated in a clear, concise manner and enclose all appropriate documentation. Include your full name, the insurance company name, your policy number and ID, any test results, doctor's statements, etc. *Expressly state what action you want your HMO to take to solve the problem.*

- ☐ Don't be afraid to ask your physician to contact the HMO on your behalf.

- ☐ If your problem is not solved, you should appeal your grievance to another level. Unfortunately, most HMO grievance procedures have several levels of appeal, all of which take an inordinate amount of time. If you or a family member is ill, time is of the essence. Do not hesitate to fight for your rights outside the HMO's appeals system as well—state agencies, the press, television, congressperson. An inquiry from a member of Congress often speeds up the most sluggish state bureaucracy.

- ☐ Insist that any claim reviews be expert and neutral. Find out the credentials of the reviewers. If it's an allergy claim, it should be reviewed by an allergist, not a general practitioner, a physician who is no longer in practice, nor a new college grad with a business degree. Know the basis of your claim, and ask for citations from the medical literature.

When insurance companies and HMOs deny a charge as exceeding what is "reasonable and customary," some plan members have had success with getting a supporting letter from their physician, or seeking support from several doctors in their geographic area. County medical associations will sometimes review your charge and tell you whether they consider it reasonable and customary. Some plans will back down with this kind of documentation; others won't.

Members of managed care plans under Medicare have the legally mandated option of having Peer Review Organizations (PROs) review their treatment when there are problems. I hope this system will extend to all managed care in the near future, so keep it in mind as a potential option. To find a PRO in your area, call the Medicare hotline: 800-638-6833.

One other point: There is a phenomenon known as "rationing by inconvenience" and some HMOs have this down to a fine science. They use it by refusing to answer letters, faxes, and telephone calls from members trying to resolve disputed claims. They also use it when patients try to get an expensive prescription or treatment or seek a second opinion, only to find they must deal with specialist approvals, invalid preauthorization numbers, and conflicting information from HMO medical and member service staff. Only the very hardy can keep up the barrage of calls and letters required to get answers. In my temporary work with an HMO, I observed firsthand that plan members who took grievances to their union leader, state assembly representative, member of Congress, or senator quickly got the HMO's attention and received a speedier (though never speedy) resolution of the problem.

Whom to Notify. Your state department of insurance, your state senator, assemblyperson, member of Congress, senator, public advocate (if you have one), state attorney general, governor, local department of health, the NCQA (if the HMO sports that accreditation), the American Association of Health Plans (AAHP) if the HMO is a member. If you are a federal employee, contact the Federal Employee Health Benefit Program (FEHBP) at the Office of Personnel Management (OPM). If you receive your insurance through your employer, inform your benefits manager. The Center for Patient Advocacy Web site (http://www.patientadvocacy.org) lists additional places to lodge a complaint on a state-by-state basis in the Insurance Problems section.

If this sounds like overkill, bear in mind that HMOs sell their policies for money, so they must deliver the services they promise to provide. Too often they deliver services only if the member puts up an intense and sustained fight. Hence, over one thousand pieces of band-aid legislation in forty-nine state legislatures attempting to rectify the situation.

Suppose you purchase a sofa from a local department store, but the store then refuses to deliver it. You make a few calls; other delivery dates are scheduled but missed. You go to the store and demand to pick up the sofa, but the store personnel won't release it to you. You write to the president of the company. You report the company to the Department of Consumer Affairs and make more follow-up telephone calls. By now, two or three months have passed, and you have put a huge effort into getting the item you paid for with your hard-earned money. Finally, the sofa is delivered—with a long rip in the upholstery and minus two of the cushions. The store tells you, "Take it or leave it."

The only difference between the mythical department store and a health plan is in the potential consequences of their actions. No one dies from a torn sofa.

If that scenario really happened, your state attorney general would probably want to prosecute the department store for fraud. Is this example any different from what HMOs do to their members when they limit or refuse medical services in order to maximize financial gain? HMOs should be held as legally accountable for their actions as any other purveyor of goods or services.

More Prescription for Your Copayment

Here are three things you can do to maximize your prescription benefit.

1. Request a ninety-day supply of your medication. Copayment charges rapidly become expensive if your plan restricts you to a month's supply of medicine and you have a chronic condition or must take several medications daily. Ask if the plan provides for a ninety-day supply under special circumstances. Some plans offer the benefit but do not bother to volunteer information about it; you have to ask the right questions, then specifically request the benefit.

2. Ask your doctor to prescribe a dosage increase, which, theoretically, you could use if you needed to. That will often at least double the amount available for the same copayment.

3. Secure a prescription for a three- to six-month supply of medication from your PCP; then fill it through a mail-order pharmacy, not the in-network pharmacy. This tactic works with some point-of-service plans. Afterwards, submit the bill as a claim. Most plans will simply deduct the $2 to $10 copayment and reimburse you for 100 percent of the remainder.

Some of the discounted drug plans control their costs by limiting the time period between refills to a different (financially based) standard than your physician may use. If you are told that the drug plan won't pay for the refill for another week (although you can get it if you are willing to pay the full price), tell the pharmacist to use the "override" code. If the code is unknown, have the pharmacist call the plan's customer service number to get the code. Your doctor prescribes your medication and the frequency of the dosage, not the plan. If the refill falls within the instructions of the prescription (i.e., two tablets three times a day), or your doctor okays the refill, the plan must pay for it.

Medical Files and Privacy

On any medical form, be careful about signing blanket information dumps to health care providers. Read the authorization, cross out words that give unlimited access to your files, and insert other words as necessary to disclose only the minimum information needed to process the claim. Do not endorse a wholesale transfer of your entire chart. Here is an example of an authorization edited by someone who is on long-term disability.

> This authorizes you to give XXXXXX Company, ~~its affiliates and representatives, any information,~~ data or records you have regarding my medical history and treatment, ~~(including records to psychiatric, drug or alcohol use, and any medical condition I may now have or have had)~~ ~~and any information, data or records regarding my activities (including~~

~~records relating to my Social Security, Worker's compensation, credit, financial, earnings and employment history)~~ needed to evaluate this claim only./ ~~my claim for benefits. I understand that any~~ such information obtained may be provided only to an employee of ~~a person or agency requested by~~ XXXXXXX Company ~~to assist with this purpose.~~ for this purpose.

The edited version now reads as follows:

This authorizes you to give XXXXX Company, data or records you have regarding my medical history and treatment, needed to evaluate this claim only. Such information obtained may be provided only to an employee of XXXXX Company for this purpose.

Some states offer basic privacy protections, give their consumers the right to correct errors in their medical records, and shield data on AIDS, mental health, chemical dependency, and genetic information. However, no two state laws are alike.

The Fair Health Information Practices Bill, introduced in January 1997, proposes sensible controls such as limiting disclosures of medical records to the minimum amount necessary and requiring health care providers to create records of disclosures made. The Health Insurance Act of 1996 (Kassebaum-Kennedy legislation) laid the groundwork for a national patient database in which physicians and other health care providers will be required to put every patient's name, residence and diagnosis into a national patient database without patient consent. It set a February 1998 deadline for the Health and Human Services (HHS) to propose security standards for a "universal health identifier" capable of linking a patient's files anywhere in the health care system. The HHS Secretary has recommended to Congress that the long-used patient consent form be eliminated. Also, under HHS recommendations, law enforcement, health researchers and statisticians, public health authorities, state health data systems and employers (if your health insurance is through your employment) all will be allowed access to your medical records without your consent.

Meanwhile, it is up to you to protect your privacy, such as it is.

Disability Insurance

Even more scary than having no medical insurance is considering what can happen to the self-employed person who has a serious accident or is disabled for several months. Disability insurance was originally designed to replace a portion of your income if you could not work. However, over the years insurance companies added so many extras that the policies became virtually unaffordable to all but the affluent. Typical benefits included lifetime coverage and payment of full benefits to policyholders who could no longer work in their former occupations, but could still earn a good income doing something else.

Well, a funny thing happened on the way to the bank. These expensive policies backfired on the insurance companies around 1994, when many policyholders filed stress-related claims and began collecting full benefits for life. The problem was particularly acute in the health care industry, where the movement toward managed care had already displaced many professionals. By 1994, a number of insurers were reporting losses. Unum Corporation, one of the largest disability insurers, was the first to announce it would no longer write individual policies that carried a level premium and paid lifetime benefits. Other insurers followed suit, and the industry opened up. The current trend is back to basics, but different insurers are taking different routes. While disability insurance is now much more affordable, *the costs and coverage vary widely from company to company. You need to shop carefully.*

A note about carpal tunnel syndrome and repetitive stress injuries (RSI): Computer users need to educate themselves about these disorders and how to prevent injury. The conditions are cumulative, which means the symptoms develop over time, which in turn makes them harder to diagnose. Reference material and related organizations appear at the end of this chapter.

Evaluating Long-Term Disability Policies

Use the following information to compare policies for coverage and value.

1. **Definition of Disability.** The definition is of primary importance; policies vary. Some pay benefits if you are unable to perform the duties of your customary occupation, others only if you can engage in no gainful employment at all.

2. **Extent of Disability.** Some policies require that you be totally disabled before payments begin. Sometimes partial disability is covered for a limited time, but most often it is covered only if the partial disability follows a period of total disability for the same cause. Some policies may not require total disability before a partial disability payment.

3. **Residual Benefits.** The residual benefits feature is standard in some policies, or it can be added as a rider. The benefit allows partial payment based on your loss of income generally without prior total disability. If you are able to work, but your income is reduced because you cannot fulfill all of your job responsibilities, residual benefits can help to make up the difference in your income.

4. **Presumptive Disability.** You are presumed fully disabled and are entitled to full benefits under specified conditions, such as loss of sight, speech, hearing, or use of limbs, even if you can still perform some or all of your regular job.

5. **Size of Benefits.** Monthly benefits are calculated in terms of stable, earned income at the time of purchase. Most insurers limit benefits to 70 or 80 percent of monthly income from all sources. This is to discourage workers from remaining at home. Of particular importance is whether or not any Social Security benefits are deducted from the monthly income. For instance, if your monthly insurance benefit is $1,000 and you qualify for a $500 benefit from Social Security, it may not mean that your total income is $1,500 per month. The majority of group policies reduce their monthly payment by the amount of the Social Security payment. (It reduces the premium amount paid by the employer.) Your employer and the insurance company benefit from your Social Security payments, not you. *Be sure to check this out thoroughly.*

6. **Date of First Payment.** Benefit payments begin in anywhere from thirty days to six months. Premium payments are smaller for longer waiting periods.

7. **Length of Coverage.** Disability benefits are payable for one year, two years, five years, to age sixty-five, or for a lifetime. Premium payments are adjusted accordingly.

8. **Inflation.** A cost-of-living adjustment (COLA) can be added for an additional premium. It increases payments by a specified percentage, generally 4 to 10 percent, after each year of disability. It is an expensive option.

9. **Waiver of Premium.** This provision waives premium payments after you have been disabled for ninety days.

10. **Additional Coverage.** Some policies offer the opportunity to buy additional coverage without having to pass a medical examination or submit further evidence of insurability.

11. **Continuation of Coverage.** There are three types of renewal:

   a. Noncancelable policy gives you the right to continue a policy by timely payment of premium, and the insurance company cannot change the premiums and benefits shown in the policy.

   b. **Guaranteed renewal** means that the policy is automatically renewed with the same benefits, but that the premium may be increased if it is changed for an entire class of policyholders.

   c. **Conditional renewal** means you can be declined because of class, geographic area, or any reasons stated in the policy other than deterioration of health.

12. **Accident or Illness.** Policies can cover accidents, illness, or both. Carefully consider the ramifications of your choice. Premiums are adjusted accordingly.

Group Plans

If you are employed on a long-term project where you receive company benefits, you need to check with the benefits office to see if you are covered by a disability plan and, if so, what is available to you. Request a booklet describing the coverage. You will need to know:

- how long you must wait before the plan takes effect
- how long payments will continue during your disability
- whether the employer's plan takes other coverage (such as government programs and Social Security) into account when calculating your long-term disability pay.

State Plans

These vary widely. In some states (for example, Hawaii, New Jersey, New York, and Rhode Island), state law requires most employers to provide benefits for up to twenty-six weeks. On the other hand, California employers must provide coverage for up to fifty-two weeks.

Disability Benefits Through Social Security

Your salary and the number of years you have been covered under Social Security determine how much you can receive. Eligibility is based on being *unable to perform any gainful employment,* not just the job you were performing at the time the disability began. You must be disabled for five months, and the disability must be expected to last twelve months. *The claim processing may take up to three months.* You should file as soon as possible.

Social Security payments may be reduced by disability entitlements under other government programs such as workers' compensation, government pension, or civil service programs. Total payments cannot exceed 80 percent of average predisability earnings.

Payments are subject to federal income tax if your adjusted gross income plus any nontaxable interest income and half of your Social Security benefits exceed $25,000 (individual return) or $32,000 (joint return). Up to 85 percent are subject to federal income tax if the total—as calculated above—exceeds $34,000 (individually) or $44,000 (jointly).

Your local Social Security Administration office will furnish you with an estimate of the benefits to which you would be entitled.

Short-Term Disability Insurance

This option provides cash benefits as a partial replacement for lost wages from injuries or illnesses not connected with employment. Benefits are 50 percent of the average weekly wage, based upon the last eight weeks of employment, but not more than $170 per week. They are payable for a maximum of twenty-six weeks of disability during fifty-two consecutive weeks and begin on the eighth consecutive day of disability.

Support Services Alliance, Inc. (see page 182) offers coverage for self-employed persons in several states. To give you some idea of cost, the premium for a single person in New York City was $16.38 per month in 1997.

Temporary Employment: Federal Benefits and Regulations

If you work as a temporary employee and are not aware of the benefits and regulations I'm about to describe, I can almost guarantee someone will find a way to exploit your ignorance. This stuff may be boring, but it is necessary to know a few basics.

A provision of the Tax Reform Act of 1986 states that if temporaries perform "substantial services" (1,500 hours in a year) to a company and make up more than 5 percent of its total "lower-paid" work force, the company (or the temporary help company) may have to provide the same health and pension benefits as are given to their other employees *or pay taxes on their plan contributions.* The plan benefits to their employees will be counted as taxable income. One thousand five hundred hours represents approximately a little over 8 months of work (at forty hours per week).

The reason you must familiarize yourself with the provisions of this act is that industry abuses have not ceased just because a law was passed. When temporaries are unaware of their rights under the law, they can fall prey to unscrupulous agencies that, in collusion with their client companies, place them in long-term assignments, terminate the assignment just before the 1,500 hours are reached, and then rehire them for a miraculous resumption of the same assignment. A variation on this ploy is for the company next to hire the temporaries as "contract workers" without benefits. Additional information is summarized in Appendix C.

Microsoft Corporation challenged this law and has been locked in a five-year legal battle. Microsoft was sued by its contractor employees, who claim to have performed the same work, under exactly the same conditions, as regular employees making them "common law" employees and therefore entitled to all benefits. Frightened by the case's implications, companies and industry groups have rallied behind Microsoft. The case was expected to go before the Supreme Court, but in January 1998 the Court refused to hear the appeal. Currently under appeal in the U.S. Ninth Circuit Court of Appeals, the rulings thus far have been largely in the contractors' favor.

Continuation Insurance (COBRA)

The Consolidated Omnibus Budget Reconciliation Act of 1986 (COBRA) allows insured individuals to extend their insurance in the event of unemployment or reduced hours of work. Persons who currently have group plans through their spouse's employer can continue their coverage after divorce, death, or retirement. Spouses and children can pay premiums and continue the plan for three years. Unemployed workers can continue for eighteen months. Employers can charge an administrative fee of up to 4 percent. At the end of the three-year or eighteen-month period, people who have availed themselves of this law have the option of continuing their coverage as individuals, but not at the group rate or at the same level of coverage. The benefit here is that a worker doesn't have to go through insurability requirements or be subjected to preexisting condition restrictions.

Companies that have fewer than twenty employees or subscribe to a government, church, or self-insured plan are exempt from this law. However, some states have continuation laws that are similar to the federal one. Check with an insurance broker or with the state insurance department if you need information on a particular company.

State Benefits

Currently, pension and health care legislation on the books offer at least minimal protection to both temporary workers and leased workers. I continue to be amazed at the number of temporaries who are registered with agencies but are unaware that state laws cover them for unemployment, disability, and workers' compensation. As employees of staffing services, temporaries qualify for these insurance plans as stipulated by the laws of their state. The temporary help companies are not educating their employees about basic benefits. Request information from your state department of insurance as well as your temporary employment company.

Temping and Collecting Unemployment Insurance Benefits

You can work as a temporary while collecting unemployment benefits, provided the benefit and temp salary together do not exceed the gross amount of your weekly benefit. For instance, if your benefit is $280 weekly, and your temp income for one week is that amount or more, you will not receive a stipend for that period. On the other hand, if your temp income is $150, you would receive a $130 stipend to bring the total back to $280. The earned portion of the benefit is not lost by working; it is extended. However, it is not extended beyond four quarters (totaling one year), and the sheer weight of the paperwork you must complete to collect a stipend may flatten you in the process.

The agency also must fill out unemployment forms for temps who work for them and collect a stipend. Ethically challenged agencies have been known to offer work to those temps at a considerably reduced hourly rate, with the veiled threat to "report them to Unemployment" if the work was refused. Blackmail, the capitalist tool. Here are two suggestions to keep this from happening:

1. Discuss the mechanics of temping and collecting unemployment with both the agency and the unemployment counselors. Get specific examples of what constitutes a "refusal of work."

2. Reach an agreement with the agency on some ground rules, such as the lowest rate they will offer that you will accept; appropriate and inappropriate assignments; accepting or refusing work out of your field.

Pensions and Retirement Plans

If you earn money from agencies and self-employment, you can have an IRA as well as a Keogh plan. This is where you need specialized help. There are a number of books, certainly, but you might also consider hiring a financial planner to guide you. See the guidelines in Chapter 7 for choosing professional advisers.

Brave New World

Using two-way television systems, patients are being examined and treated by doctors and nurses hundreds of miles away. The new technology, called telemedicine, holds particular promise for those who live in rural areas or who are homebound. According to HCFA estimates, Medicare will spend about $270 million for telemedicine services in 1999 to 2003.

The use of telephone triage by HMOs to determine if members need to go to emergency rooms is commonplace.

Technology is in place that permits radiology experts to read MRIs from images sent over telephone lines.

What does all of this have to do with temporary employment or choosing a medical plan? I mention it in passing as yet another example of how technology is changing our lives and the way we conduct business. Think of it as a preliminary form of medical telecommuting or outsourcing for managed care. Let your imagination do the rest.

RESOURCES

Insurance: Membership Organizations

Alliance for Affordable Services   *Member fee $106*

This nonprofit coalition was formerly called the Alliance for Affordable Health Care. Benefits include group health, dental, and vision plans; discount purchasing plans; a prepaid legal program; and financial and other services geared to small businesses and the self-employed.

Member Services: 800-733-2242
Health Care Information: 800-366-7818 (in North Carolina: 800-441-9969)
Web site: http://www.affordableservices.org

American Association of University Women (AAUW)   *Member fee $35*

AAUW membership is open to women with a bachelor's or higher degree from a regionally accredited institution. Undergraduates may become student affiliates:

1111 16th Street, NW
Washington, DC 20036
202-785-7700

Co-op America   Member fee $25

Co-op America, in conjunction with Alternative Health Insurance Services (AHIS), offers relatively affordable insurance in most states. Co-op America works to change the way America and the world do business by building the green business sector, fighting corporate irresponsibility, empowering consumers and investors, and creating sustainable communities.

1850 M Street, NW, Suite 700
Washington, DC 20036
202-872-5307
Insurance questions: 800-331-2713 or 800-966-8467
Web site: http://www.coopamerica.org

The Home Office Association of America (HOAA)   Member fee $35

HOAA provides a variety of benefits and services, including a health insurance plan, discounts on business services, and a monthly newsletter.

HOAA
909 Third Avenue, Suite 990
New York, NY 10022
212-980-4622
Web site: http://www.hoaa.com

International Women Writers' Guild (IWWG)   Member fee $35

IWWG is an international association of women writers with membership open to any woman regardless of portfolio.

P.O. Box 810
Gracie Station
New York, NY 10028
212-737-7536
E-mail: iwwg@iwwg.com
Web site: http://www.iwwg.com

National Association for Female Executives (NAFE)   Member Fee $29

Membership benefits include discounts on business products and services, job search and resume services, networking opportunities, and access to several medical insurance plans.

NAFE
135 West 50th Street
New York, NY 10020
800-634-6233
E-mail: info@nafe.com
Web site: http://www.nafe.com

National Association of Socially Responsible Organizations (NASRO)Member Fee $10

NASRO is a member-owned, self-sustaining clearinghouse for socially responsible issues and organizations. The association's goal is to meet the needs of members of the new independent work force, and its diverse membership links over 24,000 workers, self-employed business persons, small nonprofits, and small businesses. The NASRO Co-op offers affordable health plans to small groups of two or more in all fifty states, and to individuals in twenty-two states. They publish an informative newsletter.

> 1029 Santa Barbara Street
> Santa Barbara, CA 93101
> 800-638-8113
> E-mail: info@nasro-co-op.com
> Web site: http://www.nasro-co-op.com

National Writers Union (NWU)　　　　　　Graduated member fees from $90

NWU membership is open to all qualified writers who are actively writing and publishing (or attempting to publish) their work. Dues are graduated and based on writing income; the lowest are $90 yearly. NWU has group medical (HMO) and dental insurance.

> 873 Broadway, Suite 203
> New York, NY 10003-1209
> 212-254-0279
> E-mail: nwu@nwu.org
> Web site: http://www.nwu.org/nwu

Support Services Alliance, Inc. (SSA)　　　　　　　Member fee $40

SSA is an association of approximately 10,000 small business owners and sole proprietors. The annual membership fee quoted is for a sole proprietor with no employees. SSA provides a variety of useful services to small business, among them group health insurance programs in several states, group dental insurance, vision care, and short-term disability plans.

> P.O. Box 130
> 102 Prospect Street
> Schoharie, NY 12157
> 800-836-4772

National Association of Part-Time and Temporary Employees (NAPTE) Member fee $10

NAPTE lobbies Congress and state legislatures on behalf of part-time, temporary, and contract employees. Membership offers access to discounted medical and other services, product discounts, newsletters, and regular information on the issues affecting part-time and temporary employment. Through the Capella Care Card, NAPTE members save 20 to 30 percent on most major medical, dental, vision, chiropractic, hearing, and prescription services in their provider network. The additional membership fee to Capella is around $10 monthly.

NAPTE
P.O. Box 3805
Shawnee, KS 66203
913-962-7740

The Capella Group 1615
West Abram Street, Suite 110
Arlington, TX 76013
888-411-3588

Working Today   *Member fee $10*

This nonprofit organization is designed to meet the needs and promote the interests of the contemporary work force through education, advocacy, and service. Benefits include access to comprehensive health and dental benefits and free, prepaid legal assistance. The access to medical insurance is linked to an associate membership in the National Writers Union (an additional $45 per year).

P.O. Box 1261
Old Chelsea Box Station
New York, NY 10113-9998
212-366-6066
E-mail: working1@tiac.net
Web site: http://www.workingtoday.com

Temporary/Short-Term Medical Insurance

National Association of Temporary Staffing Services (NATSS)

The plan can be purchased in segments of 30 to 180 days; it covers spouses under sixty-five and dependent children under nineteen. It requires a $250 deductible "each illness or accident"; it then covers 80 percent for the first $5,000, and subsequently 100 percent up to $1 million. It can be renewed once for another six months, but any illness claimed in the initial period is now considered "preexisting."

NAPTE (see above) has the same plan that is often offered to new college graduates, and it is very similar to the NATSS plan described above.

Alternative Health Insurance Services (see Co-op America) offers temporary plans in several states.

Discounted Prescription Drugs (Mail Order)

AARP Pharmacy Service   800-456-2277

DPD Action Pharmacy   800-452-1976

MediMall   800-922-3444

Discounted Contact Lenses (Mail Order)

1-800-CONTACTS   800-266-8228

Credentialing (Doctors)

The American Board of Medical Specialties   800-776-2378

The board has a physician verification system where you can check to see if your specialist received the required training.

American Medical Association Physician Select Database   312-464-4982

Medi-NET   888-ASK-MEDI

There is a fee for this service.

State Medical Boards

Check the state government listings in your telephone book.

Credentialing: HMOs

American Association of Health Plans (AAHP)

1129 20th Street, NW
Washington, DC 20036
202-778-3200

National Committee for Quality Assurance (NCQA)

2000 L Street, Suite 500
Washington, DC 20036
888-275-7585, 202-955-5697
Web site: http://ncqa.org

State Insurance Commissioners

Alabama: 334-269-3550
Alaska: 907-349-1230
Arizona: 602-912-8400
Arkansas: 501-686-2945
California: 800-927-4357
Colorado: 303-894-7499
Connecticut: 203-297-3800
Delaware: 800-282-8611
District of Columbia: 202-724-7424
Florida: 800-342-2762
Georgia: 404-656-2070
Hawaii: 800-468-4644
Idaho: 208-334-2560
Illinois: 217-782-4515
Indiana: 317-232-2395
Iowa: 515-281-5705
Kansas: 800-432-2484

Kentucky: 502-564-3630
Louisiana: 504-342-5300
Maine: 207-582-8707
Maryland: 800-492-6116
Massachusetts: 617-727-3357
Minnesota: 612-296-6848
Mississippi: 601-359-3569
Missouri: 800-332-6148
Montana: 406-444-2040
North Carolina: 800-662-7777
North Dakota: 800-247-0560
Nebraska: 402-471-2201
Nevada: 800-992-0900
New Hampshire: 800-852-3416
New Jersey: 609-292-5317
New Mexico: 505-827-4500
New York: 800-342-3736

Ohio: 800-686-1526
Oklahoma: 800-522-0071
Oregon: 503-378-4271
Pennsylvania: 717-787-5173
Puerto Rico: 809-722-8686
Rhode Island: 401-222-2223
South Carolina: 800-768-3467
South Dakota: 605-773-3563
Tennessee: 800-342-4029

Texas: 512-322-2266
Utah: 801-538-3800
Vermont: 802-828-3301
Virginia: 800-552-7945
Virgin Islands: 809-774-2991
Washington: 800-562-6900
West Virginia: 800-642-9004
Wisconsin: 608-266-3585
Wyoming: 307-777-7401

Peer Review Organizations (PRO)

PROs will review the treatment when there are Medicare-related managed care problems. This review is mandated by law. To find a PRO in your area, call the Medicare hotline (800-638-6833).

Continuation Health Insurance (COBRA)

Pension and Welfare Benefits Administration
Division of Technical Assistance and Inquiries
200 Constitution Avenue, NW, Room N5625
Washington, DC 20210

Consumer Groups/Organizations

People's Medical Society

This is a nonprofit consumer health organization dedicated to the principles of better, more responsive, and less expensive medical care. Membership includes a subscription to the newsletter. They have excellent books and publications.

462 Walnut Street
Allentown, PA 18102
610-770-1670

Consumer Rights/Advocacy

AARP Managed Care Advocacy   ☺ **Free**

For information, call regional AARP offices.
Northeast: 617-723-7600
Southeast: 404-888-0077
Midwest: 312-714-9800
West: 206-526-7918
Southwest: 214-265-4060

Center for Patient Advocacy   ☺ **Free**

The Center provides assistance to people having trouble with their managed care plan. You can speak to a patient advocate who will help you find the appropriate resources to aid your fight. They do not, however, furnish either legal or medical advice.

The Web site provides extensive useful information for consumers who want to fight back.

1350 Beverly Road, Suite 108
McLean, VA 22101
800-846-7444
Web site: http://www.patientadvocacy.org

Center for the Study of Services

This nonprofit organization was established in 1974 by the U.S. Department of Consumer Affairs and the Consumers Union. It published the *Consumer's Guide to Health Care Services,* the results of a 1995 national survey of 72,000 HMO members rating their access to care and quality of care and more than twenty other specifics. Has other publications and ratings on hospitals.

800-475-7283
Web site: http://www.checkbook.org

Choosing Quality: Finding the Health Plan that's Right for You ☺ **Free**

National Committee for Quality Assurance's (NCQA) list of accredited HMOs and accreditation summary reports. Send your request with a self-addressed, stamped envelope.

NCQA Publications Center
P.O. Box 533, Attn: CB
Annapolis Junction, MD 20701-0533
Web site: http://www.ncqa.org

Compromising Your Drug of Choice ☺ **Free**

This report by the City of New York Public Advocate's Office following a six-month investigation showed that physicians and pharmacists are being systematically pressured to rewrite or switch prescriptions to cheaper medications favored by drug marketing middlemen retained by the health insurance plans.

Public Advocate's Office
City of New York
1 Centre Street, 15th floor
New York, NY 10007
212-669-7200.

HMO Consumers at Risk: States to the Rescue ☺ **Free**

An overview of managed care legislative activity from the Families USA Foundation. You can write to the foundation or download the information at no cost from the Web site. (The charge is $15 if they send you the printed report.)

Families USA
1334 G St., NW
Washington, DC 20002
Web site: http://epn.org/families.html

Managed Care: An AARP Guide ☺ **Free**

Request stock number D15595.
AARP Fulfillment EE01070
601 E Street, NW
Washington, DC 20049

Information Services

Wilkinson Benefit Consultants

This fee-based database information service sells information only, not insurance. It provides printouts of health insurance options based on your requirements. Call for a schedule of fees and services.

800-296-3030

Online Resources

Health Law ☺ **Free**

Ober, Kaler, Grimes & Shriver maintain a home page with newsletter and articles on current legal issues in health law.

Web site: http://www.ober.com

Medicare HMO Shopping ☺ **Free**

Tips on choosing wisely.
Web site: http://www.healthcare-disclose.com

Consumer Reports

In 1996, the monthly consumer advocacy magazine published a comprehensive look at HMOs in two installments. Their Web site has a sampling of recent articles from their publications, as well as information about helpful agencies on the Web. Full access to *Consumer Reports Online* costs the same as the subscription price of the magazine.

101 Truman Avenue
Yonkers, NY 10703-1057
914-378-2000
Web site: http://www.ConsumerReports.org

Mediconsult.com ☺ **Free**

This site is a professionally moderated, consumer-focused virtual medical center offering detailed medical and drug information and support.

Web site: http//www.mediconsult.com

Medmark ☺ **Free**

Medmark, by Ildo Shin, M.D., contains the largest and most extensive list of medical resource Web sites.

Web site: http://www.medmark.org

PubMed   ☺ **Free**

Maintained by the National Library of Medicine, it offers free searches using sophisticated software that lets you ask questions using nontechnical terms. You can see summaries of articles, but you will need to go to a medical library for complete reports.
Web site: http://www.nlm.nih.gov

Books

The HMO Health Care Companion, Alan G. Raymond, HarperCollins, 1994.
The HMO Survival Guide, Sue Berkman, Random House, 1997.
HMOs and the Breakdown of Medical Trust, George Anders, Houghton Mifflin Company, 1996.

Carpal Tunnel Syndrome and RSI

If you use a computer (and who doesn't these days) educate yourself about repetitive stress injuries (RSI), the fastest-growing disability of this decade. Prevention is much easier than cure.

Books

The Computer User's Survival Guide, Joan Stigliani, O'Reilly and Associates, Sebastopol, CA, 800-998-9938.
Conquering Carpal Tunnel Syndrome and Other Repetitive Strain Injuries: A Self-Care Program, Sharon Butler, Advance Press, 1996 1708 Lancaster Avenue, #321, Paoli, PA 19301, 800-909-9795.
Repetitive Strain Injury: A Computer User's Guide, Emil Pascaarelli, M.D., and Deborah Quilter, John Wiley & Sons, 1994.

Organizations

The Association for Repetitive Motion Syndromes (ARMS)

Founded by National Writers Union member Stephanie Barnes, ARMS maintains a national clearinghouse of RSI information and the most comprehensive listing of local RSI support groups around the country. It also publishes a quarterly newsletter.
707-571-0397

Labor Occupational Health Program (LOHP)

LOHP, at the University of California at Berkeley Center for Occupational and Environmental Health, offers health and safety training, information, and technical assistance to workers and health professionals.
510-642-5507

National Institute of Occupational Safety and Health   ☺ **Free**

The Institute publishes newsletters and tip sheets on how to avoid on-the-job injuries, including RSI and eyestrain. Call to hear a list of topics and order by fax or mail.
800-356-4674

RSI Action

RSI Action uses education, outreach, and advocacy to promote accommodations for injured workers and to educate medical personnel about the treatment and other needs of people with RSIs. The organization is pushing for a federal ergonomics standard, and it is developing a guide for people who want to start support/action groups of their own. The campaign is organized by the Coalition on New Office Technology (CNOT), a Massachusetts labor-community coalition that advocates for the rights of women office workers. CNOT has developed an outreach manual for injured workers to help others who want to start similar groups elsewhere.

617-247-6827

Evaluating Indemnity Health Insurance

When looking for medical coverage, use the questions below to gather the information needed to make an informed decision.

1. What is the maximum dollar amount of coverage? If it isn't unlimited, it should be in range of $1 to $2 million.
2. Is the deductible one that you can afford? Is there a carryover at the end of the year? Generally speaking, the higher the deductible, the lower the premium; but that must be weighed against out-of-pocket expenses. For this reason, don't automatically take the highest deductible you can afford without figuring in the total out-of-pocket for the year and the cap on the policy.
3. Choose a policy with a yearly deductible rather than a per-usage deductible.
4. Are the copayment provisions at least 80 percent/20 percent?
5. Does the policy restore any portion of the maximum benefits once you are well? Some policies will restore all or partial benefits after a period where no claims are submitted.
6. What is the stop-loss amount? This is the expense ceiling beyond which you stop paying anything toward your medical expense, preventing the 20 percent copayments adding up to an exorbitant amount of money. Some policies pay 100 percent of claims after $5,000, others less.
7. Is the policy noncancelable and guaranteed renewable or conditionally renewable? A conditionally renewable policy means the company would have to cancel all policies in the state and no longer do health insurance in the state. A good group policy will not necessarily increase its premiums every year. *Ask about the recent premium history.*
8. Are all hospital/doctor expenses covered, or are specific services excluded? Look for a policy that covers outpatient care. The trend is for more and more medical and surgical procedures to be performed in outpatient settings.
9. Look for coverage that begins with the first day of hospitalization, including room and board, doctors' visits and any medical/surgical procedures.
10. If you must cut corners, look for a no-frills major medical policy that pays most doctors' and hospital bills but excludes routine physicals or prescription drugs.
11. How does it handle preexisting conditions? Some policies will cover them after a waiting period.

12. To what extent are emergency room visits covered?

13. Look for policies that can be extended to a spouse or a dependent without a large increase in premium.

14. Pay your premium annually or semiannually if you can. It costs less than monthly payments.

15. Check to see if you are covered away from home in case you need medical treatment while you are traveling.

16. Check exclusions. Common ones are prescription drugs, alcoholism, mental health, ambulances, private-duty nursing.

17. Check restrictions on benefits. These are sometimes referred to as cost-containment clauses.

18. Remember, there is a ten-day "free look" period after you receive the policy during which you can get a refund if you decide it's not right for you.

19. Is the plan offered by company that is committed to health insurance as a specialty, has an A or A+ rating by A. M. Best & Co., and has at least $100 million in assets?

Indemnity Health Plan Coverage

Comprehensive plans should include the following:

Blood and components (transfusions)
Cosmetic surgery (result of accident/injury)
Dental treatment (result of accident/injury)
Diagnostic tests (x-rays, laboratory)
Durable medical equipment (hospital bed, wheelchair rental)
Home health care
Obstetric services
Outpatient treatment services (chemotherapy, radiation therapy)
Prescription drugs
Private-duty nursing
Prosthetic appliances (limbs, eyes, orthopedic braces)
Psychiatric care services
Radiation therapy
Rehabilitation services
Respiratory therapy
Room and board (semiprivate)
Second surgical opinion
Skilled nursing facility care
Special care beds: intensive care
Surgery and supplies
Surgery: surgeon/assistant surgeon fees, supplies
Therapist services: occupational, physical, respiratory, speech
Transportation (ambulance)

Surgical insurance should include the following:

Allergy testing
Anesthesia: anesthesiologist/anesthetist fees, supplies
Chemotherapy (including cost of drugs)
Chiropractic care
Consultation services
Diagnostic services (in nonhospital settings)
Doctors' visits: office, hospital, emergency room, home
Electrocardiogram (EKG)
Electroencephalogram (EEG)
Emergency accident care
Immunizations
Newborn care (routine)
Obstetric services (pre- and postnatal care)
Oral surgeon's fee
Oxygen/oxygen supplies
Pathologist's fee (laboratory)
Physical examinations
Physical therapy
Physician/surgeon services
Podiatry care
Prescription drugs
Psychiatric care services
Radiation therapy, radiologist's fees, supplies
Second surgical opinion
Surgery and supplies
Surgery: surgeon/assistant surgeon fees, supplies
Therapist services: occupational, physical, respiratory, speech
Transportation (ambulance)

10 *Legislative Watch*

Many bills now before state legislatures and Congress will eventually affect how our work is regulated in the future. This chapter summarizes the ones I am watching. By the time this book is on the shelves, a proliferation of new legislation may have been introduced; some bills included here will have stalled in committee; others will have been placed on an ice floe and given a shove. The process of turning a bill into law is fraught with opportunity to delay and derail.

How Does a Bill Become Law?

Slowly.

A member of Congress introduces a new bill to the House or the Senate. After its introduction, the bill is given a number or title by the clerk of the House, then it is assigned to the Senate or House committee into whose particular domain it falls. Next comes the opinion parade. Interested parties and members of Congress present their views on the merits or failings of the proposed legislation before the committee. The committee debates the bill and may propose amendments to it. The bill is voted on and, if it is passed, returned to the clerk of the House for the next step in the process. If it is defeated, the committee may table it, thus killing its further consideration. *And this is the just the first reading. There are two more.*

The second reading is to the House and it is performed by the clerk. The House then debates it and suggests amendments. The third reading takes place after debate, when a vote is called for and the title of the bill is read before the vote. If the bill passes, it is sent to the other house, where it is again debated, possibly amended, then voted on. If it passes with amendments, a joint congressional committee forms (with members from both House and Senate) to reach a compromise between the two versions of the bill. If the bill does not pass the second house, it dies. If the compromise version passes, the President can still veto it. But, that's a story for another day.

Web sites where you can locate bills by subject matter and track what is of interest to you are listed at the end of the chapter. These sites will link you to others for commentary about the pros, cons, and potential ramifications of various statutes. The abbreviation "H.R." followed by a number means the bill originated in the House of Representatives; "S" followed by a number means it originated in the Senate.

State legislation uses "H" and "S" for the state house and senate along with "A" for the state assembly. The sponsor's party is abbreviated "R" for Republican and "D" for Democrat.

Although this section lists only work-related legislation, you can also use its resources to learn what your state is doing to regulate HMOs. New bills in this area are too frequent and numerous for me to try and list them here.

Proposed Federal Legislation

Topic: Compensatory Time

Working Families Flexibility Act H.R. 1
Proposes to allow eligible employees (those who have worked at least 1,000 hours) to take compensatory time instead of overtime, up to a maximum of 160 hours of comp time per year.

Sponsor: Ballenger (R-North Carolina)

Status: Passed the House on March 19, 1997. The Clinton administration and organized labor oppose the bill, fearing that employers will coerce employees into accepting comp time in lieu of overtime pay.

Family Friendly (as in Peacekeeper Missile) **Workplace Act S. 4**
Senate version of H.R. 1

Sponsor: Ashcroft (R-Missouri)

Status: Passed Senate Labor and Human Resources Committee March 19, 1997. Senate failed to cut off debate, on June 4, 1997.

Topic: Contingent Work Force

National Commission on Fairness in the Workplace Act S. 1453
If passed, it will create a commission of nine members to study part-time employment and the issues of wages, benefits, earning potential, and productivity. Three wil be appointed by the President, three will be appointed by the senate president pro tem, and three appointed by the speaker of the House.

Sponsor: Dodd (D-Connecticut)

Status: Introduced into the Senate Labor and Human Resources Committee on November 7, 1997.

Topic: Overtime Compensation Exemption

White Collar Reform H.R. 647
Amends Fair Labor Standards Act (FLSA) by expanding the exemptions of salaried employees from overtime payment to include those who make $40,000 or more per year. If an employee does not work an entire year, the compensation would be annualized to reflect what the earnings would have been for the full year. Repeals the requirement that administrative employees' duties be related to management policies or general business operation in order for the employee to be exempt from overtime pay. Provides that deductions from pay for absences of less than a full day shall not be considered in determining whether an employee is an exempt employee.
Sponsor: Petri (R-Wisconsin)
Status: Introduced into the House Education and the Workforce Committee, February 1998.

Topic: Multi-Employer Welfare Arrangements (MEWAs)

Expansion of Portability and Health Insurance Coverage Act H.R. 1515
Allows small employers to pool together under trade and professional associations to purchase affordable health insurance coverage for employees. Establishes rules governing MEWAs and exempts them from state regulations.
Sponsor: Fawell (R-Illinois)
Status: Passed the House Education and the Workforce Committee, June 1997.
Expansion of Portability and Health Insurance Coverage Act S.729
Senate version of H.R. 1515
Sponsor: Hutchinson (R-Arkansas)
Status: Introduced into the Senate Labor and Commerce Committee, May 1997. Hearing held October 1997.

Topic: Health Insurance Tax Deduction for Self-Employed

H.R. 1145
Increases the deduction allowed for health insurance costs for self-employed individuals and their dependents.
Sponsor: Talent (R-Missouri)

Status: Introduced into the House Ways and Means Committee March 1997; incorporated into budget bill, August 1997.

Topic: Independent Contractors

H.R. 2642

Replaces the current IRS twenty-point test for determining whether a worker is an employee or independent contractor with an eight-point test. An individual will be considered an employee unless all eight requirements are met.

Sponsor: Visclosky (D-Indiana)

Status: Introduced into the House Ways and Means Committee, October 1997.

S. 473

Amends the Internal Revenue Code to determine whether a worker is an employee or independent contractor. Establishes that a service provider will not be considered an employee if (1) the provider can realize a profit or loss, can incur unreimbursed expenses, and makes a time-limited or task-limited agreement with the service recipient; (2) the provider has a principal place of business, does not primarily provide service at a single service recipient's facilities, pays fair rent for the use of the recipient's facilities, or operates primarily with equipment not supplied by the recipient; and (3) there is a written contract stating that the provider will not be treated as an employee for federal tax purposes.

Sponsor: Bond (R-Missouri)

Status: Introduced into the Senate Finance Committee March 1997. Similar provisions stripped from budget bill August 1997.

Proposed State Legislation

Unemployment Insurance for Temporary Workers

Alabama	H. 474
Illinois	H. 1153
Michigan	H. 5303
Tennessee	H. 566 and S. 741
Vermont	H. 236

Mandatory Benefits for Temporary Workers

Connecticut   S. 274

Requires employers to pay contingent workers the same wages as full-time workers. Defines contingent worker to include leased employees and employees of temporary help firms.

Status: Introduced by Joint Labor and Public Employees Committee; hearing scheduled, February 1998.

Illinois   H. 1195

Requires employers to provide part-time employees with the same benefits as full-time employees on a prorated basis. The benefits to be made available will include all employer-sponsored insurance and pension benefits, health services, child care services, and vacation time. Defines a part-time employee to mean an individual who has worked at least twenty-five hours per week during at least eight months of the preceding year. Applies to all employers with 500 or more employees.

Status: Introduced February 1997, passed Committee.

Rhode Island   H. 8049

Requires employers to provide part-time employees with the same wages and benefits as full-time employees on a prorated basis. Defines a part-time employee as an employee who works for a particular employer for less than twenty hours per week. Requires the director of the Employment Security Department to conduct an annual study of unemployment and underemployment in the state. The study is to include an analysis of "jobs in which workers, although seeking full-time and/or permanent work, are forced to accept part-time and/or temporary positions."

Sponsor: Committee Chair Rep. Faria

Status: Introduced into House Labor Committee; hearing scheduled February 1998.

Rhode Island   H. 8263

Requires employers to provide staffing firm employees with the same benefits as full-time employees on a prorated basis, pay them the same wages, and hire them after three months.

Sponsor: Committee Chair Rep. Faria

Status: Introduced into House Labor Committee February 1998.

Tennessee   H. 1561 & S. 1420

Requires temporary help firms to provide insurance benefits to any temporary employees working more than thirty days.

Status: Both introduced in February 1997. H. 1561 assigned to House Consumer and Employee Affairs Committee. S. 1420 not assigned to committee.

Hourly Rate Information

California   S. 1743

Requires a temporary help firm to inform its employees of the hourly rate paid by the client for the firm's services.

. **Status:** Introduced into the Senate Industrial Relations Committee February 1998.

Independent Contractors

New York   A. 02989

Amends the labor law in relation to independent contractor classification.

Preventing Employers from Replacing Older Workers with Younger Workers for Less Money.

California SB   1098 and SB 2192 "spot bill."

(A spot bill is introduced to hold a spot open in the current legislative session.)

Professional Employer Organizations (leasing companies)

Legislation pending on various issues such as workers' compensation and licensing requirements in

Florida	H. 1947
Georgia	H. 26 and S. 126
Massachusetts	H. 881
Mississippi	H. 1382 and S. 2522
New York	A. 2851
Rhode Island	H. 5252

Studies and Task Forces

Massachusetts   S. 1839

Requires the state Department of Labor and Workforce Development to conduct a study of the contingent workforce as part of an examination to determine a "livable" wage.

Status: Introduced June 1997; passed to Senate Ways and Means Committee.

Washington   SCR 8407

Established a task force to study contingent work force. Appears to have future regulation in mind.

Status: Introduced into the Senate Commerce and Labor Committee February 1997. Hearings held, passed committee.

Welfare Reform

Ohio   H. 406

Prohibits the state from referring individuals to temporary help firms.

Status: Introduced into the House Commerce and Labor Committee, April 1997. Still stalled in hearings as of February 1998.

ONLINE RESOURCES

State/Federal Legislators

Center for Responsive Politics   http://www.crp.org

This Web site furnishes information on government lobbyists, such as who hired them, how much money they spend, their areas of interest, and whether they worked in certain government positions in the previous two years. Campaign contributions also can be tracked through the site's "Do-It-Yourself Congressional Investigation Kit." Pick an interest area (i.e. ATM fees, gun control) and find out who got money, how much, and how they voted.

Congressional Quarterly   http://voter.cq.com

CQ American Voter Hotlist will link you to legislative, executive, and judicial branches; political parties (best known and lesser known); documents; indexes; activism; and potpourri. There is a place to rate your representative, and you can complete a questionnaire to inform the representative of your opinion on specific issues.

Federal Election Commission   http://www.fec.gov

This site gives campaign contribution data as well.

Thomas Legislative Guide   http://www.thomas.loc.gov

The *Thomas* (as in Thomas Jefferson) *Legislative Guide* is produced by the Library of Congress. It includes a directory that will help you locate state legislative information sites and quick-link to them. It is not limited to the workplace, and it features a search engine to locate bills.

Political Commentary

The Labor Home Page   http://www.heritage.org

The conservative Heritage Foundation sponsors this site. It is a good place to find conservative commentary about Occupational Safety and Health Administration, the TEAM (Teamwork for Employees and Managers) Act, and Flex-Time.

Labor Policy Association   http://www.lpa.org/lpa/index.html

The association membership consists of senior human resource executives from major U.S. corporations. It is a good place to look for legislative issues that are not particularly "worker-friendly."

Afterword

A Sign of the Times

In April 1998, Cafe Ke'ilu ("Cafe Make Believe") opened in a trendy section of Tel Aviv, Israel, with tables, chairs, plates, silverware, menus and servers, but no food or drink. Explained manager Nir Caspi (who calls the experience "conceptual dining"), people come to be seen and to meet people, but not for the actual food. The menu, designed by top-rated chef (and owner) Phillipe Kaufman, lets diners order some of the world's most exquisite dishes (eel mousse, salad of pomegranates, if in season), "served" on elegant (but empty) platters.

Reported in Funny Times, August 1998, "News of the Weird." (Real news collected from the mainstream press by Chuck Shepherd, P.O. Box 8306, St. Petersburg, Florida 33738.)

Virtual Reality

One of the factors used to judge the health of a nation's economy is its productivity rate; that is, the rate of how much national income is generated from an average hour of work. Only when a nation's workers *produce more* in a given amount of time, can wages rise across the board and increase the standard of living.

For almost 100 years until the early 1970s, American productivity rose each year at an average of over two percent. The rate for this decade holds steady at 1.2 percent, almost unchanged from the mid-1970s. While optimistic government officials proudly report the creation of more than 300,000 jobs per month, they neglect to mention that the bulk of this labor is going into efforts to make one gadget *seem different* from another (through design, advertising and marketing), not into increasing the total output of gadgets. Companies are putting great effort into holding onto customers, or luring them from another company, but more goods are not being produced. Poof! Busyness becomes *virtual productivity!*

The media have labeled ours a treadmill economy; one that is going nowhere fast. As we skip over the hill and through the woods into the next century, does virtual prosperity await us as we strive for an image of success in our virtual careers? A bit of a conundrum, isn't it?

We must think of our career business as a tapestry to be woven with threads from many sources, each bringing its uniqueness to the overall design, the diversity of the whole enhancing the strength, richness, and vibrancy of the final work of art.

It is my hope that *Executive Temp* helps you to design a personal, successful, *and real* career business, whatever the economy.

I enjoy hearing from readers. Please feel free to share anecdotes, ask questions, or make suggestions. Let me hear from you.

e-mail: diane_tempstrategy@compuserve.com

snail mail: Diane Thrailkill
c/o Random House, Inc.
Reference & Information Publishing
201 E. 50th Street
New York, NY 10022

APPENDIX A *Resources A to Z*

*R*esources mentioned throughout the book are listed here alphabetically along with the other A to Z topics (actually B to W). You will find books, organizations, and Web sites grouped together under each subject. The ☺ **Free** symbol signals free samples or services. The ✓ symbol alerts you to another area or source to check out. Whenever you write for information or samples, including a self-addressed label helps to speed up the process of mailing the item(s) back to you.

Resources *not* included in this section but appearing elsewhere are:

- Resources connected to medical and disability insurance appear at the end of Chapter 9.

- Temporary help agency tests and software tests are located at the end of Chapter 3.

- Web sites for current state and federal legislation appear at the end of Chapter 10.

- Appendix B lists the twenty IRS qualifiers for independent contractor status.

- Appendix C summarizes the Tax Reform Act of 1986 (TRA) as it pertains to temporary employment.

Resource Headings

Barter
Better Business Bureau
Brochures and mailing pieces
Business card brochures
Business cards, letterhead, forms
Business incubators
Business information databases (on-
line)
Business names
Business planning
Business software (online)
Checks and checking accounts
Cheap checks (mail order)
Computer user groups
Computer viruses
Computers (reference books, glos-
saries)
Computers and printers
Computers: online technical help
Consulting/freelancing
Consumer information
Credit
Credit bureaus
Credit cards
Credit: debt collection
Credit unions
Directories
Entrepreneurial centers
Entrepreneurs
Fee setting
Financial information
Financial planners
Government (federal)
Home-based businesses
Home offices
Hotlines (U.S. government)

Independent contractors
Insurance (business)
Insurance quotes
Job (project/employment) search
Lawyers/legal (business)
Lawyers/legal (general)
Lawyers/legal (labor law)
Legal forms
Legal information software
Logos
Magazines (discounted)
Mail (U.S. Postal Service)
Marketing/publicity
Membership organizations (self-
employed, temporaries, and part-
time)
Money management
Networking
Newsletters (business)
Office supplies and equipment
Office supplies and equipment: "green"
(environmentally friendly)
Organize yourself/time management
Portfolio (skills)
Sheltered workshops (disabled work-
ers)
Small business
Social Security
Speakers/speaking
Tax advice
Telecommuting
Telephone rate comparisons
Telephone services and products
Television (business programming)
Writers/writing

BARTER

In one form or another, barter has been used to conduct business since the beginning of time. What may have begun as a simple exchange of services between two people has evolved into a nationwide network of professional exchanges creatively using a vast array of goods and services as barter currency.

Barter Advantage, Inc. (BAI)

Founded in 1981, BAI is a New York trade exchange whose members use barter credits instead of cash to conduct transactions.
1751 Second Avenue, Suite 103
New York, NY 10128
212-534-7500

BarterNews

This quarterly magazine reports barter industry news. The publisher is Robert Meyer.
P.O. Box 3024
Mission Viejo, CA 92690
714-831-0607

National Association of Trade Exchanges (NATE)

NATE represents the barter industry and sixty-five nationwide trade exchanges. It will refer individuals looking for a barter exchange to one in their area.
27801 Euclid Avenue, Suite 610
Euclid, OH 44132
216-732-7171

BETTER BUSINESS BUREAU (ONLINE)

The Web site provides access to publications, "Alerts and News," a business library, information, and other outside resources for business as well as for consumers. You can file a complaint online.
Council of Better Business Bureaus, Inc.
4200 Wilson Boulevard, Suite 800
Arlington, VA 22203-1804
703-276-0100
Web site: http://www.bbb.org/

BROCHURES AND MAILING PIECES

These authors offer expert help designing brochures and mailing pieces to market your services.

Related Books

Advertising from the Desktop, Elaine Floyd and Lee Wilson, Ventana Press, 1994.
The Art and Business of Creative Self-Promotion, Jerry Herring and Mark Fulton, Watson-Guptill Publications, 1987.

Better Brochures, Catalogs and Mailing Pieces, Jane Maas, St. Martin's Press, 1981.
Creating Brochures and Booklets, Val Adkins, North Light Books, 1994.
Do-It-Yourself Advertising and Promotion, Fred E. Hahn and Kenneth G. Mangun,
    John Wiley & Sons, 1997.
Fresh Ideas in Promotion 2, Betsy Newberry, North Light Books, 1996.
How to Produce Creative Publications, Thomas Bivins and William E. Ryan, NTC
    Business Books, 1990.
The Non-Designer's Design Book, Robin Williams, Peachpit Press, 1994.

BUSINESS CARD BROCHURES

Infocard

The Infocard is a unique business card–size brochure that allows you to include
as many as eight panels of useful information about your business.

Adnet
9426 Parkfield Drive
Austin, TX 78758
800-582-3638
E-mail: adnet@onr.com
Web site: http://www.infocard1.com

BUSINESS CARDS, LETTERHEAD, FORMS

All of the following companies have free catalogues featuring a variety of business
cards, stationery, greeting cards, forms, and labels that can be used with a computer
and laser or inkjet printer.

Deluxe Business Forms and Supplies

P.O. Box 35100
Colorado Springs, CO 80935-3510
800-328-0304

The Drawing Board

P.O. Box 2944
Hartford, CT 06104-2944
800-527-9530

Paper Access

23 West 18th Street
New York, NY 10011
212-463-7035

PaperDirect

P.O. Box 618
205 Chubb Avenue
Lyndhurst, NJ 07071-0618
800-272-7377

Paper Showcase

P.O. Box 8465
Mankato, MN 56002-8465
800-287-8163

Quill Corporation

100 Schelter Road
Lincolnshire, IL 60069–3621
800-789-1331
Request the Desktop Publishing catalogue.

The Stationery House

1000 Florida Avenue
Hagerstown, MD 21741
800-422-7331

BUSINESS INCUBATORS

Incubators provide new small businesses with low-cost office space in addition to offering business advice and financing leads.

National Business Incubator Association (NBIA)

NBIA will refer you to the incubator nearest you.
20 East Circle Drive, Suite 190
Athens, OH 45701
614-593-4331

BUSINESS INFORMATION DATABASES (ONLINE)

American Business Information

http://www.abii.com

Dow Jones

http://www.dowjones.com

Dun & Bradstreet

http://www.dbisna.com

Hoover's

> http://www.hoovers.com

Infotrieve

> http://www.infotrieve.com

LEXIS-NEXIS

> http://www.lexix-nexis.com

PR Newswire

> http://www.prnewswire.com

BUSINESS NAMES

Namestormers   ☺ Free

Namestormers offers consulting services as well as proprietary software to assist you in the selection of the right name for your business.

You can download an abbreviated name development checklist from the Web site, or you can request it by telephone.

512-267-1814

Web site: http://www.namestormers.com

BUSINESS PLANNING

Related Books

The Business Planning Guide: Creating a Plan for Success in Your Own Business, David H. Bangs, Jr., Upstart Publishing Company, Inc., 7th edition, 1995. Includes examples, forms and worksheets. A diskette with plan templates is available separately.

The Complete Book of Business Plans, Joseph A. Covello and Brian J. Hazelgren, Sourcebooks, 1997.

Great Idea! Now What? Howard Bronson and Peter Lange, Sourcebooks, 1995.

How to Write a Business Plan, Mike McKeever, Nolo Press, 4th edition, 1997. Shows how to write a business plan for a new or expanding business. Also has a streamlined method for writing a plan in one day.

Related Resources

American Woman's Economic Development Corporation (AWED)

AWED is a nonprofit corporation dedicated to helping women become successful entrepreneurs. It runs low-cost programs underwritten by both public and private sectors and will help its program participants secure financing. AWED has established regional centers in Washington, DC and Los Angeles.

71 Vanderbilt Avenue
New York, NY 10169
212-692-9100

The Small Business Administration (SBA) ☺ **Free**

The SBA publishes self-help guides on business topics. It also operates 950 small business development centers where information on all aspects of entrepreneurship is available. Copies of *The Resource Directory for Small Business Management,* which catalogues the self-help guides is available at SBA regional offices. Call 800-826-5722 for the location of one nearest you, as well as a list of services, videos and publications.

Regional offices will send you a Small Business Start-up Information Package that is full of pertinent and helpful information.

Service Corps of Retired Executives (SCORE) ☺ **Free**

SCORE provides free counseling to small businesses at 750 locations nationwide. Call for the location of the office nearest you.

800-634-0245

SBA Office of Women's Business Ownership

These are special SBA programs backing women entrepreneurs. Call for more information.

202-205-6673

✓ **Additional Sources to Check Out**

✓ Columns in your local newspaper devoted to small business will often carry announcements of what is available in the community.

✓ Chambers of commerce sponsor and/or subsidize training. Check their online directory to find one near you, or check the Yellow Pages of your telephone directory.

✓ Entrepreneurial Centers connected with local colleges have seminars and training programs.

BUSINESS SOFTWARE (ONLINE)

Billing Manager Software

Web site: http://www.mrtec.com/

Debt Analysis Software

Web site: http://www.shareware.com/EdFeature/CurrentFeature/1,6,352-1,00.html

Desktop Publishing Templates and Tips

Web site: http://desktopPublishing.com

CHECKS AND CHECKING ACCOUNTS

Since 1995, New York has had a Lifeline Banking Law. As a result, all banks offering personal consumer checking accounts must also offer a limited checking account (eight transactions a month). These accounts require no minimum balance, and the bank may not charge more than $3 per month as a fee. A person with one of these accounts may not have any other accounts with that bank. However, it *is* an inexpensive source for an additional checking account at another, different bank. If you do not live in New York, check with your state banking department or your local banks for similar legislation or accounts.

CHEAP CHECKS

Order your checks by telephone and pay a fraction of what your bank will charge. Checks for laser and ink jet printers are available also.

Artistic Checks	800-224-7621
The Check Gallery, Inc.	800-354-3540
Checks in the Mail	800-733-4443
The Check Store	800-4CHECKS
Current	800-533-3973
Custom Direct	800-272-5432

COMPUTER USER GROUPS

The best way to avoid hardware and software problems is to consult an electronic discussion group prior to making your purchase. Find out if any of their members have had difficulties with the product or with the company's technical support.

Association of Personal Computer User Groups

The association maintains a database of user groups. By calling their number, you can search by area code or state for a group near you. They will also furnish information on starting your own user group.
914-876-6678

Long Island PC Users Group

Web site: http://www.li.net/~lipcug

New York PC Users Group

212-984-0626

User Group Connection

This is a support organization for Apple Computer user groups. The membership benefits are a bimonthly newsletter and discounts on computer products and supplies. They will help you find a nearby group.

P.O. Box 67249
Scotts Valley, CA 95067-7249
800-538-9696

COMPUTER VIRUSES

Online Resources

Anti Virus and Virus Hoax

Web site: http://www.symantic.com

AVP Virus Encyclopedia

Web site: http://www.avp.ch/avpve

CIAC

U.S. Department of Energy Computer Incident Advisory Capability (CIAC) has detailed information on viruses and virus hoaxes.

510-422-8193
E-mail: ciac@llnl.gov
Web site: http://ciac.llnl.gov

National Computer Security Association

Web site: http://www.ncsa.com

Virus Hoax Library

Web site: http://www.nai.com/services/support/hoax/hoax.asp

Virus Info Listing

Web site: http://www.nai.com/vinfo

Software (Commercial)

Viruscan (McAfee/Network Associates)

Web site: http://www.mcafee.com
408-988-3832

PC-cillin (Touchstone)

714-969-7746
Web site: http://www.checkit.com

Norton AntiVirus *(Symantec)*

800-441-7234
Web site: http:/www.symantec

COMPUTERS AND PRINTERS

Related Books

The Computer Glossary, Alan Freedman, Amacom, 7th edition, 1998.
The PC User's Pocket Dictionary, Peter Dyson, Sybex, 2nd edition, 1998.
Illustrated Book of Terms and Technologies, Publishers of Smart Computing Magazine, Sandhill's Publishing, 1998.
Illustrated Computer Dictionary for Dummies, Dan Gookin and Sandra Hardin Gookin, IDG Books, 3rd edition, 1998.

Precision Computer

Here is a resource that I recommend wholeheartedly. My last three systems came from Precision Computer. They offer a full array of services and have been in business and at the same location since 1988, but I have only dealt with them by telephone, fax, and mail. One-third of their customers are small business owners and home office workers. I think they have the best prices, and their service can't be beat. Everyone I have referred to them has been happy with both prices and service. Visit their Web site for more information. If you call, ask for Nancy Chin.

2415 Lemoine Avenue
Fort Lee, NJ 07024
201-947-7866
Web site: http://www.precisioncomp.com

American Computer Exchange *(AmCoEx)*

Serves as a matchmaker for buyers and sellers.
800-786-0717

Apple Computer

Web site: http://store.apple.com (note: *no* "www" prefix)
Sells everything Mac; new, closeouts, and refurbished equipment. Will let you "build" your own PC.

Boston Computer Exchange

Serves as a matchmaker for buyers and sellers.
800-262-6399

Compac Works

Sells overstocks and refurbished computers.
800-318-6919
Web site: http://www.compacworks.com

Dell Computer

Desktops, notebooks, other gear. Will let you "build" your own PC.
Web site: http://www.dell.com

Gateway 2000

Desktops, portables, printers, monitors, refurbished gear.
Web site: http://www.gateway.com

Hewlett-Packard Advantage Center

Sells remanufactured business computers and printers.
800-373-4357

IBM PC Factory Outlet

Sells overstocks and refurbished computers.
800-426-7015

COMPUTERS: ONLINE TECHNICAL HELP

Build Your Own PC

Web site: http://www.verinet.com/pc

PC Mechanic

Web site: http://www.pcmech.pair/com

CONSULTING/FREELANCING

Related Books

The Complete Guide to Consulting Contracts: How to Understand, Draft, and Negoti-ate Contracts That Work, Herman Holtz, Upstart Publishing Company, 2nd edi-tion, 1995.

Freelancing Made Simple, Larry E. Hand, Doubleday, 1995.

How to Become a Successful Consultant in Your Own Field, Hubert Bermont, Prima Publishing, 1994.

How to Succeed as an Independent Consultant, Herman Holtz, John Wiley & Sons, 1993.

The Independent Consultant's Q&A Book, Lawrence W. Tuller, Bob Adams, Inc., 1993.

Marketing Your Consulting or Professional Services, David Karlson, Crisp Publica-tions, 1993.

Organizations

American Consultants League

This educational association assists its membership in the setting up and management of a consulting business. It has more than one thousand members. Dues are $96 per year.

1290 N. Palm Avenue, Suite 112
Sarasota, FL 34236
813-952-9290

Consultant's National Resource Center

The center offers courses, software, and publications for consultants and professional service marketers.

301-791-9332

Online Resources

Janet Ruhl's Computer Consultant's Resource Page

The Web site has terrific information for *all* consultants/freelancers/contract workers, although the focus is on computer consulting.

Web site: http://www.realrates.com

NetProCon

This membership organization is dedicated to helping consultants market their services and manage their practices. It furnishes access to training, seminars, conferences, database, software, products, and services useful to consultants and independent contractors.

Web site: http://www.netprocon.com

CONSUMER INFORMATION

Consumer Information Catalogue   ☺ **Free**

This catalogue of the U.S. General Services Administration lists free and low-cost booklets on a variety of topics, such as employment, federal programs, money, taxes, credit, financial planning, and small business. Write for a free copy.

Consumer Information Center
6C-4, P.O. Box 100
Pueblo, CO 81002

Center for the Study of Services   ☺ **Free**

The Web site has information on where to find the lowest prices for services and products. Through an ongoing national survey of retailers, more than 5,000 products are listed. This nonprofit organization was established in 1974 by the U.S. Department of Consumer Affairs and the Consumers Union. It also published the

Consumer's Guide to Health Care Services ($12), the results of a 1995 national survey of 72,000 HMO members rating their access to care and quality of care and more than twenty other specifics.

> 800-475-7283
> Web site: http://www.checkbook.org

Consumer Reports

Consumer Reports publishes articles on a variety of topics of interest to consumers. On their Web site you can obtain general buying advice, find out how to contact a manufacturer, review the latest product recalls and safety alerts, read a sampling of recent articles from other Consumer Union publications, and find links to agencies on the Web that may be helpful to you as a consumer—all at no cost. Full access to Consumer Reports Online costs the same as the subscription price of the magazine.

> 101 Truman Avenue
> Yonkers NY 10703-1057
> 914-378-2000
> Web site: http://www.ConsumerReports.org

CREDIT

Related Books

Credit Repair, attorney Robin Leonard, Nolo Press, 1996. Includes worksheets and sample letters.

The Guerrilla Guide to Credit Repair, Todd Bierman and Nathaniel Wice, St. Martin's Press, 1994. Step-by-step guide with sample letters.

Money Troubles: Legal Strategies to Cope with Your Debts, attorney Robin Leonard, Nolo Press, 1997. Includes worksheets and sample letters.

Counseling Organization

National Foundation for Consumer Credit

> The foundation gives referrals to local consumer credit counselors.
> 800-388-2227

Software (commercial)

Credit Manager

EZ Legal Books sells Credit Manager, "a complete credit and collection system of over 150 letters, agreements, notices, memos and other documents to help you get paid every time."

> 384 South Military Trail
> Deerfield Beach, FL 33442
> 954-480-8933

CREDIT BUREAUS

The three largest credit reporting agencies are listed below. Credit bureaus are prohibited by law from charging more than $8 for a copy of your report.

Experian (TRW)   800-682-7654

Trans Union Corporation   800-888-4213

Equifax   800-685-1111

CREDIT CARDS

No Annual Fee/No Late Fee

USAA Federal Savings Bank   800-922-9092

United National Bank   800-242-7600

Broadway National Bank   800-531-7650
   Available in Texas only.

Generous Grace Period

American Express/Centurion Bank Optima (True Grace)   800-467-8462

Citizens Bank   800-438-9222

Low Rates

First USA Bank   800-347-7887
   6.9 percent for six months, then 13.9 percent fixed rate.

Bank of Boston   800-252-2273
   6.4 percent for six months, then 12 percent variable rate.

KeyBank   800-539-2969

   Their KeySmart card rewards users who pay off more of their balance. Clear 5 percent or more of amount owed, and KeyBank calculates the next month's interest at its lowest rate (range 8.9 to 11.9 percent).

Grace Periods on Cash Advances

Arkansas Federal Credit Card Services   800-477-3348

Fidelity National Bank   800-753-2900

Finding Low-Rate and No-Fee Cards

Money magazine and *Barron's* financial weekly both list credit cards with the current lowest annual percentage rates in each issue.

CardTrak

Send $5.00 by mail for a list of low-rate and no-fee cards, or check an abbreviated list free on the Internet.

Box 1700
Frederick, MD 21702
Web site: http://www.cardtrak.com

Bankcard Holders of America

Lists cards with no annual fee, cards with low interest rates, and secured cards. The charge for nonmembers is $4.

540-389-5445

CREDIT: DEBT COLLECTION AND THE LAW

✓ The Fair Debt Collection Practices Act, enacted in 1977, stipulates what "collectors" (what you are when trying to collect from a client) can and cannot do.

What Collectors Can Do

1. Reach a debtor by mail, telephone, telegram, or fax.

2. Charge interest and a collection fee if state law allows. Such fees must be outlined in their first notice, but not in subsequent correspondence.

3. Talk to other people (neighbors, relatives) but only to ask where debtors live or work. Collectors may not reveal that a debtor is in debt.

What Collectors Cannot Do

1. Call before 8:00 A.M. or after 9:00 P.M.

2. Call a debtor at work if they know the employer disapproves and the debtor is an employee (not business owner, of course).

3. Contact a debtor if the debtor demands in writing that collectors stop. However, they can notify a debtor if they or the creditors intend to take some specific action, such as a lawsuit.

4. Contact a debtor if notified by same within thirty days of the first notice that the debt is an error. Collectors then have to prove that debt is owed. They do not have to notify a debtor if a bill is paid.

5. Make empty threats about wages seizure or filing a lawsuit. Collector must intend to do so.

6. Threaten violence, use profane language, pose as lawyers or government officials, write to a debtor by postcard, call without identifying themselves, or publicize the debt (except to a credit bureau).

Fighting back

If you are the debtor and you think a collector has violated the law, you can notify the attorney general of your state or the Federal Trade Commission.

CREDIT UNIONS

Credit unions are member-owned, not-for-profit financial cooperatives, formed to promote thrift by offering a fair return on savings, making loans at competitive interest rates, and providing other financial services. Members are united by a common bond, such as their employment, place of worship, or residence. There are approximately 12,000 credit unions in the United States, and some of them have open membership.

Credit Union National Association

Provides information about credit unions in all states.
800-358-5710

DIRECTORIES

Directory of Executive Temporary Placement Firms, Kennedy Publications, updated yearly.
Directory of Temporary Firms, Kennedy Publications, updated yearly.
National Trade and Professional Associations in the United States, Columbia Books, updated yearly.
National Directory of Women-Owned Business Firms, Gale Business Research Services. A guide to organizations, agencies, institutions, and programs for women. Call 800-877-GALE or check your local library.
The Women's Business Resource Guide, Barbara Littman, Contemporary Books, 1996. This national directory of more than 800 programs, resources, and organizations for women offers guidance in such areas as training, business financing, membership organizations, and selling to the government.

ENTREPRENEURIAL CENTERS

These are also called Small Business Development Centers (SBDCs) and are usually campus-based. The centers bring together the resources of the university, the private sector, and government to counsel and train small businesses in resolving organizational, financial, marketing, technical, and other problems. The SBA Small Business Start-Up Information Package (free from your regional SBA office) will include a list of the centers in your region.

ENTREPRENEURS

Related Books

The E-Myth, Michael E. Gerber, HarperBusiness, 1990.
The E-Myth Revisited, Michael E. Gerber, Harper Business, 1995.
The Frugal Entrepreneur, Terri Lonier, Portico Press (800-222-7656), 1996.
Working Solo: The Real Guide to Freedom and Financial Success with Your Own Business, Terri Lonier, John Wiley & Sons, 2nd edition, 1998.
Working Solo Sourcebook: Essential Resources for Independent Entrepreneurs, Terri Lonier, John Wiley & Sons, 2nd edition, 1998. This well-written guide gives information on 1,200 important business resources.

Online Resources

Entrepeneur's Wave   http://www.en-wave.com

This resource has built an online library of thousands of small business books on sale at discounted prices. You can also chat with authors.

FEE SETTING

Related Books

The Contract and Fee-Setting Guide for Consultants and Professionals, Howard Shenson, John Wiley & Sons, 1990.
National Writers Union Guide to Freelance Rates and Standard Practice, National Writers Union, Betterway Books, 1995.
Priced to Sell, Herman Holtz, Upstart Publishing Company, 1996.
Selling Your Services, Robert Bly, Henry Holt, 1992.

FINANCIAL

Business Funding Directory

Includes sources of potential funding for both the government and private sector. Users must complete a detailed online form to receive a list of possible sources.
Web site: http://www.businessfinance.com

Catalog of Public Information Materials   ☺ **Free**

This catalogue, available from the Federal Reserve System, lists most publications and audiovisual materials prepared by the twelve Federal Reserve Banks and the Board of Governors of the Federal Reserve System. These materials are designed to increase public understanding of the functions and operations of the Federal

Reserve System, monetary policy, financial markets and institutions, consumer finance, and the economy. Call the Federal Reserve Bank in your district to request a copy.

Atlanta:	404-521-8020
Boston:	617-973-3459
Chicago:	312-322-5111
Cleveland:	216-579-3079
Dallas:	214-922-5254
Kansas City:	816-881-2683
Minneapolis:	612-340-2446
New York:	212-720-6134
Philadelphia:	215-574-6115
Richmond:	804-697-8109
St. Louis:	314-444-8808/8809
San Francisco:	415-974-2246

First Step Software Series   ☺ **Free**

The National Business Association (NBA) offers free software that gives an orientation to the SBA guaranteed loan program and helps to determine the likelihood of your getting one. Call to request the software, a newsletter, and/or membership information.

800-456-0440

Web site: http://www.nationalbusiness.org

SBA Financial Programs

Furnishes information on guaranteed loans [LowDocumentation Loan (LowDoc), FA$TRAK Loan, Microloan] to small businesses that have been denied financing from a commercial lender.

800-827-5722

Web site: http://www.sbaonline.sba.gov

The Small Business Financial Resource Guide   ☺ **Free**

This 150-page book of useful financial information is available from MasterCard International, Corporate Products Department.

914-249-2000

Web site: http://www.mastercard.com

Related Book

Money Smart Secrets for the Self-Employed, Linda Stern, Random House, 1997.

A practical guide full of great tips to maximize your income while minimizing taxes.

FINANCIAL PLANNERS

Background Checks/Complaints

Mortgage Asset Research Institute $39 fee

  800-822-0416

CFP Board of Standards

  888-237-6275

National Association of Securities Dealers Regulation

  800-289-9999

North American Securities Administrators Association

  888-846-2722

Securities and Exchange Commission

  800-732-0330

Referrals

American Institute of Certified Public Accountants (AICPA)

  888-999-9256
  Web site: http://www.aicpa.org

American Society of CLU and ChFC

  888-243-2258

Institute of Certified Financial Planners (ICFP)

  800-282-7526
  Web site: http://www.icfp.org

International Association for Financial Planning (IAFP)

  800-945-4237
  Web site: http://www.iafp.org

National Association of Personal Financial Advisors (NAPFA)

  888-333-6659
  Web site: http://www.napfa.org

GOVERNMENT (FEDERAL)

Related Books

Government Giveaways for Entrepeneurs, Matthew Lesko, InfoUSA, 5th edition, 1996. Regularly updated guide to money sources and free expertise.

Government on the Net, James Evans, Nolo Press, 1997.
Selling to Uncle Sam, Clinton Crownover, Mark Hendricks, McGraw-Hill, 1993.

Related Online Business Resources

U.S. Business Advisor

Interactive online resource for all types of business information and assistance from the federal government.
Web site: http://www.business.gov

SBA Online

Provides information about SBA programs, field offices, business development services, government contracting opportunities, and more.
Web site: http://www.sbaonline.sba.gov

FedWorld®

National Technical Information Service network that connects users electronically to over 150 computer bulletin board systems and searchable databases operated by the U.S. government. Users can view documents, download information, and order publications.
Recorded information: 703-487-4608
Web site: http://www.fedworld.gov

Federal Reserve Bank of New York

Link to other Federal Reserve research and Web sites.
Web site: http://www.ny.frb.org

HOME-BASED BUSINESSES

Related Books

The Complete Work at Home Companion, Herman Holtz, Prima Publishing, 1994.
Homemade Money, Barbara Brabec, Betterway Books, 5th edition, 1994.
Comprehensive guide to anything and everything connected to home-based businesses. Excellent reference for anyone who is self-employed.
How to Run Your Own Home Business, Coralee Smith Kern and Tammara Hoffman Wolfgram, National Textbook Company, 1990.
Making It on Your Own: Surviving and Thriving on the Ups and Downs of Being Your Own Boss, Sarah and Paul Edwards, St. Martin's Press, 1991.
Marketing for the Home-Based Business, Jeffery P. Davidson, Bob Adams, Inc., 1993.

Related Newsletters

Earning Power in the Home

Bimonthly newsletter with a special column for individuals with disabilities, $10 per year.

Patricia Galbraith, editor
P.O. Box 368
Weatherford, TX 76086
817-594-4415

Home Business Report

Monthly newsletter, $24 per year.
Rick Kerner, editor
The Kerner Group, Inc.
3231 Forks Street
Easton, PA 18042
800-972-6664

Mind Your Own Business at Home

Bimonthly newsletter, $30 per year.
Coralee Smith Kern, editor
Coralee Smith Kern Publishing
Box 14850
Chicago, IL 60614
312-472-8116

Related Organizations

American Association of Home Based Businesses (AAHBB)
Member fee $90

AAHBB is a nonprofit, national association offering support to home-based businesses. There are approximately 100 independently organized local chapters addressing the specific needs of their individual members. The benefits include discounted long-distance telephone service, merchant status for credit cards, prepaid legal services, and advocacy on Capitol Hill (related issues such as the passage of the home office deduction and full deductibility of health insurance premiums).

P.O. Box 10023
Rockville, MD 20849-0023
800-447-9710
Web site: http://www.aahbb.org

Home Business Institute (HBI)   *Member fee $49*

This organization has more than 40,000 members in home-based businesses. Benefits are discounts on products, services, prescription drugs.

David Hanania
P.O. Box 301
White Plains, NY 10605-0301
914-946-6600

HOME OFFICE

Related Books

The Home Office and Small Business Answer Book, Janet Attard, Henry Holt & Company, 1993.

Paper Clips to Printers, Dean and Jessica King, Penguin Books, 1996. This is a terrific reference source, full of information on how to manage your home office efficiently and economically.

The Work-at-Home Sourcebook, Lynie Arden, Live Oak Publications, 6th edition, 1996.

Related Organizations

The Home Office Association of America (HOAA)   *Member fee $35*

HOAA provides a variety of benefits and services, including a health insurance plan, discounts on business services, and a monthly newsletter.

909 Third Avenue, Suite 990
New York, NY 10022
212-980-4622
Web site: http://www.sohocentral.com

SOHO America   *Member fee $48*

SOHO offers a newsletter, discounts on office supplies, services and magazine subscriptions, twenty-four hour computer help by telephone, and more.

2626 East 82nd Street, Suite 325
Minneapolis, MN 55425
800-495-SOHO
Web site: http://www.org/sohoamerica

HOTLINES (U.S. GOVERNMENT)

Consumer Product Safety Commission

800-638-2772

Department of Labor (Small Business Specialist)

202-219-9154

Federal Information Center
>   800–688–9889
>   310–722–9000

Federal Trade Commission (FTC)
>   202-326-2258

Social Security
>   800-771-1213

INDEPENDENT CONTRACTORS

Related Books

Wage Slave No More: The Independent Contractor's Legal Guide, attorney Stephen Fishman, Nolo Press, 1997. Along with "everything an independent contractor should know," it includes a disk with model contracts, business correspondence, and business/legal forms.

Related Organizations

Professional Association of Contract Employees (PACE)

PACE is a service organization developed as an umbrella, "employer of record" company to provide a home base and corporate infrastructure for contract professionals. Presently, its membership is limited to contract workers who carry out assignments in California.
>   Web site: http://www.pacepros.com

The Contract Employee's Handbook

The Web site is PACE's inaugural project. It is full of essential information (on legal issues, benefits, etc.) and resources. It also lists agencies that openly disclose and discuss the assignment billing rate as well as the agency percentage of such rate.
>   Web site: http://www.cehandbook.com

Working Today   *Member fee $10*

Working Today is a nonprofit organization promoting the interests of the contemporary work force through education, advocacy and service. Benefits include access to comprehensive health and dental benefits and free prepaid legal assistance. The medical insurance is linked to associate membership in the National Writers Union (for an additional $45 per year).
>   P.O. Box 1261
>   Old Chelsea Box Station
>   New York, NY 10113-9998
>   212-366-6066
>   E-mail: working1@tiac.net
>   Web site: http://www.workingtoday.com

INSURANCE (BUSINESS)

Insurance Information Institute   ☺ **Free**

The Institute produces insurance information books and brochures for small and midsize businesses.

Some of the publications are free. Call or write for further information.

110 William Street
New York, NY 10038
212-669-9200

Insurance InLinea

Provides useful information on all forms of insurance for small business. It is maintained by a nationwide group of insurance agents.

Web site: http://www.inlinea.com/

INSURANCE QUOTES

These companies will find the lowest rates for you, but they charge a fee. Call them for rate schedules and a list of their services.

AccuQuote

800-442-9899

Insurance Information Inc. (fee)

800-472-5800

MasterQuote of America

800-337-5433

Quotesmith

800-556-9393

SelectQuote

800-343-1985

TermQuote

800-444-8376

Online Resources

InsureMarket   *http://www.insuremarket.com*

InsWeb   *http://www.insweb.com*

Quotesmith   *http://www.quotesmith.com*

RightQuote   *http://www.rightquote.com*

JOB (PROJECT/EMPLOYMENT) SEARCH

Online Resources

America's Job Bank

A service of the U.S. Labor Department and state employment agencies, AJB has 600,000 job openings offered by 9,500 employers and recruiting firms. Also provides direct hyperlinks to 1,354 employer Web sites and 450 other job banks and private employment agencies on the Internet.

Web site: http:/www.ajb.dni.us

Career Mosaic

http://www.careermosaic.com

Career Path

Contains the listings of twenty-eight major newspapers, updated daily.
http://www.careerpath.com

E-Span

http://www.espan.com

Exec-U-Net

http://www.clickit.com/touch/execunet/executive.htm

Job Center

http://www.jobcenter.com

JobWeb

Set up by college consortium.
http://www.jobweb.org

Monster Board

http://www.monster.com

Online Career Center

http://www.occ.com

TOP jobs–USA

http://www.fiber.net

Related Services

Career Magazine

General career support.
Web site: http://www.careermag.com

✓ For specific company information check out Business Information Databases (online) on page 205.

LAWYERS/LEGAL (BUSINESS-RELATED)

Books

The Complete Small Business Legal Guide, Robert Friedman, Dearborn, 1993. Includes forms and templates. Very thorough coverage, good checklists.

How to Form Your Own "S" Corporation and Avoid Double Taxation, Ted Nicholas, Upstart Publishing, 1995.

155 Legal Do's and Don'ts for the Small Business, Paul Adams, John Wiley & Sons, 1996. Pitfalls to avoid on a variety of subject areas.

Online Resources

Business Filings

Extensive information on business entities. Discounted prices on incorporations, trademark searches, and registration services.

214 North Henry Street, Suite 201
Madison, WI 53703
Web site: http://www.bizfilings.com

Corporate Creations

Discounted incorporation and trademark searches and registration services.
800-672-9110
Web site: http://www.corpcreations.com

Court TV Small Business Law Center

Access to lawyer search, QuickForm Contracts, FIND-SVP Legal Research Service. Quick links to ten additional small business sites. Information on dealing with lawyers, business organization, intellectual property.

Web site: http://www.courttv.com/legalhelp/business

LAWYERS/LEGAL (GENERAL)

Related Books

Everybody's Guide to Small Claims Court, attorney Ralph Warner, Nolo Press, 7th edition, 1997.

Law on the Net, James Evans, Nolo Press, 2nd edition, 1997. Book with CD-ROM.

Legal Research: How to Find and Understand the Law, attorneys Stephen Elias and Susan Levinkind, Nolo Press, 7th edition, 1997. Provides information on conducting specific legal inquiries on the Internet, including how to find recent statutes.

Mad at Your Lawyer, attorney Tanya Starnes, Nolo Press, 1997.

Nolo's Everyday Law Book: Answers to Your Most Frequently Asked Legal Questions, by the editors of Nolo Press, 1997.

Organizations/Publishers

HALT: An Organization for Legal Reform

HALT publishes manuals and books to help consumers handle their own legal affairs and become informed users of legal services. It also provides attorney referrals to people who are bringing charges against attorneys. Call or write for a catalogue of publications.

1319 F Street NW, Suite 300
Washington, DC 20004
202-347-9600

Nolo Press

Nolo Press is the largest publisher of self-help law books and a name synonymous with high quality and user-friendly books and software. The publications categories are Money and Consumer Matters; Going to Court; Family Matters and Seniors; Homeowner, Landlord, Tenant; Intellectual Property; Business and Workplace; Estate Planning; General Interest. Request a catalogue of titles by telephone or via the Web site.

800-992-NOLO (in California 800-445-NOLO)
Web site: http://www.nolo.com

LAWYERS/LEGAL (LABOR LAW)

Related Books

The Employer's Legal Handbook, attorney Fred S. Steingold, Nolo Press, 2nd edition, 1997.
Guide to Workplace Law, The American Bar Association, Random House, 1997.
Major Laws Administered by the U.S. Department of Labor Which Affect Business
U.S. Department of Labor, Room S-1004
200 Constitution Avenue, NW
Washington, DC 20210.
Send a self-addressed mailing label with your request. ☺ **Free**

Organization

National Employee Rights Institute (NERI) ☺ **Free**

This nonprofit organization helps both employed and unemployed individuals to understand, enforce, and expand their rights in the workplace by furnishing information and access to employment advocates.

Write or e-mail for a copy of the booklet *A Self-Help Guide for the Newly Unemployed.*

600 Harrison Street, Suite 535
San Francisco, CA 94107
E-mail: ptobial@igc.apc.org

LEGAL FORMS

Books

The Complete Book of Business and Legal Forms, Lynne Ann Frasier, Sourcebooks, 1997.
101 Law Forms for Personal Use, attorney Robin Leonard and Marcia Stewart, Nolo
    Publishing, 1997. Includes a diskette of forms.

Online Resources

Legaldocs from USA Law Publications, Inc.

Legaldocs has a variety of legal forms online. Some are free and some carry a
nominal charge, ranging from $1.50 to $24.95.

Web site: http://www.legaldocs.com

LEGAL INFORMATION SOFTWARE

Kiplinger's Small Business Attorney

800-813-7940

Nolo Legal Software

800-445-NOLO, (in California: 800-992-NOLO)
Web site: http://www.nolo.com

Parsons Technology

800-779-6000
Web site: http://www.parsonstech.com

Quicken Family Lawyer
Quicken Business Law Partner
The ABA Family Legal Guide

LOGOS

Logo SuperPower

This product is a graphics database of over two thousand images that can be
worked and combined to create logos. It is not a software program, but rather high-
quality artwork created just for logos. It is used inside a drawing program such as
FreeHand or Corel Draw. Available for Macintosh, Windows, Quark Xpress, and Page-
maker.

Decathlon Corporation
4100 Executive Park Drive, #16
Cincinnati, OH 45241
800-648-5646

MAGAZINES (DISCOUNTED)

Below Wholesale Magazines

Discounts over 500 consumer and trade titles.
1909 Prosperity Street
Reno, NV 89502
800-800-0062

MAIL (U.S. POSTAL SERVICE)   ☺ Free

Two free services from the U.S. Postal Service:

1. They will revamp your mailing list by adding the proper abbreviations, correcting misspellings of locations, and adding four-digit suffixes to your zip codes.

2. The Postal Service also has a free IBM-compatible disk that helps you evaluate the most cost-effective way to send your mail. The disk is called "The Mail Flow Planning System." Call for more information. 800-238-3150

MARKETING/PUBLICITY

Related Books

Getting Publicity, Tana Fletcher, Julia Rockler, Self-Counsel Press, 1995.
Marketing Without Advertising, Michael Phillips and Salli Raspberry, Nolo Press, 2nd edition, 1997.
The New Publicity Kit, Jeanette Smith, John Wiley & Sons, 1995.
Uncommon Marketing Techniques, Jeffrey Dobkin, Danielle Adams Publishing Company, 1997.
Which Ad Pulled Best?, Philip Burton, Scott Purvis, NTC Business Books, 8th edition, 1996.

Marketing Experts

Jay Conrad Levinson and Dr. Jeffrey Lant are both prolific writers on the topic of marketing and self-promotion. Levinson writes the Guerrilla Marketing series; both produce audiotapes, newsletters, and Web sites. I found Levinson's books especially helpful. Check your library and bookstore or their Web sites for a complete listing of their books, products, and services or contact them directly.

Jay Conrad Levinson
Guerrilla Marketing International
260 Cascade Drive, Box 1336
Mill Valley, CA 94942
800-748-6444 (in California call 415-381-8361)
http://www.guerrila.com

Dr. Jeffrey Lant
JLA Publications
P.O. Box 38-2767
Cambridge, MA 02238
617-547-6372
http://www.worldprofit.com

MEMBER ORGANIZATIONS

Self-Employed

National Association for the Self-Employed   *Member fee $72*

NASE maintains a business library and a hotline offering free business advice. The association offers discounts on legal and debt collection services, office supplies, printing, long-distance, and travel. It maintains a lobbying staff in Washington, DC to advocate on behalf of small business.

2121 Precinct Line Road
Hurst, TX 76054
800-232-6273

Small Business

National Business Association (NBA)   *Member fee $144*

This nonprofit organization's mission is to assist small business owners to achieve their personal and professional goals. NBA offers an array of benefits and discounts to members in addition to publishing a newsletter.

P.O. Box 700728
Dallas, TX 75370
800-456-0440
Web site: http://www.nationalbusiness.org

National Federation of Independent Business (NFIB)

NFIB considers itself an advocacy organization for small business (as opposed to a special interest group). It has an audited membership of 600,000, ranging from one-person cottage enterprises to firms with hundreds of employees. Its membership votes five times a year on federal issues, once a year on state issues. NFIB lobbyists carry the results to the Congress and state legislatures.

Contact either of the following offices.

Public Policy Headquarters   Membership Support Headquarters
600 Maryland Avenue, SW   53 Century Boulevard, Suite 300
Washington, DC 20024   Nashville, TN 37214
202-554-9000   800-634-2669 (800-NFIBNOW)
Web site: http://www.nfibonline.com/

National Small Business United (NSBU) ☺ **Free**

NSBU considers itself an advocacy organization for small business (as opposed to a special interest group). Formed in 1937, it has more than 65,000 members through its chapters and affiliate organizations. It is active on legislative issues before the Congress, and its members testify periodically on Capitol Hill. Offers services and discounts to its members.

A thirty-day trial membership is available to potential new members.

1156 15th Street, NW, Suite 1100
Washington, DC 20005
202-293-8830
Web site: http://www.nsbu.org

Temporaries and Part-Time Workers

National Association of Part-Time and Temporary *Member fee $10* Employees (NAPTE)

A nonprofit organization that voices the interests of part-time, temporary, and contract employees to state legislatures and the Congress. Membership entitles access to discounted medical and other services, product discounts, newsletters, and periodic information on issues affecting part-time and temporary employment.

P.O. Box 3805
Shawnee, KS 66203
913-962-7740

✓ Also check membership organizations under *Consulting/Freelancing* and *Independent Contractors*, as well as the ones that appear at the end of Chapter 9.

MONEY MANAGEMENT

Related Books

The Frugal Entrepreneur, Terri Lonier, Portico Press, 1996.
Creative ways to save time, energy, and money in your business.
Money Smart Secrets for the Self-Employed, Linda Stern, Random House, 1997. A practical guide full of great tips to maximize your income while minimizing taxes.
If Time Is Money, No Wonder I'm Not Rich, Mary L. Sprouse, Simon & Schuster, 1993.

Commercial Software

Managing Your Money (MECA Software)
Quicken Money Management (Intuit)

NETWORKING

Related Books

127 Ways to Build a Powerful Network (booklet $5 ppd.), Pamela Murray, Many Waters Publishing, P.O. Box 1996, Walla Walla, WA 99362, 509-525-5436, e-mail: PamMurray@aol.com.

Pam is a popular keynote speaker, trainer, and consultant who helps businesses and individuals with the people side of success. She has also written *Secrets of Master Networkers: How to Build a Powerful Business Network; The New Success: How to Redefine, Create and Survive Your Own Success,* and *The Twelve Practices.*

How to Work a Room, Susan RoAne, 1997, Warner Books, 1998, and Renaissance Audiotape.

The Secrets of Savvy Networking, Susan RoAne, Warner Books, 1993, and Renaissance Audiotape.

What Do I Say Next?, Susan RoAne, Warner Books, 1997, Time-Warner Audiotape.

For more information about Susan RoAne's programs, books, or audiotapes, contact

The RoAne Group.
320 Via Casitas, Suite 310
Greenbrae, CA 94904
415-239-2224
415-461-6172 (fax)
E-mail: SRoAne2224@aol.com

Business Tip Groups

These are for-profit enterprises that charge membership fees for the privilege of joining a group of local professional people who meet to help each other find more business. Local chapters typically number from ten to forty people. To avoid competition no profession is represented more than once.

Business Network Int'l. (BNI)

BNI has 600 chapters, mostly in North America, a few in Britain.
199 South Monte Vista Avenue, Suite 6
San Dimas, CA 91773-3080
800-825-8286 (inside Southern California, 909-305-1818)
Web site: http://www.bninet.com

LeTip International, Inc.

Founded in 1978, LeTip is the pioneer networking organization. There are over 400 chapters in the U.S. and Canada.
4901 Morena Boulevard, Suite 703
San Diego, CA 92117
619-490-2747

The Small Business Network

This knowledge network of professionals helps its members obtain the information they need to start, develop, and maintain a successful small business.

1341 Ancona Drive
La Verne, CA 91750
800-825-8286

Commercial Software

ACT!

This is a popular networking/contact management software by Symantec. You can order a trial copy (database limited to twenty-five) online.

Web site: http://www.symantec.com

NEWSLETTERS (BUSINESS)

The Accidental Entrepreneur

Dixie Darr is both the editor and publisher of this bimonthly newsletter for anyone who has been ". . . fired, retired, laid off, reduced-in-force, downsized, rightsized, outsourced, bought out, or fed up with corporate life." The newsletter is full of useful information on a variety of topics—and it is fun to read. Note: Only the sample copy is free.

3421 Alcott Street
Denver, CO 80211
E-mail: sknkwrks@ix.netcom.com

Disgruntled ☺ **Free**

Combines news, features, satire, and commentary about the "darker" side of the world of work. It consistently has a variety of useful information for independent contractors and temporaries in spite of its occasional negative tone.

Web site: http://www.disgruntled.com

Working Solo eNews ☺ **Free**

Free e-mail newsletter designed to bring tips and news about the world of *Working Solo* to your e-mailbox.

Web site: http://www.workingsolo.com

OFFICE SUPPLIES AND EQUIPMENT

Recently, I read that Office Depot and Staples were carving the United States up into "territories." They have grown so big they are acting like countries. Possibly, their fight for dominance will keep prices lower for a short time where a community has both stores. I hate to think what will happen when they are our only choice. In the meantime, I continue to shop by catalogue with Quill Corporation, as I have for the past ten or so years. I think catalogues are great time-savers. Quill has the best overall selection and prices for the products I use. Their service is exceptional, and their employees, whom I deal with only by telephone, are knowledgeable and actually seem to like their jobs. Check out Quill's Web site library for useful publications on business topics such as organizing a home office or a filing system.

Supplies/Equipment Catalogues

Request copies from the companies below.

Quill Corporation

> 717-272-6100
> Web site: http://www.quillcorp.com

Reliable Office Supply

> 800-735-4000

Staples, Inc.

> 508-370-8500

Viking Office Products

> 800-421-1222

Organizing/Planning Catalogues

Hold Everything

> A large selection of items, furniture, shelving to organize the office and home.
> 800-421-2264

Caddylak Systems

> Planning aids.
> 510 Fillmore Avenue
> Tonawanda, NY 14150
> 800-523-8060

OFFICE SUPPLIES AND EQUIPMENT: "GREEN" (ENVIRONMENTALLY FRIENDLY)

Related Publications

The Business Environmental Handbook, Martin Westerman, PSI Research, 800-228-2275.

Includes templates to help determine office energy use, waste production, and more.

Co-op America's National Green Pages   http://www.greenpages.com

> http://www.coopamerica.com
> Updated annually, $7.95. 800-58-GREEN

The GreenBusiness Letter   800-955-GREEN   http://www.enn.com/gbl
GreenClips   E-mail newsletter greenclips@aol.com
Green Guide on Trimming Office Waste
    http://www.pnl.gov:2080/esp/greenguide
Official Green Buying Guide, Green Seal Organization, http://www.greenseal.org
    Tips on "greenest" copiers, fax machines, other equipment and supplies
    202-588-8400
The Official Recycled Products Guide   800-267-0707
    Comprehensive nationwide listing of recycled products, updated twice a year.
The Smart Office, A. K. Townsend. Comprehensive sourcebook for "greening" an of-
    fice.
    Sustainable Development Corp.
    P.O. Box 623
    Olney, MD 20830
    301-774-0917
    Web site: http://www.smartoffice.com

ORGANIZE YOURSELF/TIME MANAGEMENT

Related Books

*If You Haven't Got the Time to Do It Right, When Will You Find the Time to Do It
    Over?,* Jeffrey J. Mayer, Simon & Schuster, 1990.
Organizing Your Home Office for Success, Lisa Kanarek, Penguin Books, 1993.
Organized to Be the Best, Susan Silver, Adams-Hall Publishing, 3rd edition, 1995.
Taming the Paper Tiger, Barbara Hemphill, Kiplinger's Books and Tapes, 1990.
Time Management for Dummies, Jeffrey J. Mayer, IDG Books, 1995.
Winning the Fight Between You and Your Desk, Jeffrey J. Mayer, HarperBusiness, 1993.

Organization

The National Association of Professional Organizers

    1604 North Country Club Road
    Tucson, AZ 85716
    602-322-9753

PORTFOLIO (SKILLS)

Book

Portfolio Power: The New Way to Showcase All Your Job Skills and Experiences, Martin
    Kimeldorf, Peterson's, 1997. This excellent resource takes you step by step
    through the process of creating professional portfolios on paper (or electroni-
    cally) and shows you how to use them to your best advantage. It has a section
    for ex–military personnel.

SHELTERED WORKSHOPS (DISABLED WORKERS)

Many entrepreneurs have had great success using disabled workers from sheltered workshops to do a variety of projects for a reasonable amount of money. These resources will help you find a workshop in your area.

Job Accommodation Network

P.O. Box 468
Morgantown, WV 26505
800-526-7234

President's Committee on Employment of the Handicapped

1111 20th Street, NW
Washington, DC 20036
202-653-5044
✓ Check in the Yellow Pages under Sheltered Workshops as well as under Social Service Agencies.

SMALL BUSINESS

Online Resources

AmEx Small Business Exchange

Offers personalized advice from small business adviser Alice Bredin in addition to articles and advice on business planning, day-to-day management, and taxes.
Web site: http://www.americanexpress.com/smallbusiness

Smart Business Supersite

Has articles, checklists, and books on a variety of topics. Site offers an interactive message board and a reminder service for online events.
Web site: http://www.smartbiz.com

SOCIAL SECURITY

Related Book

Social Security, Medicare and Pensions: Get the Most Out of Your Retirement and Medical Benefits, Joseph L. Matthews and Dorothy M. Berman, Nolo Press, 6th edition, 1997.

Social Security Hotline

800-771-1213

SPEAKERS/SPEAKING

Related Organizations

National Speakers Association (NSA)

This international association of more than 3,800 members is dedicated to advancing the art and value of experts who speak professionally.

1500 South Priest Drive
Tempe, AZ 85281
602-968-2552
Web site: http://www.nsaspeaker.org

Toastmasters International

Nearly three million people have participated in the Toastmasters program globally. There are more than 8,000 clubs in over fifty countries. Many clubs are listed with their local chamber of commerce, and most communities have a chapter. The world headquarters is located in Rancho Santa Margarita, California.

Web site: http://www.toastmasters.com

Training for Speakers

Anne Miller–Chiron Associates, Inc.

Presentation and sales skills seminars. Corporate clients only, no individual clients. Anne is the author of *Presentation Jazz: How to Make Presentations $ing*, Amacom, 1998, and *365 Sales Tips for Winning Business*, Perigee, 1998.

Box 624
New York, NY 10163
212-876-1875
E-mail: amspeak@aol.com
Web site: http://www.chironassoc.com

Dottie Walters–Walters Speakers Services

P.O. Box 1120
Glendora, CA 91740
626-335-8069

TAX ADVICE

Internal Revenue Service Helplines

All purpose number for answers to questions.
800–829–1040
Information on a variety of topics or to check the status of a refund.
800–829–4477

Related Books

Being Self-Employed, Holmes F. Crouch, Allyear Tax Guides, 1994.

Dealing with the IRS, Scott Miller and Thomas Guy, Creek Bend Publishing Company, 1992.

Disagreeing with the IRS, Holmes F. Crouch, Allyear Tax Guides, 1993.

The Ernst & Young Income Tax Guide, Ernst and Young, John Wiley & Sons, yearly updates.

H&R Block Income Tax Guide, H&R Block, Fireside, yearly updates.

How to Pay Zero Taxes, Jeff Schnepper, ed., McGraw-Hill, 1998.

How to Beat the IRS at Its Own Game: Strategies to Avoid and Fight an Audit, Amir D. Aczel, Four Walls Eight Windows, 1995.

J. K. Lasser's Your Income Tax, J. K. Lasser Institute, Macmillan General Reference, 1998.

101 Tax Loopholes for the Middle Class, Sean Smith, Bantam Doubleday Dell, 1998.

Stand Up to the IRS, Frederick Daily, Nolo Press, 1994.

Tax Planning for the One-Person Business, James Bucheister, Rayve Productions, Inc., 1994.

What the IRS Doesn't Want You to Know, Martin Kaplan and Naomi Weiss, Random House, 3rd edition, 1997.

Your Tax Questions Answered, Ed Slott, Plymouth Press, 1998.

Online Resources

AARP Tax-Aide   ☺ **Free**

Sites are also located in libraries and at community centers throughout the United States. For the one nearest you, call twenty-four hours a day, seven days a week.

888-227-7669

Web site: http://www.aarp.org/taxaide/home.html

Coopers & Lybrand

Comprehensive taxpayer questions and answers. Links to other sites.

Web site: http://www.taxnews.com/tnn_public

Deloitte & Touche

Extensive help and worksheets

Web site: http://www.dtonline.com

Ernst & Young

General tax help.

Web site: http://www.ey.com/us/tax/eyustax.html

Internal Revenue Service   ☺ **Free**

All IRS publications and forms.

Web site: http://www.irs.ustreas.gov

J. K. Lasser

Tax preparation/tax law changes.
Web site: http://www.mcp.com/mgr/lasser

State Forms ☺ **Free**

Download forms from every state that has a personal income tax.
Web site: http://www.1040.com/state.htm

TELECOMMUTING

Online Resources

Idea Cafe

Web site: http://www.ideacafe.com

New York Telecommuting Advisory Council (NYTAC)

Web site: http://www.nyworks.com

NYTAC Telecommute Links

Web site: http://www.telecommute.org

TELEPHONE RATE COMPARISONS

Long Distance Rate Survey ☺ **Free**

Consumer Action
116 New Montgomery Street, Suite 233
San Francisco, CA 94105
415-777-9635
Send a self-addressed, stamped business envelope to Consumer Action with your request.

Tele-Tips Long Distance Comparison Chart

Find the cheapest plan in your area. The comparisons are published by the Telecommunications Research & Action Center (TRAC) and are available for residential ($5) or small business customers ($7). Send a self-addressed envelope with $0.55 postage along with your check.
TRAC
P.O. Box 27279
Washington, DC 20005
202-408-1130

TeleWorth   ☺ **Free**

This Internet telecommunications agency based in Austin, Texas, offers a free, unbiased routing system to analyze potential long-distance carriers. You enter basic calling pattern information from your telephone bill into its TeleRate service, and TeleWorth recommends the four best long-distance companies and plans for you.

    800-789-2534
    Web site: http://www.teleworth.com

TELEPHONE SERVICES AND PRODUCTS   ☺ **Free**

Consulting services, resource guides, and newsletters. Browse online or call and ask about their home office/small office centers or programs.

Ameritech

    800–967–5543
    http://www.ameritech.com

AT&T

    800–473–7687
    http://www.att.com/truechoice

Bell Atlantic

    800–867–6000
    http://www.bacom

BellSouth

    800–356–3094
    http://www.bellsouth.com

Southern New England

    800–466–3633
    http://www.snet.net

Southwestern Bell

    800–347–5893
    http://www.sbc.com

U.S. West

    800–898–9675
    http://www.uswest.com

Catalogue

Hello Direct

Telephone and telecommunications products.
800–444–3556

Online Software

PhoneMiser

A computer program that routes each call you make to the cheapest of ten carriers. You can download the program from the Internet at no cost, but to use it requires an adapter and additional software.
888–843–6473
Web site: http://www.phonemiser.com

Follow Me Service

With Follow Me Service, an electronic voice answers and asks for the caller's name. It offers the choice of leaving a message or holding while the system tries to track you down from the three locations you previously programmed into the system. Check with specific vendors for details.

AT&T and MCI

Check your local telephone book.

TPS Call Sciences

379 Thornall Street, Suite 1100 West Tower
Edison, NJ 08837
732–494–5800

Wildfire Communications

81 Hartwell Avenue
Lexington, MA 02173
781–778–1500

TELEVISION: BUSINESS PROGRAMS

Here is a *minuscule* sampling of the valuable business and career counseling programming that is available on television.

AARP Works

AARP Works teaches job search skills to midlife and older workers through a series of workshops offered at more than seventy sites nationwide. AARP Works is also carried on Mind Extension University, the educational cable television network.

AARP Work Force Programs
601 E St. NW
Washington, DC 20049
800–777–MIND (6463)
To register for the cable series, call between 9 A.M. and 8 P.M. EST.

Bloomberg Small Business

Covers news, strategies, how to achieve success, etc. in the business world. USA
Network. Call for local schedule.
Bloomberg Television
P.O. Box 888
Princeton, NJ 08542
800–395–2488
E-mail: smallbiz@bloomberg.com

Small Business 2000   ☺ **Free**

This is a weekly, half-hour public television program on how to start, run, and
grow a business. Everyone connected with the program, on air and off, is a small business owner.
Viewers may request two guides: *Starting and Growing a Business* from Bottom
Line/Business and *The Small Business Financial Resource Guide* from MasterCard (see
description page 218).
504–737–0089
E-mail: sb2000@sb2000.com

WRITERS/WRITING

Ann Cefola, Corporate Writer/Editor

Specialties: articles, brochures, newsletters, and press releases. Writing workshops
(see below), professional coaching for freelancers.
914–793–0917
914–771–9363 (fax)
E-mail: Annogram@aol.com

Renee Marks Cohen, Technical Writer/Editor

Specialties: medicine, business. Media: abstracts, articles, books, brochures, case
studies, grant proposals, newsletters, proceedings. Project coordination, publicity, research.
30 Lake Street, 5C
White Plains, NY 10603
914–949–6026
914–946–8263 (fax)

Organization

National Writers Union (NWU)

If you are looking for a writer, NWU maintains a national job hotline.
212–254–0279 (East Coast)
510–839–0110 (West Coast)
510–839–6092 (Hotline)
Web site: http://www.nwu.org/nwu
E-mail: nwu@nwu.org

Workshop

Breaking into Corporate Writing

This three-hour workshop teaches writers how to shape their current skills and experience for the business market. Covers building a portfolio, attracting clients, setting fees, and managing business relationships.
Ann Cefola
Jumpstart LLC
914–793–0917
914–771–9363 (fax)
E-mail: Annogram@aol.com

APPENDIX B *The Twenty Qualifying Rules for Independent Contractors*

Questionable cases are decided on an individual basis by performance in the following categories.

1. **Instructions:** Independent contractors work without being told when, where, or how to do the work.

2. **Training:** Independent contractors come onto the job with their skills in place. They would not receive training from the client.

3. **Integration:** They are not a part of the daily routine; business can operate without a contractor's services.

4. **Performance:** They may assign others to do work.

5. **Cost of goods/assistants:** Independent contractors hire, train, supervise, and pay assistants; they pay for materials as part of their contract.

6. **Work relationship:** They have a different relationship than the employees who perform work frequently at recurring intervals as part of an ongoing relationship with the company.

7. **Schedule:** Independent contractors set their own schedule and hours.

8. **Hours worked:** They are available to work for multiple companies rather than one only.

9. **Work location:** Independent contractors are not restricted to working on company premises.

10. **Work sequence:** They do their work in whatever sequence they determine is best.

11. **Accountability:** Independent contractors are not accountable to client for daily activities.

12. **Payment method:** Independent contractors usually are paid by the job or on straight commission rather than hourly, weekly, monthly, or annually.

13. **Expenses:** They pay their own business and travel expenses (but bill company for them when they are part of a project).

14. **Tools:** Independent contractors supply their own tools or equipment.

15. **Investment:** They make a significant investment in equipment or facilities needed to perform services.

16. **Profit or loss:** Independent contractors do not receive a salary. They either make a profit or suffer a loss.

17. **Number of business customers:** They may work for multiple companies at any one time.

18. **Availability:** They are available to work for multiple companies.

19. **Termination:** Independent contractors must be paid if they produce the results specified in the contract. Employees can be fired.

20. **Right to quit:** Independent contractors are legally obligated to meet contract terms, which can include a clause to end the work relationship.

APPENDIX C *Summary of Tax Reform Act of 1986 (TRA)*

An important piece of legislation you should know about is the Tax Reform Act of 1986 (TRA), which provides safeguards for temporary and leased employees. TRA eliminated the tax shelter for top-heavy pension plans. It provides for a number of "tests" to be applied to determine whether a company's health insurance and pension plans are nondiscriminatory. It prohibits a company from excluding leased employees from pension plans if they make up more than 20 percent of its work force. It raises the employer (leasing company) contributions to employees' pension funds from 7.5 to 10 percent. In addition, emerging case law supports the view that the typical staff leasing arrangement establishes a coemployer relationship between the leasing service and the client company. This joint-employer arrangement includes joint liabilities for discriminatory hiring and other violations of labor laws, which tends to make it less attractive to companies. A further disincentive is that a company relinquishes the day-to-day control of its leased employees to the third-party leasing company in exchange for the administrative services it provides.

Employee leasing is the method by which the concept of temporary services is placed within the body of the regular work force of a corporation or company. The corporation will terminate a group of employees, who will then be hired by a third party—the leasing company—and leased back to their original company. The leasing company takes over the day-to-day personnel administration: the hiring, firing, payroll, benefits, workers' compensation, and unemployment insurance premiums. Until 1986, this arrangement owed much of its appeal to the "safe harbor" it provided employers from normal pension obligations. Thus, a company could provide generous pension benefits to executives while excluding the bulk of its work force, the leased employees.

Section 414(n) of the Tax Reform Act applies to temporaries. Temp agencies must include their temp employees in the "tests" of their own pension and health insurance plans. However, the exclusions exempt a sizable chunk of temporaries from any coverage. Excluded are employees

- of less than six months (for health insurance)
- of less than one year (for pension plans)
- under the age of twenty-one
- who work less than 17.5 hours weekly
- who are covered under a collective bargaining agreement.

Index

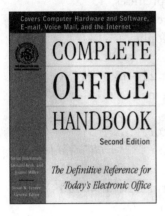